The
Gospels
and the
Letters of Paul

The Gospels and the Letters of Paul

An Inclusive-Language Edition

Translated and Edited by
Burton H. Throckmorton, Jr.

Foreword by
Arthur O. Van Eck

The Pilgrim Press
Cleveland, Ohio

Published in 1992 by The Pilgrim Press, Cleveland, Ohio 44115

© 1992 by Division of Christian Education, National Council of the Churches of Christ in the U.S.A.

Scripture based on *An Inclusive-Language Lectionary, Readings for Years A, B, and C*, © 1986, 1987, 1988 by the Division of Education and Ministry, National Council of the Churches of Christ in the U.S.A. These lectionary texts plus the additional passages not included in the lectionary and here translated by Burton H. Throckmorton, Jr., are based on the Revised Standard Version of the Bible, New Testament Section, © 1946, 1971 by the Division of Education and Ministry, National Council of the Churches of Christ in the U.S.A.

Book design by Patricia Kellis.

Printed in the United States of America

The paper used in this publication is acid free and meets the minimum requirements of American National Standard for Information Sciences-Permanence of Paper for Printed Library Materials, ANSI Z39.48–1984

97   96   95   94   93   92   5   4   3   2   1

Library of Congress Cataloging-in-Publication Data

Bible, N.T. Gospels. English. Throckmorton. 1992
   The gospels and the letters of Paul : an inclusive language
edition / translated and edited by Burton H. Throckmorton, Jr. ;
foreword by Arthur O. Van Eck.
    p. cm.
   ISBN 0-8298-0925-2 (alk. paper)
   1. Nonsexist language—Religious aspects—Christianity.
I. Throckmorton, Burton Hamilton, 1921– . II. Bible. N.T.
Epistles of Paul. English. Throckmorton. 1992. III. Title.
BS2553.T49 1992
225.5′209—dc20   92-19339
                CIP

For
Marguerite Jewell Barrows,
who led me to the Bible
and who is never far away

Contents

Foreword

An Inclusive-Language Lectionary (AILL), Year A of which was first published in 1983, had a significant impact on the life of the church in this country. It was not the first inclusive-language lectionary to be published, nor was it to be the last, but it was much noticed. The publication of Year A, prepared by a committee under the auspices of the Division of Christian Education of the National Council of the Churches of Christ in the U.S.A., was accompanied with a news conference, press release, and national coverage in all major newspapers and news magazines. This was followed by many discussions in both religious and secular media, on radio talk shows, and national television. AILL was appreciated, resisted, celebrated, lamented, but not ignored. It caught the public's attention, and a great deal of discussion ensued regarding the appropriateness of inclusive language, in both the liturgical and private use of the scriptures.

The late Percel Alston, a staff member of the United Church Board for Homeland Ministries, indicated that *An Inclusive-Language Lectionary* was the most powerful educational intervention into the life of the United Church of Christ that he had ever experienced. Alston went on to explain that it made an impact not simply upon the language used in the Sunday morning services of worship, but also on individual lives and congregational lives at the point of theology, authority, church government, formal Christian education, and pastoral concerns. There was no way that these issues could be overlooked when a person, or a congregation, began to take seriously the use of inclusive language, and the values and commitments behind that language.

People struggled with questions about God, about Jesus the Christ, about humankind, about the nature of creation. Church educators were challenged to provide seminars and classes that explored these issues.

Pastors experienced an increase in pastoral counseling. New guide-lines were developed for curriculum writers and educators. Denomina-tional assemblies engaged the issues and made statements. *An Inclusive-Language Lectionary* made an impact.

The Inclusive-Language Lectionary Committee solicited and encour-aged feedback on what it had done in the first edition of Year A, and on what it did in subsequent editions. As a result of these inquiries, many changes were made, beginning with the first edition of Year B, and con-tinuing in the second editions of the three-year cycle. Examples of such changes include:

- "Sovereign One" for "Lord" in the Old Testament, which appeared in the first edition of Year A, was replaced by "Sovereign" with "Lord" in brackets in Year B, and in the second editions of Years A, B, and C as an alternative reading.

- Sometimes "Lord" appeared as "God" in the New Testament in the first edition of Year A (such as at Matthew 9:38), and was corrected to "Sovereign" with "Lord" in brackets.

- Where the committee had introduced "God" into the text in place of the masculine pronoun of the RSV (such as in Romans 8:20, where AILL has "by the will of *God* who subjected it"), subsequent editions have "by the will of *the one* who subjected it."

In short, the committee made many changes as it went along, changes in judgment and changes where there had been errors of translation.

AILL is now completed. But even if one were to possess the whole three-year cycle of AILL, in three volumes, one would still have only about 47 percent of the New Testament in inclusive language. Further-more, one would have that 47 percent of the New Testament in three different volumes: for example, John 1:29–34 appears in one book of AILL, John 1:35–42 appears in another, John 1:43–51 does not appear at all, and John 2:1–11 appears in a third book.

What is clearly needed is a version of the whole Bible in inclusive language. Perhaps such a volume will be made available in this decade. Surely an inclusive-language New Testament will be produced. In many respects, the development of such an inclusive-language Bible will be a continuation and an affirmation of the values and commitments behind *An Inclusive-Language Lectionary*.

Meanwhile, the United Church of Christ, through The Pilgrim Press, is offering this volume, which includes the four Gospels (Matthew, Mark, Luke, and John), and all the Pauline letters, excluding the Pas-torals (1 and 2 Timothy and Titus). This volume, an adaptation of the Revised Standard Version of the New Testament, is a response to the expressed need to have at least the most significant and most widely read books of the New Testament available in their entirety in inclusive language. It has been prepared by Professor Burton H. Throckmorton, Jr., a member of the Inclusive-Language Lectionary Committee and vice-chair of the editorial committee.

ARTHUR O. VAN ECK
Director, Bible Translation and Utilization
National Council of the Churches of Christ (U.S.A.)

Preface

This book has been prepared for all those people who want to read and hear their New Testament scriptures in language that does not offend them. How can words that hurt be heard as the saving Word of God? That question arises with startling power in home after home, church after church, Sunday after Sunday, throughout our entire country. It also arises in conversations and in theological discussions about whether or not the church is so inherently and irremediably androcentric and patriarchal that women must forever remain second to men in the body of Christ. That discussion will continue; but meanwhile various attempts are being made to provide believers with versions of scripture in inclusive language, on the assumption that, as Paul says, with God there is no partiality, and in Christ there is not male and female.

Work on *An Inclusive-Language Lectionary* was begun in 1981; and that was preceded by three years of conversations about what might be done to ameliorate the harshness of the Revised Standard Version, which was conceded by many at that time to be the foremost version of the Bible in English. The three-year cycle of that lectionary is, of course, available; but one has to have three different books and three different indexes in order to locate what, in total, is less than 50 percent of the New Testament. This kind of spotty, disconnected arrangement of biblical texts, all of them totally out of sequence and dispersed among three different volumes, can hardly meet the need for an inclusive version of the scriptures.

This particular volume includes what are probably the most read books of the New Testament—the four Gospels and Paul's letters (with the exception of the so-called Pastoral Epistles)—in inclusive language. We send it out to the churches and to individuals in the hope that the many believers and others who read, study, and meditate on the New Testament for their own varying reasons will be able to read it and hear it in language that is as inclusive of women as of men, and that is also not offensive either to people of color or to those with disabling conditions.

This is not the place to argue for the legitimacy of such a translation, or to justify the particular ways in which it has been done here. We have followed the general practices worked out by the Inclusive-Language Lectionary Committee, with a few exceptions. For example, "multitude(s)" has been replaced by the more usual "crowd(s)"; and "Lord" is retained for the Greek word *Kyrios*, used frequently in the New Testament for both God and Christ.

Finally, while the English of this translation is based on the Revised Standard Version of the New Testament (second edition 1971), and not on the New Revised Standard Version published in 1990, it occasionally departs from the RSV, primarily in references to times of the day, to distances, and to amounts of money, where contemporary American idiom is called for. In addition to these changes, a small number of infelicitous or outmoded expressions that one occasionally encounters in the RSV have been replaced by alternative translations.

An appendix discusses briefly the most important words and phrases used in this translation in the interest of inclusivity.

BURTON H. THROCKMORTON, JR.
Bangor Theological Seminary

The Gospels

Matthew

1 The book of the genealogy of Jesus Christ, the son of David, the son of Abraham.

2 Abraham was the father of Isaac, and Isaac the father of Jacob, and Jacob the father of Judah and his brothers, ³and Judah the father of Perez and Zerah by Tamar, and Perez the father of Hezron, and Hezron the father of Ram, ⁴and Ram the father of Amminadab, and Amminadab the father of Nahshon, and Nahshon the father of Salmon, ⁵and Salmon the father of Boaz by Rahab, and Boaz the father of Obed by Ruth, and Obed the father of Jesse, ⁶and Jesse the father of David the king.

And David was the father of Solomon by the wife of Uriah, ⁷and Solomon the father of Rehoboam, and Rehoboam the father of Abijah, and Abijah the father of Asa, ⁸and Asa the father of Jehoshaphat, and Jehoshaphat the father of Joram, and Joram the father of Uzziah, ⁹and Uzziah the father of Jotham, and Jotham the father of Ahaz, and Ahaz the father of Hezekiah, ¹⁰and Hezekiah the father of Manasseh, and Manasseh the father of Amos, and Amos the father of Josiah, ¹¹and Josiah the father of Jeconiah and his brothers, at the time of the deportation of Babylon.

12 And after the deportation to Babylon: Jeconiah was the father of Shealtiel, and Shealtiel the father of Zerubbabel, ¹³and Zerubbabel the father of Abiud, and Abiud the father of Eliakim, and Eliakim the father of Azor, ¹⁴and Azor the father of Zadok, and Zadok the father of Achim, and Achim the father of Eliud, ¹⁵and Eliud the father of Eleazar, and Eleazar the father of Matthan, and Matthan the father of Jacob, ¹⁶and Jacob the father of Joseph the husband of Mary, of whom Jesus was born, who is called Christ.

17 So all the generations from Abraham to David were fourteen generations, and from David to the deportation to Babylon fourteen

generations, and from the deportation to Babylon to the Christ fourteen generations.

18 Now the birth of Jesus Christ took place in this way. When Jesus' mother Mary had been betrothed to Joseph, before they came together she was found to be with child of the Holy Spirit; 19and her husband Joseph, being a just man and unwilling to put her to shame, resolved to divorce her quietly. 20But at the time Joseph considered this, an angel of God appeared to him in a dream, saying, "Joseph, son of David, do not fear to take Mary your wife, for that which is conceived in her is of the Holy Spirit; 21she will bear a child, whose name you shall call Jesus, for this child will save the people from their sins." 22All this took place to fulfill what God had spoken by the prophet:

> 23"A virgin shall conceive and bear a child,
> whose name shall be called Emmanuel"

(which means, God with us). 24When Joseph woke from sleep, he did as the angel of God had commanded, and married Mary, 25but knew her not until she had borne a child; and Joseph named the child Jesus.

2 Now when Jesus was born in Bethlehem of Judea in the days of Herod the king, magi from the East came to Jerusalem, saying, 2"Where is the one who has been born king of the Jews? For we have seen his star in the East, and have come to worship him." 3And hearing this, Herod the king was troubled, and all Jerusalem as well; 4and assembling all the chief priests and scribes of the people, he inquired of them where the Messiah was to be born. 5They told Herod, "In Bethlehem of Judea; for so it is written by the prophet:

> 6'And you, O Bethlehem, in the land of Judah,
> are by no means least among the rulers of Judah;
> for from you shall come a ruler
> who will govern my people Israel.'"

7 Then Herod summoned the magi secretly, inquired from them what time the star appeared, 8and sent them to Bethlehem, saying, "Go and search diligently for the child, and when you have found him bring me word, that I too may come and worship him." 9When they had heard the king they went their way; and the star which they had seen in the East went before them, till it came to rest over the place where the child was. 10When they saw the star, they were overjoyed; 11and going into the house they saw the child with Mary his mother, and they fell down and worshiped him. Then, opening their treasures, they offered the child gifts, gold and frankincense and myrrh. 12And being warned in a dream

not to return to Herod, they departed to their own country by another way.

13 Now when the magi had departed, an angel of God appeared to Joseph in a dream and said, "Rise, take the child and his mother, and flee to Egypt, and remain there till I tell you; for Herod is about to search for the child, to kill him." ¹⁴And Joseph rose and took the child and his mother by night, and departed to Egypt, ¹⁵remaining there until the death of Herod. This was to fulfill what God had spoken by the prophet, "Out of Egypt have I called my child."

16 Then when Herod saw that he had been tricked by the magi, he sent and killed all the male children in Bethlehem and in all that region who were two years old or under, reckoning from the date given him by the magi. ¹⁷Then was fulfilled what was spoken by the prophet Jeremiah:

> ¹⁸"A voice was heard in Ramah,
> wailing and loud lamentation,
> Rachel weeping for her children;
> she refused to be consoled,
> because they were no more."

19 But when Herod died, an angel of God appeared in a dream to Joseph in Egypt, saying, ²⁰"Rise, take the child and his mother, and go to the land of Israel, for those who sought the child's life have died." ²¹And Joseph rose and took the child and his mother, and went to the land of Israel. ²²But hearing that Archelaus reigned over Judea in place of his father Herod, Joseph was afraid to go there, and being warned in a dream, withdrew to the district of Galilee. ²³And Joseph went and dwelt in a city called Nazareth, that what was spoken by the prophets might be fulfilled, "There shall come forth a Nazarene."

3 In those days came John the Baptist, preaching in the wilderness of Judea, ²"Repent, for the dominion of heaven is at hand." ³For this is the one spoken of by the prophet Isaiah,

> "The voice of one crying in the wilderness:
> Prepare the way of the Lord,
> make the paths of the Lord straight."

⁴Now John wore a garment of camel's hair, and a leather girdle around his waist; and his food was locusts and wild honey. ⁵Then Jerusalem and all Judea and all the region about the Jordan went out to him, ⁶and they were baptized by him in the river Jordan, confessing their sins.

7 But seeing many of the Pharisees and Sadducees coming for baptism, John said to them, "You brood of vipers! Who warned you to flee from the wrath to come? ⁸Bear fruit that befits repentance, ⁹and do not

presume to say to yourselves, 'We have Abraham as our father'; for I tell you, God is able from these stones to raise up children to Abraham. ¹⁰Even now the axe is laid to the root of the trees; every tree therefore that does not bear good fruit is cut down and thrown into the fire.

11 "I baptize you with water for repentance, but the one who is coming after me is mightier than I, whose sandals I am not worthy to carry; that one will baptize you with the Holy Spirit and with fire. ¹²With winnowing fork in hand, that one will clear the threshing floor and gather the wheat into the granary, but will burn the chaff with unquenchable fire."

13 Then Jesus came from Galilee to the Jordan to be baptized by John. ¹⁴John would have prevented Jesus, saying, "I need to be baptized by you, and do you come to me?" ¹⁵But Jesus answered, "Let it be so now; for thus it is fitting for us to fulfill all righteousness." Then John consented. ¹⁶And having been baptized, Jesus went up immediately from the water, and the heavens were opened and Jesus saw the Spirit of God descending like a dove, and alighting on him. ¹⁷ And there was a voice from heaven, saying, "This is my beloved Child, with whom I am well pleased."

4 Then Jesus was led up by the Spirit into the wilderness to be tempted by the devil. ²Having fasted forty days and forty nights, Jesus was hungry. ³And the tempter came and said to Jesus, "If you are the Child of God, command these stones to become loaves of bread." ⁴But Jesus answered, "It is written,

'One shall not live by bread alone,
but by every word that proceeds from the mouth of God.' "

⁵Then the devil took Jesus to the holy city, and set him on the pinnacle of the temple, ⁶and said, "If you are the Child of God, throw yourself down; for it is written,

'God will give the angels charge of you,'

and

'On their hands they will bear you up,
lest you strike your foot against a stone.' "

⁷Jesus said to the devil, "Again it is written, 'You shall not tempt the Lord your God.' " ⁸Again, the devil took Jesus to a very high mountain, and showed him all the nations of the world and the glory of them; ⁹and the devil said to Jesus, "All these I will give you, if you will fall down and worship me." ¹⁰Then Jesus said to the devil, "Be gone, Satan! for it is written,

'You shall worship the Lord your God,
and God only shall you serve.' "

[11]Then the devil left Jesus, and angels came and ministered to him.

12 Now having heard that John had been arrested, Jesus withdrew into Galilee; [13]and leaving Nazareth, he went and dwelt in Capernaum by the sea, in the territory of Zebulun and Naphtali, [14]that what was spoken by the prophet Isaiah might be fulfilled:

[15]"The land of Zebulun and the land of Naphtali,
toward the sea, across the Jordan,
Galilee of the Gentiles—
[16]the people who sat without light
have seen a great light,
and for those who sat in the region and shadow of death
light has dawned."

[17]From that time Jesus began to preach, saying, "Repent, for the dominion of heaven is at hand."

18 Then walking by the Sea of Galilee, Jesus saw two brothers, Simon who is called Peter, and Andrew his brother, casting a net into the sea; for they were fishers. [19]And Jesus said to them, "Follow me, and I will make you fishers of human beings." [20]Immediately they left their nets and followed him. [21]And going on from there Jesus saw two other brothers, James the son of Zebedee and his brother John, in the boat with Zebedee their father, mending their nets, and Jesus called them. [22]Immediately they left the boat and their father, and followed Jesus.

23 And Jesus went about all Galilee, teaching in their synagogues, preaching the gospel of the dominion of heaven, and healing every disease and every infirmity among the people. [24]So Jesus' fame spread throughout all Syria, and they brought him all the sick, those afflicted with various diseases and pains, people with demons or epilepsy, people who were paralyzed, and Jesus healed them. [25]And great crowds followed Jesus from Galilee and the Decapolis and Jerusalem and Judea and from beyond the Jordan.

5 Seeing the crowds, Jesus went up on the mountain and sat down; and the disciples came up. [2]And Jesus taught them, saying:

3 "Blessed are the poor in spirit, for theirs is the dominion of heaven.

4 "Blessed are those who mourn, for they shall be comforted.

5 "Blessed are the meek, for they shall inherit the earth.

6 "Blessed are those who hunger and thirst for righteousness, for they shall be satisfied.

7 "Blessed are the merciful, for they shall obtain mercy.

8 "Blessed are the pure in heart, for they shall see God.

9 "Blessed are the peacemakers, for they shall be called children of God.

10 "Blessed are those who are persecuted for righteousness' sake, theirs is the dominion of heaven.

11 "Blessed are you when others revile you and persecute you and utter all kinds of evil against you falsely on my account. [12]Rejoice and be glad for your reward is great in heaven, for so they persecuted the prophets who were before you.

13 "You are the salt of the earth; but if salt has lost its taste, how shall its saltness be restored? It is no good for anything except to be thrown out and trampled under foot.

14 "You are the light of the world. A city set on a hill cannot be hidden. [15]No one lights a lamp and puts it under a bushel, but on a stand, and it gives light to all in the house. [16]Let your light so shine before others, that they may see your good works and give glory to God your Father and Mother who is in heaven.

17 "Think not that I have come to abolish the law and the prophets; I have come not to abolish them but to fulfill them. [18]For truly, I say to you, till heaven and earth pass away, not an iota, not a dot, will pass from the law until everything is accomplished. [19]Whoever then relaxes one of the least of these commandments and teaches others so, shall be called least in the dominion of heaven; but whoever does them and teaches them shall be called great in the dominion of heaven. [20]For I tell you, unless your righteousness exceeds that of the scribes and Pharisees, you will never enter the dominion of heaven.

21 "You have heard that it was said in ancient times, 'You shall not kill; and whoever kills shall be liable to judgment.' [22]But I say to you that everyone who is angry with a neighbor shall be liable to judgment; whoever insults a neighbor shall be liable to the council, and whoever says, 'You fool!' shall be liable to the hell of fire. [23]So if you are offering your gift at the altar, and there remember that your neighbor has something against you, [24]leave your gift there before the altar and go; first be reconciled to your neighbor, and then come and offer your gift. [25]Make friends quickly with your accuser, while you are going to court, lest your accuser hand you over to the judge, and the judge to the guard, and you be put in prison; [26]truly, I say to you, you will never get out till you have paid the last penny.

27 "You have heard that it was said, 'You shall not commit adultery.' [28]But I say to you that any one of you who looks at another lustfully has already committed adultery in your heart. [29]If your right eye causes you to sin, pluck it out and throw it away; it is better that you lose one of your members than that your whole body be thrown into hell. [30]And if your right hand causes you to sin, cut it off and throw it away; it is

better that you lose one of your members than that your whole body go into hell.

31 "It was also said, 'Whoever divorces his wife, let him give her a certificate of divorce.' ³²But I say to you that everyone who divorces his wife, except on the ground of unchastity, forces her into adultery; and whoever marries a divorced woman commits adultery.

33 "Again you have heard that it was said in ancient times, 'You shall not swear falsely, but shall perform to God what you have sworn.' ³⁴But I say to you, Do not swear at all, either by heaven, for it is the throne of God, ³⁵or by the earth, for it is God's footstool, or by Jerusalem, for it is the city of the great Ruler. ³⁶And do not swear by your head, for you cannot make one hair white or black. ³⁷Let what you say be simply 'Yes' or 'No'; anything more than this comes from evil.

38 "You have heard that it was said, 'An eye for an eye and a tooth for a tooth.' ³⁹But I say to you, Do not resist one who is evil. But if anyone strikes you on the right cheek, turn the other also; ⁴⁰and if anyone would sue you and take your coat, give your cloak as well; ⁴¹and if anyone forces you to go one mile, go two miles. ⁴²Give to the one who begs from you, and do not refuse anyone who would borrow from you.

43 "You have heard that it was said, 'You shall love your neighbor and hate your enemy.' ⁴⁴But I say to you, Love your enemies and pray for those who persecute you, ⁴⁵so that you may be children of God who is in heaven; for God makes the sun rise on the evil and on the good, and sends rain on the just and on the unjust. ⁴⁶For if you love those who love you, what reward have you? Do not even the tax collectors do the same? ⁴⁷And if you salute only your neighbors, what more are you doing than others? Do not even the Gentiles do the same? ⁴⁸You, therefore, must be perfect, as God your heavenly Father and Mother is perfect.

6 "Beware of practicing your piety before others in order to be seen by them; for then you will have no reward from God your Father and Mother who is in heaven.

2 "Thus, when you give alms, sound no trumpet before you, as the hypocrites do in the synagogues and in the streets, that they may be praised by others. Truly, I say to you, they have received their reward. ³But when you give alms, do not let your left hand know what your right hand is doing, ⁴so that your alms may be in secret; and God who sees in secret will reward you.

5 "And when you pray, you must not be like the hypocrites; for they love to stand and pray in the synagogues and at the street corners, that they may be seen by others. Truly, I say to you, they have received their reward. ⁶But when you pray, go into your room and shut the door and pray to God who is in secret; and God who sees in secret will reward you.

7 "And in praying do not heap up empty phrases as the Gentiles do; for they think that they will be heard for their many words. [8]Do not be like them, for God knows what you need before you ask. [9]Pray then like this:

> God, our Father and Mother, who is in the heavens,
> May your name be made holy.
> [10]May your dominion come,
> And your will be done,
> On the earth as it is in heaven.
> [11]Give us today the bread we need;
> [12]And forgive us our debts,
> As we have forgiven our debtors;
> [13]And do not put us to the test,
> But rescue us from evil.

[14]For if you forgive people their trespasses, God in heaven also will forgive you; [15]but if you do not forgive people their trespasses, neither will God forgive your trespasses.

16 "And when you fast, do not look dismal, like the hypocrites, for they disfigure their faces that their fasting may be seen by others. Truly, I say to you, they have received their reward. [17]But when you fast, anoint your head and wash your face, [18]that your fasting may not be seen by others but by God who is in secret; and God who sees in secret will reward you.

19 "Do not lay up for yourselves treasures on earth, where moth and rust consume and where thieves break in and steal, [20]but lay up for yourselves treasures in heaven, where neither moth nor rust consumes and where thieves do not break in and steal. [21]For where your treasure is, there will your heart be also.

22 "The eye is the lamp of the body. So, if your eye is sound, your whole body will be full of light; [23]but if your eye is not sound, your whole body will be full of darkness. If then the light in you is darkness, how great is the darkness!

24 "No one can serve two masters; for a person will either hate the one and love the other, or will be devoted to the one and despise the other. You cannot serve God and mammon.

25 "Therefore I tell you, do not be anxious about your life, what you will eat or what you will drink, nor about your body, what you will put on. Is not life more than food, and the body more than clothing? [26]Look at the birds of the air: they neither sow nor reap nor gather into barns, and yet God your heavenly Father and Mother feeds them. Are you not of more value than they? [27]And which of your by being anxious can add one cubit to your span of life? [28]And why are you anxious about clothing? Consider the lilies of the field, how they grow; they neither toil

nor spin; [29]yet I tell you, even Solomon in all his glory was not arrayed like one of these. [30]But if God so clothes the grass of the field, which today is alive and tomorrow is thrown into the oven, will God not much more clothe you, O you of little faith? [31]Therefore do not be anxious, saying, 'What shall we eat?' or 'What shall we drink?' or 'What shall we wear?' [32]For the Gentiles seek all these things; and God your heavenly Mother and Father knows that you need them all. [33]But seek first God's dominion and God's righteousness, and all these things shall be yours as well.

34 "Therefore do not be anxious about tomorrow, for tomorrow will be anxious for itself. Let the day's own trouble be sufficient for the day.

7 "Judge not, that you be not judged. [2]For with the judgment you pronounce you will be judged, and the measure you give will be the measure you get. [3]Why do you see the speck that is in your neighbor's eye, but do not notice the log that is in your own eye? [4]Or how can you say to your neighbor, 'Let me take the speck out of your eye,' when there is the log in your own eye? [5]You hypocrite, first take the log out of your own eye, and then you will see clearly to take the speck out of your neighbor's eye.

6 "Do not give dogs what is holy; and do not throw your pearls before swine, lest they trample them under foot and turn to attack you.

7 "Ask, and it will be given you; seek, and you will find; knock, and it will be opened to you. [8]For everyone who asks receives, and one who seeks finds, and to one who knocks it will be opened. [9]Or what parent among you, if your child asks for bread, will give a stone? [10]Or if the child asks for a fish, will give a serpent? [11]If you then, who are evil, know how to give good gifts to your children, how much more will God who is in heaven give good things to those who ask! [12]So whatever you wish that others would do to you, do the same to them; for this is the law and the prophets.

13 "Enter by the narrow gate; for the gate is wide and the way is easy, that leads to destruction, and those who enter by it are many. [14]For the gate is narrow and the way is hard, that leads to life, and those who find it are few.

15 "Beware of false prophets, who come to you in sheep's clothing but inwardly are ravenous wolves. [16]You will know them by their fruits. Are grapes gathered from thorns, or figs from thistles? [17]So, every sound tree bears good fruit, but the bad tree bears evil fruit. [18]A sound tree cannot beat evil fruit, nor can a bad tree bear good fruit. [19]Every tree that does not bear good fruit is cut down and thrown into the fire. [20]Thus you will know them by their fruits.

21 "Not everyone who says to me, 'Lord, Lord' will enter the dominion of heaven, but those who do the will of God my Father and Mother

who is in heaven. [22]On that day many will say to me, 'Lord, Lord, did we not prophesy in your name, and cast out demons in your name, and do many mighty works in your name?' [23]And then will I declare to them, 'I never knew you; depart from me, you evildoers.'

24 "Everyone then who hears these words of mine and does them will be like someone wise enough to build a house upon the rock; [25]and the rain fell, and the floods came, and the winds blew and beat upon that house but it did not fall, because it had been founded on the rock. [26]And everyone who hears these words of mine and does not do them will be like the fool who built a house upon the sand; [27]and the rain fell, and the floods came, and the winds blew and beat against that house, and it fell and great was the fall of it."

28 And when Jesus finished these sayings, the crowds were astonished at the teaching, [29]for Jesus taught them as one who had authority, and not as their scribes.

8 When Jesus came down from the mountain, great crowds followed; [2]and a person with leprosy came up and knelt down and said, "Lord, if you will, you can make me clean." [3]And Jesus stretched out his hand and touched the person, saying, "I will; be clean." And immediately the leprosy was cleansed. [4]And Jesus said to the one who had been cleansed, "See that you say nothing to anyone; but go, show yourself to the priest, and offer the gift that Moses commanded, for a proof to the people."

5 When Jesus entered Capernaum, a centurion came up and begged Jesus, [6]saying, "Lord, my servant is lying paralyzed at home, in terrible distress." [7]And Jesus said to the centurion, "I will come and heal your servant." [8]But the centurion answered, "Lord, I am not worthy to have you come under my roof; but only say the word, and my servant will be healed. [9]For I am a person under authority, with soldiers under me; and I say to some, 'Go,' and they go, and to others, 'Come,' and they come; and to my slaves I say 'Do this,' and they do it." [10]Jesus, having heard this, marveled, and said to those who followed, "Truly, I say to you, not even in Israel have I found such faith. [11]I tell you, many will come from east and west and sit at table with Abraham, Isaac, and Jacob in the dominion of heaven, [12]while the children of the dominion will be thrown into outer darkness; there people will weep and gnash their teeth." [13]And to the centurion Jesus said, "Go; as you have believed, let it be done for you." And the servant was healed at that very moment.

14 And having entered Peter's house, Jesus saw Peter's mother-in-law lying sick with a fever; [15]and Jesus touched her hand, and the fever left her, and she rose and served Jesus. [16]That evening they brought to Jesus many who were possessed with demons; and Jesus cast out the spirits with a word, and healed all who were sick. [17]This was to

fulfill what was spoken by the prophet Isaiah, "The servant took our infirmities and bore our diseases."

18 Now Jesus, seeing great crowds gathered around, gave orders to go over to the other side. ¹⁹And a scribe came up and said to Jesus, "Teacher, I will follow you wherever you go." ²⁰And Jesus answered, "Foxes have holes, and birds of the air have nests; but the Human One has nowhere to lie down and sleep." ²¹Another of the disciples said to Jesus, "Lord, let me first go and bury my father." ²²But Jesus answered, "Follow me, and leave the dead to bury their own dead."

23 And when Jesus got into the boat, the disciples followed. ²⁴And there arose a great storm on the sea, so that the boat was being swamped by the waves; but Jesus was asleep. ²⁵And they went and woke Jesus, saying, "Save, Lord; we are perishing." ²⁶And Jesus said to them, "Why are you afraid, O you of little faith?" Then Jesus rose and rebuked the winds and the sea; and there was a great calm. ²⁷And they marveled, saying, "What kind of a person is this, that even winds and sea obey?"

28 And Jesus, having gone to the other side, to the country of the Gadarenes, was met by two people with demons, coming out of the tombs, who were so fierce that no one could pass that way. ²⁹And they cried out, "What have you to do with us, O Child of God? Have you come here to torment us before the time?" ³⁰Now a herd of many swine was feeding at some distance from them. ³¹And the demons begged Jesus, "If you cast us out, send us away into the herd of swine." ³²And Jesus said to them, "Go." So they came out and went into the swine; and amazingly, the whole herd rushed down the steep bank into the sea, and perished in the waters. ³³The swineherds fled, and going into the city they told everything, and what had happened to the people with demons. ³⁴Then the whole city came out to meet Jesus; and when they saw Jesus, they begged him to leave their neighborhood.

9 And getting into a boat Jesus crossed the sea and came to his own city. ²Just then some people came up and brought to Jesus a person who was paralyzed, lying on a bed; and seeing their faith, Jesus said to the person, "Take heart, my child; your sins are forgiven." ³Then some of the scribes said to themselves, "This person is blaspheming." ⁴But Jesus, knowing their thoughts, said, "Why do you think evil in your hearts? ⁵For which is easier, to say, 'Your sins are forgiven,' or to say, 'Rise and walk'? ⁶But that you may know that the Human One has authority on earth to forgive sins"—Jesus said to the person who had been paralyzed—"Rise, take up your bed and go home." ⁷And the person rose and went home. ⁸When the crowds saw it, they were afraid, and they glorified God, who had given such authority to human beings.

9 Passing on from there, Jesus saw someone called Matthew sitting

at the tax office; and Jesus said to him, "Follow me." And Matthew rose and followed Jesus.

10 And as Jesus sat at table in the house, many tax collectors and sinners came and sat down with him and the disciples. [11]And when the Pharisees saw this, they said to the disciples, "Why does your teacher eat with tax collectors and sinners?" [12]But hearing this, Jesus said, "Those who are well have no need of a physician, but those who are sick. [13]Go and learn what this means, 'I desire mercy, and not sacrifice.' For I came not to call the righteous, but sinners."

14 Then the disciples of John came to Jesus, saying, "Why do we and the Pharisees fast, but your disciples do not fast?" [15]And Jesus said to them, "Can the wedding guests mourn as long as the bridegroom is with them? The days will come, when the bridegroom is taken away from them, and then they will fast. [16]And no one puts a piece of unshrunk cloth on an old garment, for the patch tears away from the garment, and a worse tear is made. [17]Neither is new wine put into old wineskins; if it is, the skins burst, and the wine is spilled, and the skins are destroyed; but new wine is put into fresh wineskins, and so both are preserved."

18 While Jesus was speaking to them, a ruler came in and knelt down, saying, "My daughter has just died; but come and lay your hand on her, and she will live." [19]And Jesus and the disciples rose and followed him. [20]And at that moment, a woman, who had suffered from a hemorrhage for twelve years, came up from behind and touched the fringe of Jesus' garment; [21]for she said to herself, "If I only touch Jesus' garment, I shall be made well." [22]Jesus turned and, seeing her, said, "Take heart, daughter; your faith has made you well." And instantly the woman was healed. [23]And having come to the ruler's house, and seeing the flute players, and the crowd making a tumult, [24]Jesus said, "Depart; for the girl is not dead but sleeping." And the people began to laugh. [25]But when the crowd had been put outside, Jesus went in and took the girl by the hand, and she arose. [26]And the report of this went through all that district.

27 As Jesus went on from there, two blind people followed after, crying aloud, "Have mercy on us, Child of David." [28]And when Jesus entered the house, the two came up; and Jesus said to them, "Do you believe that I am able to do this?" They answered, "Yes, Lord." [29]Then Jesus touched their eyes, saying, "According to your faith let it be done to you." [30]And their eyes were opened. And Jesus sternly charged them, "See that no one knows it." [31]But they went away and spread Jesus' fame through all that district.

32 Just as they were going away, a person with a demon who could not speak was brought to Jesus. [33]And when the demon had been cast out, the person spoke; and the crowds marveled, saying, "Never was

anything like this seen in Israel." ³⁴But the Pharisees said, "Jesus casts out demons by the prince of demons."

35 And Jesus went about all the cities and villages, teaching in their synagogues and preaching the gospel of the dominion of heaven, and healing every disease and every infirmity. ³⁶Seeing the crowds, Jesus had compassion for them, because they were harassed and helpless, like sheep without a shepherd. ³⁷Then Jesus said to the disciples, "The harvest is plentiful, but the laborers are few; ³⁸pray therefore to the Lord of the harvest, to send out laborers into the harvest."

10 And Jesus summoned the twelve disciples and gave them authority over unclean spirits, to cast them out, and to heal every disease and every infirmity. ²The names of the twelve apostles are these: first, Simon, who is called Peter, and Andrew his brother; James the son of Zebedee, and John his brother; ³Philip and Bartholomew; Thomas and Matthew the tax collector; James the son of Alphaeus, and Thaddaeus; ⁴Simon the Cananaean, and Judas Iscariot, who betrayed Jesus.

5 These twelve Jesus sent out, charging them, "Go nowhere among the Gentiles, and enter no town of the Samaritans, ⁶but go rather to the lost sheep of the house of Israel. ⁷And preach as you go, saying, 'The dominion of heaven is at hand.' ⁸Heal those who are sick, raise the dead, cleanse those who have leprosy, cast out demons. You received without paying, give without pay. ⁹Take no gold, nor silver, nor copper in your belts, ¹⁰no bag for your journey, nor two tunics, nor sandals, nor a staff; for those who labor deserve their food. ¹¹And whatever town or village you enter, find out who is worthy in it, and stay there until you depart. ¹²As you enter the house, salute it. ¹³And if the house is worthy, let your peace come upon it; but if it is not worthy, let your peace return to you. ¹⁴And if anyone will not receive you or listen to your words, shake off the dust from your feet as you leave that house or town. ¹⁵Truly, I say to you, it shall be more tolerable on the day of judgment for the land of Sodom and Gomorrah than for that town.

16 "Notice, I send you out as sheep in the midst of wolves; so be wise as serpents and innocent as doves. ¹⁷Beware of people; for they will deliver you up to councils, and flog you in their synagogues, ¹⁸and you will be dragged before governors and rulers for my sake, to bear testimony before them and the Gentiles. ¹⁹When they deliver you up, do not be anxious how you are to speak or what you are to say; for what you are to say will be given to you in that hour; ²⁰for it is not you who speak, but the Spirit of God speaking through you. ²¹Brother will deliver up brother to death, and sister will deliver up sister; a father and mother will deliver up their child, and children will rise against parents and have them put to death; ²²and you will be hated by all for my name's

sake. But anyone who endures to the end will be saved. [23]When they persecute you in one town, flee to the next; for truly, I say to you, you will not have gone through all the towns of Israel, before the Human One comes.

24 "A disciple is not above the teacher, nor a servant above the one who is served; [25]it is enough for the disciple to be like the teacher, and the servant like the one who is served. If they have called the householder Beelzebub, how much more will they malign those of that household?

26 "So have no fear of them; for nothing is covered that will not be revealed, or hidden that will not be known. [27]What I tell you in the night utter in the light; and what you hear whispered, proclaim upon the housetops. [28]And do not fear those who kill the body but cannot kill the soul; rather fear the one who can destroy both soul and body in hell. [29]Are not two sparrows sold for a penny? And not one of them will fall to the ground without the will of God. [30]But even the hairs of your head are all numbered. [31]Fear not, therefore; you are of more value than many sparrows. [32]So everyone who acknowledges me before others, I also will acknowledge before God my Mother and Father who is in heaven; [33]but whoever denies me before others, I also will deny before God who is in heaven.

34 "Do not think that I have come to bring peace on earth; I have not come to bring peace, but a sword. [35]For I have come to set a man against his father, and a daughter against her mother, and a daughter-in-law against her mother-in-law; [36]and one's foes will be those of one's own household. [37]Whoever loves father or mother more than me is not worthy of me; and whoever loves son or daughter more than me is not worthy of me; [38]and those who do not take their own cross and follow me are not worthy of me. [39]Those who find their life will lose it, and those who lose their life for my sake will find it.

40 "Anyone who receives you receives me, and anyone who receives me receives the one who sent me. [41]Anyone who receives a prophet because that one is a prophet shall receive the reward of a prophet, and anyone who receives the righteous because they are righteous shall receive the reward of the righteous. [42]And whoever gives to one of these little ones even a cup of cold water because that little one is a disciple, truly, I say to you, the giver shall not go unrewarded."

11 Jesus, having finished instructing the twelve disciples, went on from there to teach and preach in their cities.

2 Now John, having heard in prison about the deeds of the Messiah, sent word by his disciples and [3]said to Jesus, "Are you the one who is to come, or shall we look for another?" [4]And Jesus answered them, "Go and tell John what you hear and see: [5]those who are blind receive their sight and those who are lame walk; people with leprosy are cleansed

and those who are deaf hear; the dead are raised up; and to those who are poor good news is preached. ⁶And blessed is anyone who takes no offense at me."

7 As they went away, Jesus began to speak to the crowds concerning John: "What did you go out into the wilderness to observe? A reed shaken by the wind? ⁸Why then did you go out? To see someone clothed in soft raiment? Those who wear soft raiment are in royal palaces. ⁹Why then did you go out? To see a prophet? Yes, I tell you, and more than a prophet. ¹⁰This is the one of whom it is written,

'I am sending my messenger before your face,
who will prepare your way before you.'

¹¹Truly, I say to you, among those born of women, there has risen no one greater than John the Baptist; yet one who is least in the dominion of heaven is greater than John. ¹²From the days of John the Baptist until now the dominion of heaven has suffered violence, and people of violence take it by force. ¹³For all the prophets and the law prophesied until John; ¹⁴and if you are willing to accept it, John is Elijah who is to come. ¹⁵Those who have ears to hear, let them hear.

16 "But to what shall I compare this generation? It is like children sitting in the market places and calling to their playmates,

¹⁷'We piped to you, and you did not dance;
we wailed, and you did not mourn.'

¹⁸For John came neither eating nor drinking, and they say, 'He has a demon'; ¹⁹the Human One came eating and drinking, and they say, 'Look at the glutton and drunkard, a friend of tax collectors and sinners!' Yet wisdom is justified by its deeds."

20 Jesus began to reproach the cities where most of his mighty works had been done, because they did not repent. ²¹"Woe to you, Chorazin! woe to you, Bethsaida! for if the mighty works done in you had been done in Tyre and Sidon, they would have repented long ago in sackcloth and ashes. ²²But I tell you, it shall be more tolerable on the day of judgment for Tyre and Sidon than for you. ²³And you, Capernaum, will you be exalted to heaven? You shall be brought down to Hades. For if the mighty works done in you had been done in Sodom, it would have remained until this day. ²⁴But I tell you that it shall be more tolerable on the day of judgment for the land of Sodom than for you."

25 At that time Jesus declared, "I thank you, God, my Mother and Father, Lord of heaven and earth, that you have hidden these things from the wise and understanding and have revealed them to children; ²⁶for such, O God, was your gracious will. ²⁷All things have been delivered to me by God my Father and Mother; and no one knows the Child except God, and no one knows God except the Child and anyone to whom the

Child chooses to reveal God. 28Come to me, all who labor and are heavy laden, and I will give you rest. 29Take my yoke upon you, and learn from me; for I am gentle and lowly in heart, and you will find rest for your souls. 30For my yoke is easy, and my burden is light."

12 At that time Jesus went through the grainfields on the sabbath; and the disciples were hungry, and began to pluck ears of grain and to eat. 2But when the Pharisees saw it, they said to Jesus, "Look, your disciples are doing what is not lawful to do on the sabbath." 3Jesus answered, "Have you not read what David did, when he was hungry, and those who were with him: 4how he entered the house of God and ate the bread of the Presence, which it was not lawful for him to eat nor for those who were with him, but only for the priests? 5Or have you not read in the law how on the sabbath the priests in the temple profane the sabbath, and are guiltless? 6I tell you, something greater than the temple is here. 7And if you had known what this means, 'I desire mercy, and not sacrifice,' you would not have condemned the guiltless. 8For the Human One is Lord of the sabbath."

9 Jesus went on from there, and entered their synagogue. 10And a person was there with a withered hand. And they asked Jesus, "Is it lawful to heal on the sabbath?" so that they might accuse him. 11Jesus said to them, "Who among you, if you have one sheep and it falls into a pit on the sabbath, will not lay hold of it and lift it out? 12Of how much more value is a human being than a sheep! So it is lawful to do good on the sabbath." 13Then Jesus said to the person with the withered hand, "Stretch out your hand." And the person stretched it out, and it was restored, whole like the other. 14But the Pharisees went out and plotted how to bring about Jesus' death.

15 Jesus, aware of this, withdrew from there, and many followed; and Jesus healed them all, 16and ordered them not to make him known. 17This was to fulfill what was spoken by the prophet Isaiah:

18"Here is my servant whom I have chosen,
    my beloved with whom my soul is well pleased.
I will put my Spirit upon my servant,
    who will proclaim justice to the Gentiles.
19My servant will not quarrel or cry aloud,
    nor be heard in the streets;
20my servant will not break a bruised reed
    or quench a smoldering wick,
    till justice is brought to victory;
21and in the servant's name will the Gentiles hope."

22 Then a person who had a demon, who was blind and could not speak, was brought to Jesus, who healed the person so that the person

could both speak and see. ²³And all the people were amazed, and said, "Can this be the Child of David?" ²⁴But when the Pharisees heard it they said, "It is only by Beelzebub, the prince of demons, that this person casts out demons." ²⁵Knowing their thoughts, Jesus said to them, "Every dominion divided against itself is laid waste, and no city or house divided against itself will stand; ²⁶and if Satan casts out Satan, Satan is divided; how then will Satan's dominion stand? ²⁷And if I cast out demons by Beelzebub, by whom do your own offspring cast them out? Therefore they shall be your judges. ²⁸But if it is by the Spirit of God that I cast out demons, then the dominion of God has come upon you. ²⁹Or how can one enter a strong person's house and plunder their goods, unless one first binds the strong person? Then indeed one may plunder the house. ³⁰Anyone who is not with me is against me, and anyone who does not gather with me scatters. ³¹Therefore I tell you, people will be forgiven every sin and blasphemy, but the blasphemy against the Spirit will not be forgiven. ³²And whoever says a word against the Human One will be forgiven; but whoever speaks against the Holy Spirit will not be forgiven, either in this age or in the age to come.

33 "Either make the tree good and its fruit good; or make the tree bad, and its fruit bad; for the tree is known by its fruit. ³⁴You brood of vipers! how can you speak good, when you are evil? For out of the abundance of the heart the mouth speaks. ³⁵The good person brings forth good out of a good treasure, and the evil person out of evil treasure brings forth evil. ³⁶I tell you, on the day of judgment people will render account of every careless word they utter; ³⁷for by your words you will be justified, and by your words you will be condemned."

38 Then some of the scribes and Pharisees said to Jesus, "Teacher, we wish to see a sign from you." ³⁹But Jesus answered them, "An evil and adulterous generation seeks for a sign; but no sign will be given to it except the sign of the prophet Jonah. ⁴⁰For as Jonah was three days and three nights in the belly of the whale, so will the Human One be three days and three nights in the heart of the earth. ⁴¹The Ninevites will arise at the judgment with this generation and condemn it; for they repented at the preaching of Jonah, and see, something greater than Jonah is here. ⁴²The queen of the South will arise at the judgment with this generation and condemn it; for she came from the ends of the earth to hear the wisdom of Solomon, and see, something greater than Solomon is here.

43 "When the unclean spirit has gone out of a person, it passes through waterless places seeking rest, but it finds none. ⁴⁴Then it says, 'I will return to my house from which I came.' And when it comes it finds the house empty, swept, and put in order. ⁴⁵Then it goes and brings with it seven other spirits more evil than itself, and they enter and dwell there; and the last state of that person becomes worse than the first. So will it be also with this evil generation."

46 While still speaking to the people, Jesus' mother and brothers stood outside, asking to speak to him.* ⁴⁸But Jesus replied to the person who told him, "Who is my mother, and who are my brothers?" ⁴⁹And pointing to the disciples, Jesus said, "Here are my mother and my brothers! ⁵⁰For whoever does the will of God my Father and Mother in heaven is my brother, and sister, and mother."

13 That same day Jesus went out of the house and sat beside the sea. ²And great crowds gathered around, so that Jesus got into a boat and sat there; and the whole crowd stood on the beach. ³And Jesus told them many things in parables, saying: "A sower went out to sow. ⁴And as the seeds were being scattered, some seeds fell along the path, and the birds came and devoured them. ⁵Other seeds fell on rocky ground, where there was little soil, and immediately they sprang up, since there was not much soil, ⁶but when the sun rose they were scorched; and since they had no root they withered away. ⁷Other seeds fell upon thorns, and the thorns grew up and choked them. ⁸Other seeds fell on good soil and brought forth grain, some a hundredfold, some sixty, some thirty. ⁹Those who have ears, let them hear."

10 Then the disciples came and said to Jesus, "Why do you speak to them in parables?" ¹¹And Jesus answered them, "To you it has been given to know the secrets of the dominion of heaven, but to them it has not been given. ¹²For to those who have will more be given, and they will have abundance; but from those who have not, even what they have will be taken away. ¹³This is why I speak to them in parables, because seeing they do not see, and hearing they do not hear, nor do they understand. ¹⁴With them indeed is fulfilled the prophecy of Isaiah which says:

'You will indeed hear but never understand,
    and you will indeed see but never perceive.
¹⁵For this people's heart has grown dull,
    they have covered their ears,
    and they have closed their eyes,
lest they should perceive with their eyes,
    and hear with their ears,
and understand with their heart,
    and turn for me to heal them.'

¹⁶But blessed are your eyes, for they see, and your ears, for they hear. ¹⁷Truly, I say to you, many prophets and righteous people longed to see

---

* Other ancient authorities insert verse 47, *Someone told him, "Your mother and your brothers are standing outside, asking to speak to you."*

what you see, and did not see it, and to hear what you hear, and did not hear it.

18 "Hear then the parable of the sower. ¹⁹When any hear the word of the dominion of heaven and do not understand it, the evil one comes and snatches away what is sown in the heart; this is what was sown along the path. ²⁰As for what was sown on rocky ground, this is the one who hears the word and immediately receives it with joy; ²¹yet having no root within, this one endures for a while, and when tribulation or persecution arises on account of the word, immediately falls away. ²²As for what was sown among thorns, this is the one who hears the word, but the cares of the world and the delight in riches choke the word, and it proves unfruitful. ²³As for what was sown on good soil, this is the one who hears the word and understands it, who indeed bears fruit, and yields, in one case a hundredfold, in another sixty, and in another thirty."

24 Jesus put a parable before them, saying, "The dominion of heaven may be compared to someone who sowed good seed in a field; ²⁵but while everyone was sleeping, an enemy came and sowed weeds among the wheat, and went away. ²⁶So when the plants came up and bore grain, then the weeds appeared also. ²⁷And the servants of the householder came and asked, 'Did you not sow good seed in your field? Why then does it have weeds?' ²⁸The householder said to them, 'An enemy has done this.' The servants replied, 'Then do you want us to go and gather them?' ²⁹But the householder said, 'No; lest in gathering the weeds you root up the wheat along with them. ³⁰Let both grow together until the harvest; and at harvest time I will tell the reapers, Gather the weeds first and bind them in bundles to be burned, but gather the wheat into my barn.'"

31 Another parable he put before them, saying, "The dominion of heaven is like a grain of mustard seed which a man took and sowed in his field; ³²it is the smallest of all seeds, but when it has grown it is the greatest of shrubs and becomes a tree, so that the birds of the air come and make nests in its branches."

33 He told them another parable. "The dominion of heaven is like leaven which a woman took and hid in three measures of meal, till it was all leavened."

34 All this Jesus said to the crowds in parables; indeed he said nothing to them without a parable. ³⁵This was to fulfill what was spoken by the prophet:

"I will open my mouth in parables,
I will utter what has been hidden since the foundation of the world."

36 Then Jesus left the crowds and went into the house. And the disciples came up, saying, "Explain to us the parable of the weeds of the

field." ³⁷Jesus answered, "The one who sows the good seed is the Human One; ³⁸the field is the world, and the good seed means the children of the heavenly dominion; the weeds are the children of the evil one, ³⁹and the enemy who sowed them is the devil; the harvest is the close of the age, and the reapers are angels. ⁴⁰Just as the weeds are gathered and burned with fire, so will it be at the close of the age. ⁴¹The Human One will send angels, and they will gather out of the world all causes of sin and all evildoers, ⁴²and throw them into the furnace of fire, where there will be weeping and gnashing of teeth. ⁴³Then the righteous will shine like the sun in the dominion of their God. Those who have ears, let them hear."

44 "The dominion of heaven is like treasure hidden in a field, which someone found and covered up; then in great joy the finder goes and sells everything and buys that field.

45 "Again, the dominion of heaven is like a merchant in search of fine pearls, ⁴⁶who, on finding one pearl of great value, went and sold everything and bought it.

47 "Again, the dominion of heaven is like a net which was thrown into the sea and gathered fish of every kind; ⁴⁸when the net was full, it was drawn ashore and people sat down and sorted the good into vessels but threw away the bad. ⁴⁹So it will be at the close of the age. The angels will come out and separate the evil from the righteous, ⁵⁰and throw them into the furnace of fire, where there will be weeping and gnashing of teeth.

51 "Have you understood all this?" They answered, "Yes." ⁵²And Jesus said to them, "Therefore every scribe who has been trained for the dominion of heaven is like a householder who brings out of the treasury what is new and what is old."

53 Having finished these parables, Jesus went away from there, ⁵⁴and coming to his own country, taught them in their synagogue, so that they were astonished, and said, "Where did this man get this wisdom and these mighty works? ⁵⁵Is not this the carpenter's son? Is not his mother called Mary? And are not his brothers James and Joseph and Simon and Judas? ⁵⁶And are not all his sisters with us? Where then did this person get all this?" ⁵⁷And they took offense at Jesus. But Jesus said to them, "A prophet is not without honor, except in the prophet's own country, and in the prophet's own house." ⁵⁸And Jesus did not do many mighty works there, because of their unbelief.

14 At that time Herod the tetrarch heard about Jesus' fame, ²and he said to his servants, "This is John the Baptist, he has been raised from the dead; that is why these powers are at work in him." ³For Herod had seized John and bound him and put him in prison, for the sake of Herodias, his brother Philip's wife; ⁴because John said to him, "It is not

lawful for you to have her." ⁵And though Herod wanted to put John to death, he feared the people, because they held John to be a prophet. ⁶But when Herod's birthday came, the daughter of Herodias danced before the company, and pleased Herod, ⁷so that he promised with an oath to give her whatever she might ask. ⁸Prompted by her mother, she said, "Give me the head of John the Baptist here on a platter." ⁹And the king was sorry; but because of his oaths and his guests he commanded it to be given; ¹⁰he sent and had John beheaded in the prison, ¹¹and his head was brought on a platter and given to the girl, and she brought it to her mother. ¹²And John's disciples came and took the body and buried it; and they went and told Jesus.

13 Jesus, having heard this, withdrew from there in a boat to a lonely place apart. But when the crowds heard it, they followed on foot from the towns. ¹⁴Going ashore, Jesus saw a great throng and had compassion on them, and healed their sick. ¹⁵When it was evening, the disciples returned, saying, "This is a lonely place, and the day is now over; send the crowds away to go into the villages and buy food for themselves." ¹⁶Jesus said, "They need not go away; you give them something to eat." ¹⁷They replied, "We have only five loaves here and two fish." ¹⁸Jesus said, "Bring them here to me." ¹⁹Then he ordered the crowds to sit down on the grass; and taking the five loaves and the two fish Jesus looked up to heaven, and blessed, and broke and gave the loaves to the disciples, and the disciples gave them to the crowds. ²⁰And they all ate and were satisfied. And they took up twelve baskets full of the broken pieces left over. ²¹And those who ate were about five thousand men, in addition to women and children.

22 Jesus made the disciples get into the boat and go on ahead to the other side, while he dismissed the crowds. ²³After dismissing the crowds, he went up on the mountain by himself to pray. When evening came, he was there alone, ²⁴but the boat by this time was several hundred yards from the land, beaten by the waves; for the wind was against them. ²⁵And very early in the morning Jesus came to the disciples, walking on the sea. ²⁶But when the disciples saw Jesus walking on the sea, they were terrified, saying, "It is a ghost!" And they cried out in fear. ²⁷But immediately Jesus spoke to them, saying, "Take heart, it is I; have no fear."

28 And Peter answered, "Lord, if it is you, bid me come to you on the water." ²⁹Jesus said, "Come." So Peter got out of the boat and walked on the water and came to Jesus; ³⁰but seeing the wind, Peter was afraid and, beginning to sink, cried out, "Lord, save me." ³¹Jesus immediately reached out and caught Peter, saying, "O you of little faith, why did you doubt?" ³²And when Jesus and Peter got into the boat, the wind ceased. ³³And those in the boat worshiped Jesus, saying, "Truly you are the Child of God."

34 And when they had crossed over, they came to land at Gennesaret. ³⁵And when the citizens of that place recognized Jesus, they sent round to all that region and brought to Jesus all who were sick, ³⁶and they begged Jesus only to touch the fringe of his garment; and as many as touched it were made well.

15 Then Pharisees and scribes came to Jesus from Jerusalem and said, ²"Why do your disciples transgress the tradition of the elders? For they do not wash their hands when they eat." ³Jesus answered them, "And why do you transgress the commandment of God for the sake of your tradition? ⁴For God commanded, 'Honor your father and your mother,' and 'One who speaks evil of father or mother must surely die.' ⁵But you say, 'If people tell their father or mother, What you would have gained from me is given to God, they need not honor their father or mother.' ⁶So, for the sake of your tradition, you have made void the word of God. ⁷You hypocrites! Well did Isaiah prophesy of you, saying:

⁸'This people honors me with their lips,
  but their heart is far from me;
⁹in vain do they worship me,
  teaching human precepts as doctrines.' "

10 And Jesus called the people together and said to them, "Hear and understand: ¹¹not what goes into the mouth defiles a person, but what comes out of the mouth is what defiles." ¹²Then the disciples came and said to Jesus, "Do you know that the Pharisees were offended when they heard this saying?" ¹³Jesus answered, "Every plant which God my heavenly Father and Mother has not planted will be rooted up. ¹⁴Let them alone; they are blind guides. And if one blind person leads another, both will fall into a pit. ¹⁵Peter said to Jesus, "Explain the parable to us." ¹⁶And Jesus said, "Are you also still without understanding? ¹⁷Do you not see that whatever goes into the mouth passes into the stomach, and so passes on? ¹⁸But what comes out of the mouth proceeds from the heart, and this is what defiles. ¹⁹For out of the heart come evil thoughts, murder, adultery, fornication, theft, false witness, slander. ²⁰These are what defile; but to eat with unwashed hands does not defile."

21 And Jesus went away from there and withdrew to the district of Tyre and Sidon. ²²And a Canaanite woman from that region came out and cried, "Have mercy on me, Lord, Child of David, my daughter is severely possessed by a demon." ²³But Jesus did not answer her a word. And the disciples came and begged Jesus, saying, "Send her away, for she is crying after us." ²⁴Jesus answered, "I was sent only to the lost sheep of the house of Israel." ²⁵But she came and knelt before Jesus, saying, "Lord, help me." ²⁶And Jesus answered, "It is not fair to take the children's bread and throw it to the dogs." ²⁷She said, "Yes, Lord, yet even

the dogs eat the crumbs that fall from their owners' table." ²⁸Then Jesus answered her, "O woman, great is your faith! Be it done for you as you desire." And her daughter was healed instantly.

29 Jesus went on from there and walked along the Sea of Galilee. And after going up on the mountain and sitting down, ³⁰great crowds came up, bringing with them those who were lame and maimed, those who were blind and could not speak, and many others, and they put them at Jesus' feet, and Jesus healed them. ³¹The throng then wondered, when they saw those who could not speak speaking, and those who had been maimed whole, and those who had been lame walking, and those who had been blind seeing; and they glorified the God of Israel.

32 Then Jesus called the disciples and said, "I have compassion on the crowd, because they have been with me now three days, and have nothing to eat; and I am unwilling to send them away hungry, lest they faint on the way." ³³And the disciples said to Jesus, "Where are we to get bread enough in the desert to feed so great a crowd?" ³⁴And Jesus said to them, "How many loaves have you?" They said, "Seven, and a few small fish." ³⁵And Jesus commanded the crowd to sit down on the ground, ³⁶and taking the seven loaves and the fish, and having given thanks, Jesus broke them and gave them to the disciples, and the disciples gave them to the crowds. ³⁷And they all ate and were satisfied; and they took up seven baskets full of the broken pieces left over. ³⁸Those who ate were four thousand men, besides women and children. ³⁹And sending away the crowds, Jesus got into the boat and went to the region of Magadan.

16 And the Pharisees and Sadducees came, and to test Jesus they asked him to show them a sign from heaven. ²Jesus answered them, "When it is evening, you say, 'It will be fair weather; for the sky is red.' ³And in the morning, 'It will be stormy today, for the sky is red and threatening.' You know how to interpret the appearance of the sky, but you cannot interpret the signs of the times. ⁴An evil and adulterous generation seeks for a sign, but no sign will be given to it except the sign of Jonah." So Jesus left them and departed.

5 When the disciples reached the other side, they had forgotten to bring any bread. ⁶Jesus said to them, "Take heed and beware of the leaven of the Pharisees and Sadducees." ⁷And they discussed it among themselves, saying, "We brought no bread." ⁸But Jesus, aware of this, said, "O you of little faith, why do you discuss among yourselves the fact that you have no bread? ⁹Do you not yet perceive? Do you not remember the five loaves of the five thousand, and how many baskets you gathered? ¹⁰Or the seven loaves of the four thousand, and how many baskets you gathered? ¹¹How is it that you fail to perceive that I did not speak about bread? Beware of the leaven of the Pharisees and Sadducees." ¹²Then they understood that Jesus did not tell them to be-

ware of the leaven of bread, but of the teaching of the Pharisees and Sadducees.

13 Now coming into the district of Caesarea Philippi, Jesus asked the disciples, "Who do people say that the Human One is?" [14]And they said, "Some say John the Baptist, others say Elijah, and others Jeremiah or one of the prophets." [15]Jesus said to them, "But who do you say that I am?" [16]Simon Peter replied, "You are the Messiah, the Child of the living God." [17]And Jesus answered Peter, "Blessed are you, Simon Bar-Jonah! For flesh and blood has not revealed this to you, but God my Father and Mother who is in heaven. [18]And I tell you, you are Peter, and on this rock I will build my church, and the powers of death shall not prevail against it. [19]I will give you the keys of the dominion of heaven, and whatever you bind on earth will be bound in heaven, and whatever you loose on earth will be loosed in heaven." [20]Then Jesus strictly charged the disciples to say to no one, "Jesus is the Messiah."

21 From that time Jesus began to show the disciples that he must go to Jerusalem and suffer many things from the elders and chief priests and scribes, and be killed, and on the third day be raised. [22]And Peter took Jesus and spoke in rebuke, "God forbid! This shall never happen to you." [23]But Jesus turned and said to Peter, "Get behind me, Satan! You are a hindrance to me; for you are not siding with God, but with humankind."

24 Then Jesus told the disciples, "If any would come after me, let them deny themselves and take up their cross and follow me. [25]For those who would save their life will lose it, and those who lose their life for my sake will find it. [26]For what advantage will it be to gain the whole world and forfeit one's life? Or what will one give in return for one's life? [27]For the Human One is to come with the angels in the heavenly glory of God, and will then repay everyone for their actions. [28]Truly, I say to you, there are some standing here who will not taste death before they see the Human One coming in power and glory."

17 And after six days Jesus took Peter and James and John his brother, and led them up a high mountain apart. [2]Jesus was transfigured before them, and his face shone like the sun, and his garments became brilliant as light. [3]And Moses and Elijah appeared to them, talking with Jesus. [4]And Peter said to Jesus, "Lord, it is well that we are here; if you wish, I will make three booths here, one for you and one for Moses and one for Elijah." [5]Peter was still speaking, when a bright cloud overshadowed them, and a voice from the cloud said, "This is my beloved Child, with whom I am well pleased; to this one you shall listen." [6]When the disciples heard this, they fell on their faces, and were filled with fear. [7]But Jesus came and touched them, saying, "Rise, and have no fear." [8]And when they lifted up their eyes, they saw no one but Jesus only.

9 And as they were coming down the mountain, Jesus commanded them, "Tell no one the vision, until the Human One is raised from the dead." ¹⁰And the disciples asked Jesus, "Then why do the scribes say that first Elijah must come?" ¹¹Jesus replied, "Elijah does come, and is to restore all things; ¹²but I tell you that Elijah has already come, and they did not know him, but did to him whatever they pleased. So also the Human One will suffer at their hands." ¹³Then the disciples understood that Jesus was speaking to them of John the Baptist.

14 And when they came to the crowd, a person came up to Jesus and kneeling before him said, ¹⁵"Lord, have mercy on my son, for he has epilepsy and suffers terribly. Often he falls into the fire, and often into the water. ¹⁶And I brought him to your disciples, and they could not heal him." ¹⁷And Jesus answered, "O faithless and perverse generation, how long am I to be with you? How long am I to bear with you? Bring him here to me." ¹⁸And Jesus rebuked the demon, and it came out of him, and the boy was cured instantly. ¹⁹Then the disciples came to Jesus privately and said, "Why could we not cast it out?" ²⁰Jesus said to them, "Because of your little faith. For truly, I say to you, if you have faith as a grain of mustard seed, you will say to this mountain, 'Move from here to there,' and it will move; and nothing will be impossible to you."*

22 As they were gathering in Galilee, Jesus said to them, "The Human One will be betrayed into human hands, ²³and will be killed, and will be raised on the third day." And they were greatly distressed.

24 When they came to Capernaum, the collectors of the temple tax went up to Peter and said, "Does not your teacher pay the tax?" ²⁵Peter said, "Yes, he does." And when Peter came home, Jesus spoke to him first, saying, "What do you think, Simon? From whom do rulers of the earth take toll or tribute? From their own people or from aliens?" ²⁶And when Peter said, "From aliens," Jesus said to him, "Then the rulers' own people are free. ²⁷However, not to give offense to them, go to the sea and cast a hook, and take the first fish that comes up, and when you open its mouth you will find a silver coin; take that and give it to them for me and for yourself."

18 At that time the disciples came to Jesus, saying, "Who is the greatest in the dominion of heaven?" ²And calling a child, Jesus put it in the midst of them, ³and said, "Truly, I say to you, unless you turn and become like children, you will never enter the dominion of heaven. ⁴Those who humble themselves like this child are the greatest in the dominion of heaven.

5 "All who receive one such child in my name receive me; ⁶but all

* Other ancient authorities add verse 21, *But this kind never comes out except by prayer and fasting.*

who cause one of these little ones who believe in me to sin, it would be better for them to have a great millstone fastened round their neck and to be drowned in the depth of the sea.

7 "Woe to the world for temptations to sin! For it is necessary that temptations come, but woe to the person by whom the temptation comes! 8And if your hand or your foot causes you to sin, cut it off and throw it away; it is better for you to enter life maimed or lame than with two hands or two feet to be thrown into the eternal fire. 9And if your eye causes you to sin, pluck it out and throw it away; it is better for you to enter life with one eye than with two eyes to be thrown into the hell of fire.

10 "See that you do not despise one of these little ones; for I tell you that in heaven their angels always behold the face of God my Father and Mother who is in heaven.* 12What do you think? If a man has a hundred sheep, and one of them has gone astray, does he not leave the ninety-nine on the mountains and go in search of the one that went astray? 13And if he finds it, truly, I say to you, he rejoices over it more than over the ninety-nine that never went astray. 14So it is not the will of God who is in heaven that one of these little ones should perish.

15 "If your neighbor in the church sins against you, go and point out the fault between the two of you alone. If your neighbor listens to you, you have gained your neighbor. 16But if your neighbor does not listen, take one or two others along with you, that every word may be confirmed by the evidence of two or three witnesses. 17If your neighbor refuses to listen to them, tell it to the church; and if your neighbor refuses to listen even to the church, let that neighbor be to you as a Gentile and a tax collector. 18Truly, I say to you, whatever you bind on earth will be bound in heaven, and whatever you loose on earth will be loosed in heaven. 19Again I say to you, if two of you agree on earth about anything they ask, it will be done for them by God my Mother and Father in heaven. 20For where two or three are gathered in my name, there am I in the midst of them."

21 Then Peter came up and said to Jesus, "Lord, how often shall my brother or sister sin against me, and I forgive them? As many as seven times?" 22Jesus answered, "I do not say to you seven times, but seventy times seven.

23 "Therefore the dominion of heaven may be compared to a king who wished to settle accounts with his servants. 24When the king began the reckoning, one servant was brought in owing ten thousand talents; 25and as the servant could not pay, the king ordered the servant to be sold, with spouse and children and all possessions, and payment to be made. 26So the servant fell down and implored, 'Have patience with me,

* Other ancient authorities add verse 11, *For the Human One came to save the lost.*

and I will pay you everything.' 27And out of pity the king released the servant and forgave the debt. 28But that same servant went out, and came upon a coworker who owed the first servant a small sum of money, and seizing the debtor by the throat said, 'Pay what you owe.' 29So the coworker fell down, pleading, 'Have patience with me, and I will pay you.' 30But the first servant refused and went and put the debtor in prison till the debt was paid. 31When the other servants saw what had taken place, they were greatly distressed, and they went and reported to their king all that had taken place. 32Then the king summoned the first servant and said, 'You wicked servant! I forgave you all that debt because you pleaded with me; 33and should not you have had mercy on your coworker, as I had mercy on you?' 34And in anger the king delivered that servant to the jailers, till the debt was paid in full. 35So also my heavenly Father and Mother will do to everyone of you, if you do not forgive your sister or brother from your heart."

19 Having finished these sayings, Jesus went away from Galilee and entered the region of Judea beyond the Jordan; 2and large crowds followed, and Jesus healed them there.

3 And Pharisees came up to Jesus and tested him by asking, "Is it lawful to divorce one's wife for any cause?" 4Jesus answered, "Have you not read that the one who made them from the beginning made them male and female, 5and said, 'For this reason a man shall leave his father and mother and be joined to his wife, and the two shall become one flesh'? 6So they are no longer two but one flesh. What therefore God has joined together, let no one put asunder." 7They said to Jesus, "Why then did Moses command us to give a certificate of divorce before releasing her?" 8Jesus said to them, "For your hardness of heart Moses allowed you to divorce your wives, but from the beginning it was not so. 9And I say to you: whoever divorces his wife, except for unchastity, and marries another, commits adultery."

10 The disciples said to Jesus,"If such is the case of a man with his wife, it is better not to marry." 11But Jesus said to them, "Not all people can receive this saying, but only those to whom it is given. 12For there are eunuchs who have been so from birth, and there are eunuchs who have been made eunuchs by others, and there are eunuchs who have made themselves eunuchs for the sake of the dominion of heaven. Those who are ready to receive this, let them receive it."

13 Then children were brought to Jesus that Jesus might lay hands on them and pray. The disciples rebuked the people; 14but Jesus said, "Let the children come to me, and do not hinder them; for to such belongs the dominion of heaven." 15And Jesus laid hands on them and went away.

16 Then a person came up to Jesus, saying, "Teacher, what good

deed must I do to have eternal life?" ¹⁷Jesus answered, "Why do you ask me about what is good? One there is who is good. If you would enter life, keep the commandments." ¹⁸The person said to Jesus, "Which ones?" And Jesus said, "You shall not kill, You shall not commit adultery, You shall not steal, You shall not bear false witness, ¹⁹Honor your father and mother, and, You shall love your neighbor as yourself." ²⁰The young person said to Jesus, "All these I have observed; what do I still lack?" ²¹Jesus answered, "If you would be perfect, go, sell what you possess and give to the poor, and you will have treasure in heaven; and come, follow me." ²²The young person, having heard this, went away sorrowful, for that person had great possessions.

23 And Jesus said to the disciples, "Truly, I say to you, it will be hard for a rich person to enter the dominion of heaven. ²⁴Again I tell you, it is easier for a camel to go through the eye of a needle than for a rich person to enter the dominion of God." ²⁵When the disciples heard this they were astonished, saying, "Who then can be saved?" ²⁶But Jesus looked at them and said to them, "With human beings this is impossible, but with God all things are possible." ²⁷Then Peter said in reply, "Well, we have left everything and followed you. What then shall we have?" ²⁸Jesus said to them, "Truly, I say to you, in the new world, when the Human One shall sit on a glorious throne, you who have followed me will also sit on twelve thrones, judging the twelve tribes of Israel. ²⁹And everyone who has left houses or brothers or sisters or father or mother or children or lands, for my name's sake, will receive a hundredfold, and inherit eternal life. ³⁰But many that are first will be last, and the last first.

20 "For the dominion of heaven is like a householder who went out early in the morning to hire laborers for the vineyard. ²After agreeing with the laborers for a usual day's pay, the householder sent them into the vineyard. ³And going out about nine o'clock the householder saw others standing idle in the marketplace, ⁴and said to them, 'You go into the vineyard too, and whatever is right I will give you.' So they went. ⁵Going out again about noon and about three o'clock, the householder did the same. ⁶And about five o'clock the householder went out and found others standing, and said to them, 'Why do you stand here idle all day?' ⁷They replied, 'Because no one has hired us.' The householder said to them, 'You go into the vineyard too.' ⁸And when evening came, the owner of the vineyard said to the steward, 'Call the laborers and pay them their wages, beginning with the last, up to the first.' ⁹And when those hired about five o'clock came, each of them received a day's pay. ¹⁰Now when the first came, they thought they would receive more; but each of them also received a day's pay. ¹¹And on receiving it they grumbled at the householder, ¹²saying, 'These last worked only one hour, and you have made them equal to us who have borne the burden

of the day and the scorching heat.' ¹³But the householder replied to one of them, 'Friend, I am doing you no wrong; did you not agree with me for a day's pay? ¹⁴Take what belongs to you, and go; I choose to give to this last as I give to you. ¹⁵Am I not allowed to do what I choose with what belongs to me? Or do you begrudge my generosity?' ¹⁶So the last will be first, and the first last."

17 And going up to Jerusalem Jesus took the twelve disciples aside, and on the way said to them, ¹⁸"See, we are going up to Jerusalem; and the Human One will be delivered to the chief priests and scribes, and will be condemned to death, ¹⁹and delivered to the Gentiles to be mocked and scourged and crucified, and will be raised on the third day.

20 Then the mother of the sons of Zebedee came up to Jesus, with her sons, and kneeling before Jesus she asked for something. ²¹And Jesus said to her, "What do you want?" She answered, "Command that these two sons of mine may sit, one at your right hand and one at your left, in your dominion." ²²But Jesus replied, "You do not know what you are asking. Are you able to drink the cup that I am to drink?" They answered, "We are able." ²³Jesus said to them, "You will drink my cup, but to sit at my right hand and at my left is not mine to grant, but it is for those for whom it has been prepared by my God." ²⁴And when the ten heard it, they were indignant at the two brothers. ²⁵But Jesus called them over and said, "You know that the rulers of the Gentiles lord it over them, and their great people exercise authority over them. ²⁶It will not be that way among you; but whoever would be great among you must be your servant, ²⁷and whoever would be first among you must be your slave; ²⁸even as the Human One came not to be served but to serve, and to give up life as a ransom for many."

29 And as they went out of Jericho, a great crowd followed Jesus. ³⁰And two blind people sitting by the roadside, when they heard that Jesus was passing by, cried out, "Have mercy on us, Child of David!" ³¹The crowd rebuked them, telling them to be silent; but they cried out the more, "Lord, have mercy on us, Child of David!" ³²And Jesus stopped and called them, saying, "What do you want me to do for you?" ³³They said, "Lord, let our eyes be opened." ³⁴And Jesus in pity touched their eyes, and immediately they received their sight and followed Jesus.

21 And when they drew near to Jerusalem and came to Bethphage, to the Mount of Olives, then Jesus sent two disciples, ²saying to them, "Go into the village opposite you, and immediately you will find a donkey tied, and a colt with it; untie them and bring them to me. ³If anyone says anything to you, you will say, 'The Lord has need of them,' and they will be sent immediately." ⁴This took place to fulfill what was spoken by the prophet, saying,

⁵"Tell this to Zion,
Your ruler is coming to you,
humble, and mounted on a donkey,
and on a colt, the foal of a donkey."

⁶The disciples went and did as Jesus had directed them. ⁷They brought the donkey and the colt, and put their garments on them, and Jesus sat on them. ⁸Most of the crowd spread their garments on the road, and others cut branches from the trees and spread them on the road. ⁹And the crowds that went before Jesus and that followed shouted, "Hosanna to the Child of David! Blessed is the one who comes in the name of the Lord! Hosanna in the highest!" ¹⁰And when Jesus entered Jerusalem, all the city was stirred, saying, "Who is this?" ¹¹And the crowds said, "This is the prophet Jesus from Nazareth of Galilee."

12 And Jesus entered the temple of God and drove out all who sold and bought in the temple, and overturned the tables of the money-changers and the seats of those who sold pigeons. ¹³And Jesus said to them, "It is written, 'My house shall be called a house of prayer'; but you make it a den of robbers."

14 And those who were blind and lame came to Jesus in the temple, and were healed. ¹⁵But when the chief priests and the scribes saw the wonderful things that Jesus did, and the children crying out in the temple, "Hosanna to the Child of David!" they were indignant; ¹⁶and they said to Jesus, "Do you hear what these are saying?" And Jesus said to them, "Yes; have you never read,

'Out of the mouth of babes and sucklings
you have brought perfect praise'?"

¹⁷And leaving them, Jesus went out of the city to Bethany and lodged there.

18 In the morning, Jesus was returning to the city and was hungry. ¹⁹And seeing a fig tree by the wayside Jesus went to it, and found nothing on it but leaves only. And Jesus said to it, "May no fruit ever come from you again!" And the fig tree withered at once. ²⁰When the disciples saw it they marveled, saying, "How did the fig tree wither at once?" ²¹Jesus answered them, "Truly, I say to you, if you have faith and never doubt, you will not only do what has been done to the fig tree, but even if you say to this mountain, 'Be taken up and cast into the sea,' it will be done. ²²And whatever you ask in prayer, you will receive, if you have faith."

23 And when Jesus entered the temple, the chief priests and the elders of the people came up as Jesus was teaching, and said, "By what authority are you doing these things, and who gave you this authority?"

24Jesus answered them, "I also will ask you a question; and if you tell me the answer, then I also will tell you by what authority I do these things. 25The baptism of John—was it of divine or human origin?" And they argued with one another, "If we say, 'Of divine origin,' Jesus will answer us, 'Then why did you not believe him?' 26But if we say, 'Of human origin,' we are afraid of the crowd for all hold that John was a prophet." 27So they answered Jesus, "We do not know." And Jesus said to them, "Neither will I tell you by what authority I do these things.

28 "What do you think? Someone who owned a vineyard had two children, and went to the first and said, 'My child, go and work in the vineyard today.' 29And the child answered, 'I will not'; but afterward repented and went. 30And the owner of the vineyard went to the second child and said the same thing; and that child answered, 'I will go,' but did not go. 31Which of the two did the will of the parent?" They said, "The first." Jesus said to them, "Truly, I say to you, the tax collectors and the harlots go into the dominion of God before you. 32For John came to you in the way of righteousness, and you did not believe him, but the tax collectors and the harlots did believe him; and even when you saw it, you did not afterward repent and believe John.

33 "Listen to another parable. There was a householder who planted a vineyard, and set a hedge around it, and dug a wine press in it, and built a tower, and let it out to tenants, and went into another country. 34When the season of fruit drew near, the householder sent servants to the tenants, to get the fruit; 35and the tenants took the servants and beat one, killed another, and stoned another. 36Again the householder sent other servants, more than the first; and they did the same to them. 37Afterward the householder sent the heir to them, the one who would inherit the vineyard, saying, 'They will respect my heir, my very own child.' 38But when the tenants saw the owner's child, they said to themselves, 'This is the heir; come, let us kill this one too and have the inheritance.' 39And they took and cast the heir out of the vineyard, and killed the heir. 40When therefore the owner of the vineyard comes, what will be done to those tenants?" 41Those hearing the parable said to Jesus, "The owner will put those evil people to a miserable death, and let out the vineyard to other tenants who will give the owner the fruits in their seasons."

42 Jesus said to them, "Have you never read in the scriptures:

'The very stone which the builders rejected
has become the head of the corner;
this was the Lord's doing,
and it is marvelous in our eyes'?

43Therefore I tell you, the dominion of God will be taken away from you and given to a nation producing the fruits of it."*

45 When the chief priests and the Pharisees heard Jesus' parables, they perceived that Jesus was speaking about them. 46But when they tried to arrest Jesus, they feared the crowds because they held Jesus to be a prophet.

22 And again Jesus spoke to them in parables, saying, 2"The dominion of heaven may be compared to a king who gave a marriage feast for his son, 3and sent servants to call those who were invited to the marriage feast; but they would not come. 4Again the king sent other servants, saying, 'Tell those who are invited, I have made ready my dinner, my oxen and my fat calves are killed, and everything is ready; come to the marriage feast.' 5But those who were invited made light of it and went off, one to a farm, another to a business, 6while the rest seized the king's servants, treated them shamefully, and killed them. 7The king was angry, and sent his troops and destroyed those murderers and burned their city. 8Then the king said to the servants, 'The wedding is ready, but those invited were not worthy. 9Go therefore to the thoroughfares, and invite to the marriage feast as many as you find.' 10And those servants went out into the streets and gathered all whom they found, both bad and good; so the wedding hall was filled with guests.

11 "But when the king came in to look at the guests, he saw someone who had no wedding garment; 12and the king said, 'Friend, how did you get in here without a wedding garment?' And the guest was speechless. 13Then the king said to the attendants, 'Let the guest be bound hand and foot and cast into the night, where there will be weeping and gnashing of teeth. 14For many are called, but few are chosen."

15 Then the Pharisees went and took counsel how to entangle Jesus in his talk. 16And they sent their disciples to Jesus, along with the Herodians, saying, "Teacher, we know that you are true, and teach the way of God truthfully, and court no one's favor; for you do not regard a person's status. 17Tell us, then, what you think. Is it lawful to pay taxes to Caesar, or not?" 18But Jesus, aware of their evil, said, "Why put me to the test, you hypocrites? 19Show me the money for the tax." And they brought him a coin. 20And Jesus said to them, "Whose likeness and inscription is this?" 21They said, "Caesar's." Then Jesus said to them, "Render therefore to Caesar the things that are Caesar's, and to God the things that are God's." 22When they heard it, they marveled; and they left Jesus and went away.

23 The same day Sadducees, who say that there is no resurrection,

---

* Other ancient authorities add verse 44, *Whoever falls on this stone will be broken to pieces; and it will crush anyone on whom it falls.*

came to Jesus and asked a question, [24]saying, "Teacher, Moses said, 'If a man dies, having no children, his brother must marry the widow, and raise up children for his brother.' [25]Now there were seven brothers among us; the first married, and died, and having no children left his wife to his brother. [26]So too the second and third, down to the seventh. [27]After them all, the woman died. [28]In the resurrection, then, to which of the seven will she be wife? For they were all married to her."

29 But Jesus answered them, "You are wrong, because you know neither the scriptures nor the power of God. [30]For in the resurrection they neither marry nor are given in marriage, but are like angels in heaven. [31]And as for the resurrection of the dead, have you not read what was said to you by God, [32]'I am the God of Abraham, and the God of Isaac, and the God of Jacob'? God is not God of the dead, but of the living." [33]And when the crowd heard it, they were astonished at Jesus' teaching.

34 But when the Pharisees heard that Jesus had silenced the Sadducees, they came together. [35]And one of them, a lawyer, asked Jesus a question, as a test. [36]"Teacher, which is the great commandment in the law?" [37]And Jesus said to him, "You shall love the Lord your God with all your heart, and with all your soul, and with all your mind. [38]This is the great and first commandment. [39]And a second is like it, You shall love your neighbor as yourself [40]On these two commandments depend all the law and the prophets."

41 Now while the Pharisees were gathered together, Jesus asked them a question, [42]saying, "What do you think of the Messiah? Whose offspring is the Messiah?" They said to Jesus, "The offspring of David." [43]Jesus said to them, "How is it then that David, inspired by the Spirit, calls the Messiah, Lord, saying,

> [44]'God said to my Lord,
>   Sit at my right hand,
>   till I put your enemies under your feet'?

[45]If David thus calls the Messiah, Lord, how can the Messiah be David's offspring?" [46]And no one was able to answer Jesus a word, nor from that day did anyone dare to ask Jesus any more questions.

23 Then Jesus said to the crowds and to the disciples, [2]"The scribes and the Pharisees sit on Moses' seat; [3]so practice and observe whatever they tell you, but not what they do; for they preach, but do not practice. [4]They bind heavy burdens, hard to bear, and lay them on people's shoulders; but they themselves will not move them with their finger. [5]They do all their deeds to be seen by others; for they make their phylacteries broad and their fringes long, [6]and they love the place of honor at feasts and the best seats in the synagogues, [7]and salutations

in the marketplaces, and hearing people call them rabbi. [8]But you are not to be called rabbi, for you have one teacher, and you are all brothers and sisters. [9]And call no one on earth by the title 'father,' for you have only one who deserves such a title, God, your heavenly Father and Mother. [10]Neither be called teachers, for you have one teacher, the Messiah. [11]The one who is greatest among you shall be your servant; [12]all who exalt themselves will be humbled, and all who humble themselves will be exalted.

13 "But woe to you, scribes and Pharisees, hypocrites! because you shut the dominion of heaven against others; for you neither enter yourselves, nor allow those who would enter to go in.* [15]Woe to you, scribes and Pharisees, hypocrites! for you traverse sea and land to make a single proselyte, and when you make one, you make it twice as much a child of hell as yourselves.

16 "Woe to you, blind guides, who say, 'If someone swears by the temple it is nothing; but whoever swears by the gold of the temple is bound by their oath.' [17]You blind fools! For which is greater, the gold or the temple that has made the gold sacred? [18]And you say, 'If someone swears by the altar, it is nothing; but whoever swears by the gift that is on the altar is bound by their oath.' [19]You blind people! For which is greater, the gift or the altar that makes the gift sacred? [20]So one who swears by the altar, swears by it and by everything on it; [21]and one who swears by the temple, swears by it and by the one who dwells in it; [22]and one who swears by heaven, swears by the throne of God and by the one who sits upon it.

23 "Woe to you, scribes and Pharisees, hypocrites! for you tithe mint and dill and cumin, and have neglected the weightier matters of the law, justice and mercy and faith; these you ought to have done, without neglecting the others. [24]You blind guides, straining out a gnat and swallowing a camel!

25 "Woe to you, scribes and Pharisees, hypocrites! for you cleanse the outside of the cup and of the plate, but inside they are full of greed and self-indulgence. [26]You blind Pharisee! first cleanse the inside of the cup and of the plate, that the outside also may be clean.

27 "Woe to you, scribes and Pharisees, hypocrites! for you are like whitewashed tombs, which outwardly appear beautiful, but within they are full of dead people's bones and all kinds of uncleanness. [28]So you also outwardly appear righteous to others, but within you are full of hypocrisy and lawlessness.

29 "Woe to you, scribes and Pharisees, hypocrites! for you build the tombs of the prophets and adorn the monuments of the righteous, [30]say-

---

* Other ancient authorities add here (or after verse 12) verse 14, *Woe to you, scribes and Pharisees, hypocrites! for you devour widows' houses and for a pretense you make long prayers; therefore you will receive the greater condemnation.*

ing, 'If we had lived in the days of our ancestors, we would not have taken part with them in shedding the blood of the prophets.' ³¹Thus you witness against yourselves, that you are children of those who murdered the prophets. ³²Fill up, then, the measure of your ancestors. ³³You serpents, you brood of vipers, how are you to escape being sentenced to hell? ³⁴Therefore I send you prophets and wise people and scribes, some of whom you will kill and crucify, and some you will scourge in your synagogues and persecute from town to town, ³⁵that upon you may come all the righteous blood shed on earth, from the blood of innocent Abel to the blood of Zechariah the son of Barachiah, whom you murdered between the sanctuary and the altar. ³⁶Truly, I say to you, all this will come upon this generation.

37 "O Jerusalem, Jerusalem, killing the prophets and stoning those who are sent to you! How often would I have gathered your children together as a hen gathers her brood under her wings, and you would not! ³⁸See, your house is forsaken and desolate. ³⁹For I tell you, you will not see me again, until you say, 'Blessed is the one who comes in the name of the Lord.'"

24 Jesus left the temple and was going away, when the disciples came to point out to him the buildings of the temple. ²But Jesus answered them, "You see all these, do you not? Truly, I say to you, there will not be left here one stone upon another, that will not be thrown down."

3 As Jesus sat on the Mount of Olives, the disciples came up privately, saying, "Tell us, when will this be, and what will be the sign of your coming and of the close of the age?" ⁴And Jesus answered them, "Take heed that no one leads you astray. ⁵For many will come in my name, saying 'I am the Messiah,' and they will lead many astray. ⁶And you will hear of wars and rumors of wars; see that you are not alarmed; for this must take place, but the end is not yet. ⁷For nation will rise against nation, and kingdom against kingdom, and there will be famines and earthquakes in various places: ⁸all this is but the beginning of the birth pangs.

9 "Then they will deliver you up to tribulation, and put you to death; and you will be hated by all nations for my name's sake. ¹⁰And then many will fall away, and betray one another, and hate one another. ¹¹And many false prophets will arise and lead many astray. ¹²And because wickedness is multiplied, most people's love will grow cold. ¹³But the one who endures to the end will be saved. ¹⁴And this gospel of the dominion will be preached throughout the whole world, as a testimony to all nations; and then the end will come.

15 "So when you see the desolating sacrilege spoken of by the prophet Daniel, standing in the holy place (let the reader understand),

¹⁶then let those who are in Judea flee to the mountains; ¹⁷let one who is on the housetop not go down to take what is in one's house; ¹⁸and let one who is in the field not turn back to take one's mantle. ¹⁹And alas for those who are with child and for those who give suck in those days! ²⁰Pray that your flight may not be in winter or on a sabbath. ²¹For then there will be great tribulation, such as has not been from the beginning of the world until now, no, and never will be. ²²And if those days had not been shortened, no human being would be saved; but for the sake of the elect those days will be shortened. ²³Then if anyone says to you, 'See, here is the Messiah!' or 'There is the Messiah!' do not believe it. ²⁴For false Messiahs and false prophets will arise and show great signs and wonders, so as to lead astray, if possible, even the elect. ²⁵Look, I have told you beforehand. ²⁶So, if they say to you, 'See, the Messiah is in the wilderness,' do not go out; if they say, 'See, the Messiah is in the inner rooms,' do not believe it. ²⁷For as the lightning comes from the east and shines as far as the west, so will be the coming of the Human One. ²⁸Wherever the corpse is, there the vultures will be gathered together.

29 "Immediately after the tribulation of those days the sun will be darkened, and the moon will not give its light, and the stars will fall from heaven, and the powers of the heavens will be shaken; ³⁰then will appear the sign of the Human One in heaven, and then all the tribes of the earth will mourn, and they will see the Human One coming on the clouds of heaven with power and great glory; ³¹and that one will send out angels with a loud trumpet call, and they will gather the elect of the Human One from the four winds, from one end of heaven to the other.

32 "From the fig tree learn its lesson: as soon as its branch becomes tender and puts forth its leaves, you know that summer is near. ³³So, also, when you see all these things, you know that the coming one is near, at the very gates. ³⁴Truly, I say to you, this generation will not pass away till all these things take place. ³⁵Heaven and earth will pass away, but my words will not pass away.

36 "But of that day and hour no one knows, not even the angels of heaven, nor God's Child, but God only. ³⁷As were the days of Noah, so will be the coming of the Human One. ³⁸For as in those days before the flood they were eating and drinking, marrying and giving in marriage, until the day when Noah entered the ark, ³⁹and they did not know until the flood came and swept them all away, so will be the coming of the Human One. ⁴⁰Then two men are in the field; one is taken and one is left. ⁴¹Two women are grinding at the mill; one is taken and one is left. ⁴²Watch, for you do not know on what day your Lord is coming. ⁴³But know this, that if the householder had known in what part of the night the thief was coming, that householder would have watched and would not have let the house be broken into. ⁴⁴Therefore you also must be ready; for the Human One is coming at an hour you do not expect.

45 "Who then is the faithful and wise servant, who has been set over the master's household, to give them their food at the proper time? ⁴⁶Blessed is that servant whose master, when he comes, will find so doing. ⁴⁷Truly, I say to you, he will set his servant over all his possessions. ⁴⁸But if that wicked servant thinks, 'My master is delayed,' ⁴⁹and begins to beat other servants, and eats and drinks with the drunken, ⁵⁰the master of that servant will come on a day the servant does not expect, and at an hour the servant does not know, ⁵¹and will punish the servant, and put the servant with the hypocrites; there people will weep and gnash their teeth.

25 "Then the dominion of heaven will be compared to ten young women who took their lamps and went to meet the bridegroom. ²Five of them were foolish, and five were wise. ³For when the foolish took their lamps, they took no oil with them; ⁴but the wise took flasks of oil with their lamps. ⁵As the bridegroom was delayed, they all slumbered and slept. ⁶But at midnight there was a cry, 'Look, the bridegroom! Come out to meet him.' ⁷Then all the women rose and trimmed their lamps. ⁸And the foolish said to the wise, 'Give us some of your oil, for our lamps are going out.' ⁹But the wise replied, 'Perhaps there will not be enough for us and for you; go rather to the dealers and buy for yourselves.' ¹⁰And while they went to buy, the bridegroom came, and those who were ready went in with him to the marriage feast; and the door was shut. ¹¹Afterward the other young women came also, saying, 'Lord, Lord, open to us.' ¹²But the bridegroom replied, 'Truly, I say to you, I do not know you.' ¹³Watch therefore, for you know neither the day nor the hour.

14 "For it will be as when someone going on a journey called in servants and entrusted to them some money, ¹⁵giving to one five talents, to another two, to another one, to each according to their ability, and then went away. ¹⁶The one who had received the five talents went at once and traded with the money, and made five talents more. ¹⁷So also, the one who had the two talents made two talents more. ¹⁸But the one who had received the one talent went and dug in the ground and hid the money. ¹⁹Now after a long time the master of those servants returned and settled accounts with them. ²⁰And the servant who had received the five talents came forward, bringing five talents more, saying, 'Master, you delivered to me five talents; here I have made five talents more.' ²¹The master said, 'Well done, good and faithful servant; you have been faithful over a little, I will set you over much; enter into the joy of your master.' ²²And the one also who had the two talents came forward, saying, 'Master, you delivered to me two talents; here I have made two talents more.' ²³The reply came, 'Well done, good and faithful servant; you have been faithful over a little, I will set you over much; enter into

the joy of your master.' ²⁴The one who had received the one talent came forward, saying, 'Master, I knew you to be a demanding person, reaping where you did not sow, and gathering where you did not winnow; ²⁵so I was afraid, and I went and hid your talent in the ground. Here you have what is yours.' ²⁶But the master answered, 'You wicked and slothful servant! You knew that I reap where I have not sowed, and gather where I have not winnowed? ²⁷Then you ought to have invested my money with the bankers, and at my coming I would have received what was my own with interest. ²⁸So take back the talent, and give it to the one who has the ten talents. ²⁹For to all who have will more be given, and they will have abundance; but from all who have not, even what they have will be taken away. ³⁰And cast the worthless servant into the outer regions, where there will be weeping and gnashing of teeth.'

31 "When the Human One comes in glory, with all the angels, then that one will sit on a glorious throne. ³²All the nations will be gathered before the Human One, who will separate them one from another as a shepherd separates the sheep from the goats, ³³placing the sheep on the right, but the goats on the left. ³⁴Then the ruler will say to those on the right, 'Come, O blessed of God my Father and Mother, inherit the dominion prepared for you from the foundation of the world; ³⁵for I was hungry and you gave me food, I was thirsty and you gave me drink, I was a stranger and you welcomed me, ³⁶I was naked and you clothed me, I was sick and you visited me, I was in prison and you came to me.' ³⁷Then the righteous will answer, 'Lord, when did we see you hungry and feed you, or thirsty and give you drink? ³⁸And when did we see you a stranger and welcome you, or naked and clothe you? ³⁹And when did we see you sick or in prison and visit you?' ⁴⁰And the ruler will answer them, 'Truly, I say to you, as you did it to one of the least of these my sisters and brothers, you did it to me.' ⁴¹Then the ruler will say to those on the left, 'Depart from me, you cursed, into the eternal fire prepared for the devil and the devil's angels; ⁴²for I was hungry and you gave me no food, I was thirsty and you gave me no drink, ⁴³I was a stranger and you did not welcome me, naked and you did not clothe me, sick and in prison and you did not visit me.' ⁴⁴Then they also will answer, 'Lord, when did we see you hungry or thirsty or a stranger or naked or sick or in prison, and did not minister to you?' ⁴⁵Then the ruler will answer them, 'Truly, I say to you, as you did it not to one of the least of these, you did it not to me.' ⁴⁶And they will go away into eternal punishment, but the righteous into eternal life."

26 Having finished all these sayings, Jesus said to the disciples, ²"You know that after two days the Passover is coming, and the Human One will be delivered up to be crucified."

3 Then the chief priests and the elders of the people gathered in the

palace of the high priest, who was called Caiaphas, ⁴and took counsel together in order to arrest Jesus by treachery and kill him. ⁵But they said, "Not during the feast, lest there be a tumult among the people."

6 Now when Jesus was at Bethany in the house of Simon who was leprous, ⁷a woman came up with an alabaster flask of very expensive ointment, and she poured it on Jesus' head, as Jesus sat at table. ⁸But when the disciples saw it, they were indignant, saying, "Why this waste? ⁹For this ointment might have been sold for a large sum, and given to the poor." ¹⁰But Jesus, aware of this, said to them, "Why do you trouble the woman? For she has done a beautiful thing to me. ¹¹For you always have the poor with you, but you will not always have me. ¹²In pouring this ointment on my body she has done it to prepare me for burial. ¹³Truly, I say to you, wherever this gospel is preached in the whole world, what she has done will be told in memory of her."

14 Then one of the twelve, who was called Judas Iscariot, went to the chief priests ¹⁵and said, "What will you give me if I deliver Jesus to you?" And they paid Judas thirty pieces of silver. ¹⁶And from that moment he sought an opportunity to betray Jesus.

17 Now on the first day of Unleavened Bread the disciples came to Jesus, saying, "Where will you have us prepare for you to eat the passover?" ¹⁸Jesus replied, "Go into the city to a certain one, and say, 'The Teacher says, My time is at hand; I will keep the passover at your house with my disciples.' " ¹⁹And the disciples did as Jesus had directed them, and they prepared the passover.

20 When it was evening, Jesus sat at table with the twelve disciples, ²¹and as they were eating, said, "Truly, I say to you, one of you will betray me." ²²And they were very sorrowful, and began to say to Jesus one after another, "Is it I, Lord?" ²³Jesus answered, "The one who has dipped a hand in the dish with me, will betray me. ²⁴The Human One goes as it is written, but woe to that person by whom the Human One is betrayed! It would have been better for that one not to have been born." ²⁵Judas, who betrayed Jesus, said, "Is it I, Teacher?" Jesus said to him, "You have said so."

26 Now as they were eating, Jesus took bread, and blessed, and broke it, and gave it to the disciples and said, "Take, eat; this is my body." ²⁷Then taking a cup, and having given thanks, Jesus gave it to them, saying, "Drink of it, all of you; ²⁸for this is my blood of the covenant, which is pᵣ·ᵣred out for many for the forgiveness of sins. ²⁹I tell you I will not drink again of this fruit of the vine until that day when I drink it new with you in the dominion of God."

30 And when they had sung a hymn, they went out to the Mount of Olives. ³¹Then Jesus said to them, "You will all fall away because of me this night; for it is written, 'I will strike the shepherd, and the sheep of the flock will be scattered.' ³²But after I am raised up, I will go before you

to Galilee." ³³Peter declared to Jesus, "Though they all fall away because of you, I will never fall away." ³⁴Jesus said to him, "Truly, I say to you, this very night, before the cock crows, you will deny me three times." ³⁵Peter said to Jesus, "Even if I must die with you, I will not deny you." And so said all the disciples.

36 Then Jesus went with them to a place called Gethsemane, and said to the disciples. "Sit here, while I go over there and pray." ³⁷And taking Peter and the two sons of Zebedee, he began to be sorrowful and troubled. ³⁸Then Jesus said to them, "My soul is very sorrowful, even to death; remain here, and watch with me." ³⁹And going a little farther Jesus fell to the ground and prayed, "God my Father and Mother, if it be possible, let this cup pass from me; nevertheless, not as I will, but as you will." ⁴⁰And he came and found them sleeping, and said to Peter, "So, could you not watch with me one hour? ⁴¹Watch and pray that you may not enter into temptation; the spirit indeed is willing, but the flesh is weak." ⁴²Again, for the second time, Jesus went away and prayed, "God my Father and Mother, if this cannot pass unless I drink it, your will be done." ⁴³And again he came and found them sleeping, for their eyes were heavy. ⁴⁴So, leaving them again, Jesus went away and prayed for the third time, saying the same words. ⁴⁵Then coming to the disciples Jesus said to them, "Are you still sleeping and taking your rest? Look, the hour is at hand, and the Human One is betrayed into the hands of sinners. ⁴⁶Rise, let us be going; see, my betrayer is at hand."

47 While Jesus was still speaking, Judas came, one of the twelve, and with him a great crowd with swords and clubs, from the chief priests and the elders of the people. ⁴⁸Now the betrayer had given them a sign, saying, "The one I will kiss is the person; seize him." ⁴⁹And Judas came up to Jesus at once and said, "Greetings, Teacher!" And Judas kissed him. ⁵⁰Jesus said to Judas, "Friend, why are you here?" Then they came up and laid hands on Jesus and seized him. ⁵¹And one of those who were with Jesus stretched out his hand and drew a sword, and struck the slave of the high priest, and cut off his ear. ⁵²Then Jesus said to the disciple, "Put your sword back into its place; for all who take the sword will perish by the sword. ⁵³Do you think that I cannot appeal to God my Father and Mother, who will at once send me more than twelve legions of angels? ⁵⁴But how then should the scriptures be fulfilled, that it must be so?" ⁵⁵At that hour Jesus said to the crowds, "Have you come out as against a robber, with swords and clubs to capture me? Day after day I sat in the temple teaching, and you did not seize me. ⁵⁶But all this has taken place, that the scriptures of the prophets might be fulfilled." Then all the disciples forsook him and fled.

57 Then those who had seized Jesus led him to Caiaphas the high priest, where the scribes and the elders had gathered. ⁵⁸But Peter followed Jesus at a distance, as far as the courtyard of the high priest, and

going inside Peter sat with the guards to see the end. ⁵⁹Now the chief priests and the whole council sought false testimony against Jesus that they might put him to death, ⁶⁰but they found none, though many false witnesses came forward. At last two came forward ⁶¹and said, "This person said, 'I am able to destroy the temple of God, and to build it in three days.' " ⁶²And the high priest stood up and said, "Have you no answer to make? What is it that these people testify against you?" ⁶³But Jesus was silent. And the high priest said to him, "I adjure you by the living God, tell us if you are the Messiah, the Child of God." ⁶⁴Jesus replied, "You have said so. But I tell you, hereafter you will see the Human One seated at the right hand of Power, and coming on the clouds of heaven." ⁶⁵Then the high priest tore his robes, and said, "He has uttered blasphemy. Why do we still need witnesses? You have now heard the blasphemy. ⁶⁶What is your judgment?" They answered, "He deserves death." ⁶⁷Then they spat in Jesus' face, and struck him; and some slapped him, ⁶⁸saying, "Prophesy to us, you Messiah! Who is it that struck you?"

69 Now Peter was sitting outside in the courtyard. And a maid came up and said, "You also were with Jesus the Galilean." ⁷⁰But Peter denied it before them all, saying, "I do not know what you mean." ⁷¹And when Peter went out to the porch, another maid saw him, and she said to the bystanders, "This one was with Jesus of Nazareth." ⁷²And again Peter denied it with an oath, "I do not know the man." ⁷³After a little while the bystanders came up and said to Peter, "Certainly you are also one of them, for your accent betrays you." ⁷⁴Then Peter began to invoke a curse on himself and to swear, "I do not know the man." And immediately the cock crowed. ⁷⁵And Peter remembered the saying of Jesus, "Before the cock crows, you will deny me three times." And Peter went out and wept bitterly.

27 When the morning came, all the chief priests and the elders of the people took counsel against Jesus to put him to death; ²and they bound him and led him away and delivered him to Pilate the governor.

3 When Judas, the betrayer, saw that Jesus was condemned, Judas repented and brought back the thirty pieces of silver to the chief priests and the elders, ⁴saying, "I have sinned in betraying innocent blood." They said, "What is that to us? See to it yourself." ⁵And throwing down the pieces of silver in the temple, Judas departed, and went and hanged himself. ⁶But the chief priests, taking the pieces of silver, said, "It is not lawful to put them into the treasury, since they are blood money." ⁷So they took counsel, and bought with them the potter's field, to bury strangers in. ⁸Therefore that field has been called the Field of Blood to this day. ⁹Then was fulfilled what had been spoken by the prophet Jeremiah, saying, "And they took the thirty pieces of silver, the price of the one on whom a price had been set by some of the chil-

dren of Israel, [10]and they gave them for the potter's field, as the Lord directed me."

11 Now Jesus stood before the governor; and the governor asked, "Are you the King of the Jews?" Jesus said, "You have said so." [12]But when accused by the chief priests and elders, Jesus made no answer. [13]Then Pilate said to him, "Do you not hear how many things they testify against you?" [14]But Jesus gave Pilate no answer, not even to a single charge; so that the governor wondered greatly.

15 Now at the feast the governor was accustomed to release for the crowd any one prisoner whom they wanted. [16]And they had then a notorious prisoner, called Barabbas. [17]So when they had gathered, Pilate said to them, "Whom do you want me to release for you, Barabbas or Jesus who is called Messiah?" [18]For he knew it was out of envy that they had delivered up Jesus. [19]Besides, while Pilate was sitting on the judgment seat, his wife sent word, "Have nothing to do with that righteous person, for I have suffered much over him today in a dream." [20]Now the chief priests and the elders persuaded the people to ask for Barabbas and destroy Jesus. [21]The governor again said to them, "Which of the two do you want me to release for you?" And they said, "Barabbas." [22]Pilate said to them, "Then what shall I do with Jesus who is called Messiah?" They all said, "Let him be crucified." [23]And Pilate said, "Why, what evil has he done?" But they shouted all the more, "Let him be crucified."

24 So when Pilate saw that nothing was being gained, but rather that a riot was beginning, he took water and washed his hands before the crowd, saying, "I am innocent of this one's blood; see to it yourselves." [25]And all the people answered, "His blood be on us and on our children!" [26]Then Pilate released for them Barabbas, and having scourged Jesus, delivered him to be crucified.

27 Then the soldiers of the governor took Jesus into the praetorium, and they gathered the whole battalion before him. [28]And they stripped him and put a scarlet robe upon him, [29]and plaiting a crown of thorns they put it on his head, and put a reed in his right hand. And kneeling down, they mocked Jesus, saying "Hail, King of the Jews!" [30]And they spat upon him, and took the reed and struck him on the head. [31]And when they had mocked Jesus, they stripped him of the robe, and put his own clothes on him, and led him away to be crucified.

32 As they went out, they came upon a Cyrenian, Simon by name, whom they compelled to carry Jesus' cross. [33]And when they came to a place called Golgotha (which means the place of a skull), [34]they offered Jesus wine to drink, mingled with gall; but after tasting it, he would not drink it. [35]And when they had crucified him, they divided his garments among them by casting lots; [36]then they sat down and kept watch over him there. [37]And over Jesus' head they put the charge against him, which read, "This is Jesus the King f the Jews." [38]Then two robbers were

crucified with him, one on the right and one on the left. [39]And those who passed by derided him, wagging their heads [40]any saying, "You who would destroy the temple and build it in three days, save yourself! If you are the Child of God, come down from the cross." [41]So also the chief priests, with the scribes and elders, mocked Jesus, saying, [42]"This one saved others, but cannot save himself. He is the King of Israel; let him come down now from the cross , and we will believe in him. [43]He trusts in God; let God deliver him now, if God desires to; for he said, 'I am the Child of God.' " [44]And the robbers who were crucified with Jesus also reviled him in the same way.

45 Now from noon there was darkness over all the land until three o'clock. [46]And about three o'clock Jesus cried with a loud voice, "Eli, Eli, lama sabachthani?" that is, "My God, my God, why have you forsaken me?" [47]And some of the bystanders hearing it said, "He is calling Elijah." [48]And one of them at once ran and took a sponge, filled it with vinegar, and put it on a reed, and gave it to Jesus to drink. [49]But the others said, "Wait, let us see whether Elijah will come to save him." [50]And Jesus cried again with a loud voice and yielded up his spirit.

51 And with that, the curtain of the temple was torn in two, from top to bottom; and the earth shook, and the rocks were split; [52]the tombs also were opened, and many bodies of the saints who had fallen asleep were raised, [53]and coming out of the tombs after Jesus' resurrection they went into the holy city and appeared to many. [54]When the centurion and those who were with him, keeping watch over Jesus, saw the earthquake and what took place, they were filled with awe, and said, "Truly this was the Child of God!"

55 There were also many women there, looking on from afar, who had followed Jesus from Galilee, ministering to him; [56]among whom were Mary Magdalene, and Mary the mother of James and Joseph, and the mother of the sons of Zebedee.

57 When it was evening, a rich man came from Arimathea, named Joseph, who also was a disciple of Jesus. [58]Joseph went to Pilate and asked for the body of Jesus. Then Pilate ordered it to be given to him. [59]And Joseph took the body, and wrapped it in a clean linen shroud, [60]and laid it in his own new tomb, which he had hewn in the rock; and he rolled a great stone to the door of the tomb, and departed. [61]Mary Magdalene and the other Mary were there, sitting opposite the sepulchre.

62 Next day, that is, after the day of Preparation, the chief priests and the Pharisees gathered before Pilate [63]and said, "Sir, we remember how that impostor, while still alive, said, 'After three days I will rise again.' [64]Therefore order the sepulchre to be made secure until the third day, lest the disciples go and steal the body, and tell the people, 'He has risen from the dead,' and the last fraud will be worse than the first." [65]Pilate

said to them, "You have a guard of soldiers; go, make it as secure as you can." ⁶⁶So they went and made the sepulchre secure by sealing the stone and setting a guard.

28 Now after the sabbath, toward the dawn of the first day of the week, Mary Magdalene and the other Mary went to see the sepulchre. ²And there was a great earthquake; for an angel of God descended from heaven and came and rolled back the stone, and sat upon it. ³The angel's appearance was like lightning, and its raiment white as snow. ⁴And for fear of the angel the guards trembled and became like dead people. ⁵But the angel said to the women, "Do not be afraid; for I know that you seek Jesus who was crucified. ⁶Jesus is not here, but has risen, as he said. Come, see the place where Jesus lay. ⁷Then go quickly and tell the disciples that Jesus has risen from the dead, and even now is going before you to Galilee. There you will see Jesus. Indeed, I have told you." ⁸So they departed quickly from the tomb with fear and great joy, and ran to tell the disciples. ⁹And then Jesus met them and said, "Hail!" And they came up and took hold of Jesus' feet and worshiped Jesus. ¹⁰Then Jesus said to them, "Do not be afraid; go and tell my followers to go to Galilee, and there they will see me."

11 While they were going, some of the guard went into the city and told the chief priests all that had taken place. ¹²And when they had assembled with the elders and taken counsel, they gave a sum of money to the soldiers ¹³and said, "Tell people, 'Jesus' disciples came by night and stole Jesus away while we were asleep.' ¹⁴And if this comes to the governor's ears, we will satisfy him and keep you out of trouble." ¹⁵So they took the money and did as they were directed; and this story has been spread among the Jews to this day.

16 Now the eleven disciples went to Galilee, to the mountain to which Jesus had directed them. ¹⁷And when they saw Jesus they worshiped Jesus; but some doubted. ¹⁸And Jesus came and said to them, "All authority in heaven and on earth has been given to me. ¹⁹Go therefore and make disciples of all nations, baptizing them in the name of God the Father and Mother, and of Jesus Christ the beloved Child, and of the Holy Spirit, ²⁰teaching them to observe all that I have commanded you; and I am with you always, to the close of the age."

Mark

1 The beginning of the gospel of Jesus Christ, the Child of God.
2 As it is written in Isaiah the prophet,

"See, I am sending my messenger before your face,
who shall prepare your way;
³the voice of one crying in the wilderness:
Prepare the way of the Lord,
make the paths of the Lord straight—"

⁴John the baptizer appeared in the wilderness, preaching a baptism of repentance for the forgiveness of sins. ⁵And all the country of Judea went out to John, and all the people of Jerusalem; and they were baptized by him in the river Jordan, confessing their sins. ⁶Now John was clothed with camel's hair, and had a leather girdle around his waist, and ate locusts and wild honey. ⁷And he preached, saying, "After me comes the one who is mightier than I, the thong of whose sandals I am not worthy to stoop down and untie. ⁸I have baptized you with water; but the one who comes will baptize you with the Holy Spirit."

9 In those days Jesus came from Nazareth of Galilee and was baptized by John in the Jordan. ¹⁰And having come up out of the water, immediately Jesus saw the heavens opened and the Spirit descending upon him like a dove; ¹¹and a voice came from heaven, "You are my beloved Child; with you I am well pleased."

12 The Spirit immediately drove Jesus out into the wilderness. ¹³And Jesus was in the wilderness forty days, tempted by Satan; and he was with the wild beasts; and the angels ministered to him.

14 Now after John was arrested, Jesus came into Galilee, preaching the gospel of God, ¹⁵and saying, "The time is fulfilled, and the dominion of God is at hand; repent, and believe in the gospel."

16 And passing along by the Sea of Galilee, Jesus saw Simon, and Andrew the brother of Simon, casting a net in the sea; for they were fishers. ¹⁷And Jesus said to them, "Follow me and I will make you become fishers of people." ¹⁸And immediately they left their nets and followed him. ¹⁹And going on a little farther, Jesus saw James the son of Zebedee and John his brother, who were in their boat mending the nets. ²⁰And immediately Jesus called them; and they left their father Zebedee in the boat with the hired help, and followed Jesus.

21 And they went into Capernaum; and immediately on the sabbath Jesus entered the synagogue and taught. ²²And they were astonished at Jesus' teaching, for he taught them as one who had authority, and not as the scribes. ²³And immediately there was in their synagogue someone with an unclean spirit ²⁴who cried out, "What have you to do with us, Jesus of Nazareth? Have you come to destroy us? I know who you are, the Holy One of God." ²⁵But Jesus rebuked the spirit, saying, "Be silent, and come out!" ²⁶And the unclean spirit, convulsing the person and crying with a loud voice, came out. ²⁷And they were all amazed, so that they questioned among themselves, saying, "What is this? A new teaching! With authority Jesus commands even the unclean spirits, and they obey." ²⁸And at once Jesus' fame spread everywhere throughout all the surrounding region of Galilee.

29 And immediately Jesus left the synagogue, and entered the house of Simon and Andrew, with James and John. ³⁰Now Simon's mother-in-law lay sick with a fever, and immediately they told Jesus of her. ³¹And Jesus came and took her by the hand and lifted her up, and the fever left her; and she served them.

32 That evening, at sundown, they brought to Jesus all who were sick or possessed with demons. ³³And the whole city was gathered together about the door. ³⁴And Jesus healed many who were sick with various diseases, and cast out many demons, and would not permit the demons to speak, because they knew him.

35 And in the morning, a great while before day, Jesus rose and went out to a lonely place, and there Jesus prayed. ³⁶And Simon and those who were with him pursued Jesus, ³⁷and they found him and said, "Everyone is searching for you." ³⁸And Jesus replied, "Let us go on to the next towns, that I may preach there also; for that is why I came out." ³⁹And Jesus went throughout all Galilee, preaching in their synagogues and casting out demons.

40 A person with leprosy came beseeching Jesus, and kneeling said to him, "If you will, you can make me clean." ⁴¹Moved with pity, Jesus reached out and touched the person, and said, "I will; be clean." ⁴²And immediately the leprosy went away and the person was made clean. ⁴³And Jesus sternly charged and sent away the one whom he had healed, ⁴⁴saying, "See that you say nothing to anyone; but go, show yourself to

the priest, and offer for your cleansing what Moses commanded, for a proof to the people." ⁴⁵But the one who had been healed went out and began to talk freely about it, and to spread the news, so that Jesus could no longer openly enter a town, but was out in the country; and people came to Jesus from every quarter.

2 And when Jesus returned to Capernaum after some days, it was reported that he was at home. ²And many were gathered together, so that there was no longer room for them, not even about the door; and Jesus was preaching the word to them. ³And some people came, bringing to Jesus a person who was paralyzed, carried by four men. ⁴And when they could not get near Jesus because of the crowd, they removed the roof above him; and when they had made an opening, they let down the pallet on which the person lay. ⁵And having seen their faith, Jesus said to the one who was paralyzed, "My child, your sins are forgiven." ⁶Now some of the scribes were sitting there, questioning in their hearts, ⁷"Why does this man speak thus? It is blasphemy! Who can forgive sins but God alone?" ⁸And immediately Jesus, perceiving in his spirit that they thus questioned within themselves, said to them, "Why do you question this way in your hearts? ⁹Which is easier, to say to the one paralyzed, 'Your sins are forgiven,' or to say, 'Rise, take up your pallet and walk'? ¹⁰But that you may know that the Human One has authority on earth to forgive sins"—Jesus said to the one who was paralyzed—¹¹"I say to you, rise, take up your pallet and go home." ¹²And the one who had been paralyzed arose, and immediately took up the pallet and went out before them all; so that they were all amazed and glorified God, saying, "We never saw anything like this!"

13 Jesus went out again beside the sea; and all the crowd gathered around, and he taught them. ¹⁴And walking on, Jesus saw Levi the son of Alphaeus sitting at the tax office, and Jesus said to him, "Follow me." And Levi rose and followed Jesus.

15 And as Jesus sat at table in Levi's house, many tax collectors and sinners were sitting with Jesus and the disciples; for there were many who followed him. ¹⁶And the scribes of the Pharisees, when they saw that Jesus was eating with sinners and tax collectors, said to the disciples, "Why does Jesus eat with tax collectors and sinners?" ¹⁷And when Jesus heard it, he said to them, "Those who are well have no need of a physician, but those who are sick; I came not to call the righteous, but sinners."

18 Now John's disciples and the Pharisees were fasting; and people came and said to Jesus, "Why do John's disciples and the disciples of the Pharisees fast, but your disciples do not fast?" ¹⁹And Jesus said to them, "Can the wedding guests fast while the bridegroom is with them? As long as they have the bridegroom with them, they cannot fast. ²⁰The

days will come, when the bridegroom is taken away from them, and then they will fast in that day. 21No one sews a piece of unshrunk cloth on an old garment; if one does, the patch tears away from it, the new from the old, and a worse tear is made. 22And no one puts new wine into old wineskins; if one does, the wine will burst the skins, and the wine is lost, and so are the skins; but new wine is for fresh skins."

23 One sabbath Jesus was going through the grainfields; and as they made their way the disciples began to pluck heads of grain. 24And the Pharisees said to Jesus, "Look, why are they doing what is not lawful on the sabbath?" 25And Jesus said to them, "Have you never read what David did, when in need and hungry, he and those who were with him: 26how David entered the house of God, when Abiathar was high priest, and ate the bread of the Presence, which it is not lawful for any but the priests to eat, and also gave it to those who were with him?" 27And Jesus said to them, "The sabbath was made for the human being, not the human being for the sabbath; 28so the Human One is lord even of the sabbath."

3 Again Jesus entered the synagogue, and a person was there who had a withered hand. 2And they watched, to see whether Jesus would heal on the sabbath, so that they might accuse him. 3And Jesus said to the one who had the withered hand, "Come here." 4Then Jesus said to them, "Is it lawful on the sabbath to do good or to do harm, to save life or to kill?" But they were silent. 5And looking around at them with anger, grieved at their hardness of heart, Jesus said to the person, "Stretch out your hand." The one with the withered hand stretched it out, and it was restored. 6The Pharisees went out, and immediately held counsel with the Herodians against Jesus, how to destroy him.

7 Jesus withdrew with the disciples to the sea, and a great crowd from Galilee followed; also from Judea 8and Jerusalem and Idumea, and from beyond the Jordan, and from about Tyre and Sidon a great crowd, hearing all that Jesus did, came to him. 9And Jesus told the disciples to have a boat ready because of the crowd, lest they should crush him; 10for Jesus had healed many, so that all who had diseases pressed near to touch him. 11And whenever the unclean spirits beheld Jesus, they fell down before him and cried out, "You are the Child of God." 12And Jesus strictly ordered them not to make him known.

13 And Jesus went up on the mountain and called those whom he desired; and they came to Jesus. 14And Jesus appointed twelve, to be with him, and to be sent out to preach 15and have authority to cast out demons: 16Simon whom Jesus surnamed Peter; 17James the son of Zebedee and John the brother of James, whom Jesus surnamed Boanerges, that is, sons of thunder; 18Andrew, and Philip, and Bartholomew, and Matthew, and Thomas, and James the son of Alphaeus, and Thad-

daeus, and Simon the Cananaean, ¹⁹and Judas Iscariot, who betrayed Jesus.

Then Jesus went home; ²⁰and the crowd came together again, so that they could not even eat. ²¹And when Jesus' family heard it, they went out to seize him, for people were saying, "He is beside himself." ²²And the scribes who came down from Jerusalem said, "Jesus is possessed by Beelzebul, and casts out the demons by the prince of demons." ²³And Jesus called them, and said to them in parables, "How can Satan cast out Satan? ²⁴If a dominion is divided against itself, that dominion cannot stand. ²⁵And if a house is divided against itself, that house will not be able to stand. ²⁶And if Satan has risen up against Satan and is divided, Satan cannot stand, but is coming to an end. ²⁷But none can enter the house of the strong and plunder their goods, without first binding the strong; then indeed they may plunder the house.

28 "Truly, I say to you, all sins will be forgiven human beings, and whatever blasphemies they utter; ²⁹but whoever blasphemes against the Holy Spirit never has forgiveness, but is guilty of an eternal sin"—³⁰for they had said, "Jesus has an unclean spirit."

31 And Jesus' mother and brothers came; and standing outside they sent to Jesus and called him. ³²And a crowd was sitting around Jesus; and they said, "Your mother and your brothers are outside, asking for you." ³³And Jesus replied, "Who are my mother and my brothers?" ³⁴And looking around on those who sat around him, Jesus said, "Here are my mother and my brothers! ³⁵Whoever does the will of God is my brother, and sister, and mother."

4 Jesus began to teach beside the sea. And a very large crowd gathered around, so that Jesus got into a boat and sat in it on the sea; and the whole crowd was beside the sea on the land. ²And Jesus taught them many things in parables, and, while teaching, was saying to them: ³"Listen! A sower went out to sow. ⁴And as the seeds were being scattered, some seed fell along the path, and the birds came and devoured it. ⁵Other seed fell on rocky ground, where it had not much soil, and immediately it sprang up, since it had no depth of soil; ⁶and when the sun rose it was scorched, and since it had no root it withered away. ⁷Other seed fell among thorns and the thorns grew up and choked it, and it yielded no grain. ⁸And other seed fell into good soil and brought forth grain, growing up and increasing and yielding thirtyfold and sixtyfold and a hundredfold." ⁹And Jesus said, "Those who have ears to hear, let them hear."

10 And when Jesus was alone, those who were there with the twelve asked concerning the parables. ¹¹And Jesus said to them, "To you has been given the secret of the dominion of God, but for those outside everything is in parables; ¹²so that they may indeed see but not perceive,

and may indeed hear but not understand; lest they should turn again, and be forgiven." [13]And Jesus said to them, "Do you not understand this parable? How then will you understand all the parables? [14]The sower sows the word. [15]And these are the ones along the path, where the word is sown; when they hear, Satan immediately comes and takes away the word which is sown in them. [16]And in the same way these are the ones sown upon rocky ground, who, when they hear the word, immediately receive it with joy; [17]and they have no root in themselves, but endure for a while; then, when tribulation or persecution arises on account of the word, immediately they fall away. [18]And others are the ones sown among thorns; they are those who hear the word, [19]but the cares of the world, and the delight in riches, and the desire for other things, enter in and choke the word, and it proves unfruitful. [20]But those that were sown upon the good soil are the ones who hear the word and accept it and bear fruit, thirtyfold and sixtyfold and a hundredfold."

21 Jesus said to them, "Is a lamp brought in to be put under a bushel, or under a bed, and not on a stand? [22]For there is nothing hid, except to be made manifest; nor is anything secret, except to come to light. [23]All who have ears to hear, let them hear." [24]And Jesus said to them, "Take heed what you hear; the measure you give will be the measure you get, and still more will be given you. [25]For to those who have will more be given; and from those who have not, even what they have will be taken away."

26 And Jesus said, "The dominion of God is as if someone should scatter seed upon the ground, [27]and should sleep and rise night and day, and the seed should sprout and grow, without the sower knowing how. [28]The earth produces of itself, first the blade, then the ear, then the full grain in the ear. [29]But when the grain is ripe, at once the one who has sown puts in the sickle, because the harvest has come."

30 And Jesus said, "With what can we compare the dominion of God, or what parable shall we use for it? [31]It is like a grain of mustard seed, which, when sown upon the ground is the smallest of all the seeds on earth; [32]yet when it is sown it grows up and becomes the greatest of all shrubs, and puts forth large branches, so that the birds of the air can make nests in its shade."

33 With many such parables Jesus spoke the word to them, as they were able to hear it; [34]he did not speak to them without a parable, but privately to his own disciples Jesus explained everything.

35 On that day, when evening had come, Jesus said to the disciples, "Let us go across to the other side." [36]And leaving the crowd, they took Jesus with them, just as he was, in the boat. And other boats were there. [37]And a great storm of wind arose, and the waves beat into the boat, so that the boat was already filling. [38]And the disciples woke Jesus, who was asleep on a cushion in the stern, and they said, "Teacher, do you not

care if we perish?" ³⁹And Jesus awoke and rebuked the wind, and said to the sea, "Peace! Be still!" And the wind ceased, and there was a great calm. ⁴⁰Jesus said to them, "Why are you afraid? Have you no faith?" ⁴¹And they were filled with awe, and said to one another, "Who then is this, whom even the wind and the sea obey?"

5 They came to the other side of the sea, to the country of the Gerasenes. ²And when Jesus had come out of the boat, a man from the tombs, with an unclean spirit, ³who lived among the tombs, met him; and no one could bind him anymore, even with a chain; ⁴for he had often been bound with shackles and chains, but the chains he wrenched apart, and the shackles he broke in pieces; and no one had the strength to subdue him. ⁵Night and day among the tombs and on the mountains he was always crying out, and bruising himself with stones. ⁶And when he saw Jesus from afar, he ran and worshiped Jesus; ⁷and crying out with a loud voice, said, "What have you to do with me, Jesus, Child of the Most High God? I adjure you by God, do not torment me." ⁸For Jesus had said, "Come out of the man, you unclean spirit!" ⁹And Jesus asked, "What is your name?" The man replied, "My name is Legion; for we are many." ¹⁰And he begged Jesus eagerly not to send them out of the country. ¹¹Now a great herd of swine was feeding there on the hillside; ¹²and they begged Jesus, "Send us to the swine, let us enter them." ¹³So Jesus gave them permission. And the unclean spirits came out, and entered the swine; and the herd, numbering about two thousand, rushed down the steep bank into the sea, and were drowned in the sea.

14 And the swineherds fled, and told it in the city and in the country. And people came to see what it was that had happened. ¹⁵And they came to Jesus, and saw the demoniac sitting there, clothed and in his right mind, the man who had had the legion; and they were afraid. ¹⁶And those who had seen it told what happened to the demoniac and to the swine. ¹⁷And they began to beg Jesus to depart from their neighborhood. ¹⁸And as Jesus was getting into the boat, the man who had been possessed with demons begged Jesus that he might be with him. ¹⁹But Jesus refused, and said, "Go home to your friends, and tell them how much the Lord has done for you, and how the Lord has had mercy on you." ²⁰And the man went away and began to proclaim in the Decapolis how much Jesus had done for him; and everybody marveled.

21 And when Jesus had crossed again in the boat to the other side, a great crowd gathered around, and Jesus was beside the sea. ²²Then one of the rulers of the synagogue came, Jairus by name, who, seeing Jesus, fell at his feet, ²³and pleaded, "My little daughter is at the point of death. Come and lay your hands on her, so that she may be made well, and live." ²⁴And Jesus went with him.

And a great crowd followed and pressed against Jesus. ²⁵And there was a woman who had had a flow of blood for twelve years, ²⁶and who had suffered much under many physicians, and had spent all that she had, and was no better but rather grew worse. ²⁷Having heard the reports about Jesus, she came up in the crowd from behind, and touched Jesus' garment. ²⁸For she said, "If I touch even his garments, I will be made well." ²⁹And immediately the hemorrhage ceased; and she felt in her body that she was healed of her disease. ³⁰And Jesus, perceiving in himself that power had gone forth from him, immediately turned about in the crowd, and said, "Who touched my garments?" ³¹And the disciples said, "You see the crowd pressing against you, and yet you say 'Who touched me?'" ³²And Jesus looked around to see who had done it. ³³But the woman, knowing what had been done to her, came in fear and trembling and fell down before Jesus, and told the whole truth. ³⁴And Jesus said to her, "Daughter, your faith has made you well; go in peace, and be healed of your disease."

35 While Jesus was still speaking, some people came from the ruler's house and said, "Your daughter is dead. Why trouble the Teacher any further?" ³⁶But ignoring what they said, Jesus said to the ruler of the synagogue, "Do not fear, only believe." ³⁷And Jesus allowed no one to follow him except Peter and James and John the brother of James. ³⁸When they came to the house of the ruler of the synagogue, Jesus saw a turmoil, and people weeping and wailing loudly. ³⁹And having entered, Jesus said to them, "Why do you make a turmoil and weep? The child is not dead but sleeping." ⁴⁰And they laughed at him. But Jesus put them all outside, and took the child's father and mother and the disciples, and went in where the child was. ⁴¹Taking her by the hand Jesus said to her, "Talitha cumi"; which means, "Little girl, I say to you, arise." ⁴²And immediately the girl got up and walked (she was twelve years of age), and they were immediately overcome with amazement. ⁴³And Jesus strictly charged them that no one should know this, and told them to give her something to eat.

6 Jesus went away from there and came to his own country; and the disciples followed. ²And on the sabbath Jesus began to teach in the synagogue; and many who heard were astonished, saying, "Where did this man get all this? What is the wisdom given to him? What mighty works are done by his hands! ³Is not this the carpenter, the son of Mary and brother of James and Joses and Judas and Simon, and are not his sisters here with us?" And they took offense at him. ⁴And Jesus said to them, "A prophet is not without honor, except in the prophet's own country, and among the prophet's own kin, and in the prophet's own house." ⁵And he could do no mighty work there, except to lay hands

upon a few sick people and heal them. ⁶And Jesus marveled because of their unbelief.

7 Jesus called the twelve, and began to send them out two by two, and gave them authority over the unclean spirits. ⁸He charged them to take nothing for their journey except a staff; no bread, no bag, no money in their belts; ⁹but to wear sandals and not put on two tunics. ¹⁰And Jesus said to them, "Wherever you enter a house, stay there until you leave the place. ¹¹And if any place will not receive you and they refuse to hear you, when you leave, shake off the dust that is on your feet for a testimony against them." ¹²So they went out and preached that people should repent. ¹³And they cast out many demons, and anointed with oil many that were sick and healed them.

14 King Herod heard of it; for Jesus' name had become known. Some said, John the baptizer has been raised from the dead; that is why these powers are at work in Jesus." ¹⁵But others said, "It is Elijah." And others said, "It is a prophet, like one of the prophets of old." ¹⁶But when Herod heard of it he said, "John, whom I beheaded, has been raised." ¹⁷For Herod had sent and seized John, and bound him in prison for the sake of Herodias, Herod's brother Philip's wife; because Herod had married her. ¹⁸For John said to Herod, "It is not lawful for you to have your brother's wife." ¹⁹And Herodias had a grudge against John, and wanted to kill him. But she could not, ²⁰for Herod feared John, knowing that he was a righteous and holy man, and Herod protected him. When Herod heard John, he was very perplexed; and yet he heard him gladly. ²¹But an opportunity came when Herod on his birthday gave a banquet for his courtiers and officers and the leading people of Galilee. ²²When Herodias' daughter came in and danced, she pleased Herod and his guests; and the king said to the girl, "Ask me for whatever you wish, and I will grant it." ²³And Herod vowed to her, "Whatever you ask me, I will give you, even half of my kingdom." ²⁴And she went out, and said to her mother, "What shall I ask?" And her mother said, "The head of John the baptizer." ²⁵And she came in immediately with haste to the king, and said, "I want you to give me at once the head of John the Baptist on a platter." ²⁶And the king was very sorry; but because of his oaths and his guests he did not want to break his word to her. ²⁷And immediately the king sent a soldier of the guard and gave orders to bring John's head. The soldier went and beheaded John in the prison, ²⁸and brought his head on a platter, and gave it to the girl; and the girl gave it to her mother. ²⁹When John's disciples heard of it, they came and took his body, and laid it in a tomb.

30 The apostles returned to Jesus, and reported all that they had done and taught. ³¹And Jesus said to them, "Come away by yourselves to a lonely place, and rest a while." For many were coming and going, and they had no leisure even to eat. ³²And they went away in the boat

to a lonely place by themselves. [33]Now many saw them going and knew them, and they ran there on foot from all the towns, and got there ahead of them. [34]Going ashore, Jesus saw a great crowd and had compassion on them, because they were like sheep without a shepherd; and Jesus began to teach them many things. [35]And when it grew late, the disciples came to Jesus and said, "This is a lonely place, and the hour is now late; [36]send them away, to go into the country and villages round about and buy themselves something to eat." [37]But Jesus answered them, "You give them something to eat." And they answered, "Shall we go and buy thousands of dollars worth of bread, and give it to them to eat?" [38]And Jesus said to them, "How many loaves have you? Go and see." And when they had found out, they said, "Five, and two fish." [39]Then Jesus commanded them all to sit down in groups on the green grass. [40]So they sat down in groups, by hundreds and by fifties. [41]And taking the five loaves and the two fish Jesus looked up to heaven, and blessed, and broke the loaves, and gave them to the disciples to set before the people; and Jesus divided the two fish among them all. [42]And they all ate and were satisfied. [43]Then they filled twelve baskets with what was left of the bread and of the fish. [44]Those who ate the loaves were five thousand men.

45 Immediately Jesus made the disciples get into the boat and go ahead to the other side, to Bethsaida, while he dismissed the crowd. [46]And after leaving them, Jesus went up on the mountain to pray. [47]And when evening came, the boat was out on the sea, and Jesus was alone on the land. [48]And Jesus saw that they were making little headway, for the wind was against them. Then very early in the morning Jesus came to them, walking on the sea, and Jesus intended to pass by them; [49]but when they saw Jesus walking on the sea they thought it was a ghost, and cried out; [50]for they all saw Jesus, and were terrified. But immediately Jesus spoke to them and said, "Take heart, it is I; have no fear." [51]And Jesus got into the boat with them and the wind ceased. And they were utterly astounded, [52]for they did not understand about the loaves, but their hearts were hardened.

53 And when they had crossed over, they came to land at Gennesaret, and moored to the shore. [54]When they got out of the boat, immediately the people recognized Jesus, [55]and ran about the whole neighborhood and began to bring sick people on their pallets to any place where they heard Jesus was. [56]And wherever Jesus came, in villages, cities, or country, they laid the sick in the market places, and begged Jesus that they might touch even the fringe of Jesus' garment; and as many as touched it were made well.

7 Now when the Pharisees gathered together to Jesus, with some of the scribes who had come from Jerusalem, [2]they saw that some of Jesus' disciples ate with hands defiled, that is, unwashed. [3](For the

Pharisees, and all the Jews, do not eat unless they wash their hands, observing the tradition of the elders; [4]and when they come from the marketplace, they do not eat unless they purify themselves; and there are many other traditions which they observe, the washing of cups and pots and vessels of bronze.) [5]And the Pharisees and the scribes asked Jesus, "Why do your disciples not live according to the tradition of the elders, but eat with hands defiled?" [6]And Jesus said to them, "Well did Isaiah prophesy of you hypocrites, as it is written,

'This people honors me with their lips,
    but their heart is far from me;
[7]in vain do they worship me,
    teaching human precepts as doctrines.'

[8]You leave the commandment of God, and hold fast human tradition."

9 Jesus said to them, "You have a fine way of rejecting the commandment of God, in order to keep your tradition! [10]For Moses said, 'Honor your father and your mother'; and, 'Whoever speaks evil of father or mother must surely die'; [11]but you say, 'If people tell their father or mother, What you would have gained from me is Corban' (that is, given to God)—[12]then you no longer permit them to do anything for their father or mother, [13]thus making void the word of God through your tradition which you hand on. And many other such things you do."

14 And Jesus called the people to him again, and said to them, "Hear me, all of you, and understand: [15]there is nothing outside a person which by going in can defile; but the things which come out are what defile."* [17]When Jesus had entered the house, and left the people, the disciples asked him about the parable. [18]And Jesus said to them, "Then are you also without understanding? Do you not see that whatever goes into anyone from outside cannot defile, [19]since it enters, not the heart but the stomach, and so passes on." (Thus Jesus declared all foods clean.) [20]And Jesus said, "What comes out of a person is what defiles. [21]For from within, out of the human heart, come evil thoughts, fornication, theft, murder, adultery, [22]coveting, wickedness, deceit, licentiousness, envy, slander, pride, foolishness. [23]All these evil things come from within, and these are what defile."

24 From there Jesus arose and went away into the region of Tyre and Sidon. And he entered a house, and did not want anyone to know it; yet Jesus could not be hidden. [25]But immediately a woman, whose little daughter was possessed by an unclean spirit, heard of Jesus, and came and fell down at Jesus' feet. [26]Now the woman was a Greek, a Syrophoenician by birth. And she begged Jesus to cast the demon out of her daughter. [27]And Jesus said to her, "Let the children first be fed,

---

* Other ancient authorities add verse 16, *"Those who have ears to hear, let them hear."*

for it is not right to take the children's bread and throw it to the dogs." ²⁸But she answered, "Yes, Lord; yet even the dogs under the table eat the children's crumbs." ²⁹And Jesus said to her, "For this saying you may go your way; the demon has left your daughter." ³⁰And she went home, and found the child lying in bed, and the demon gone.

31 Then Jesus returned from the region of Tyre, and went through Sidon to the Sea of Galilee, through the region of the Decapolis. ³²And they brought to him one who was deaf and had a speech impediment; and they begged Jesus to lay his hand upon that person. ³³And taking the person aside from the crowd privately, Jesus put his fingers into the person's ears, and spat and touched the person's tongue; ³⁴and looking up to heaven, Jesus sighed, and said, "Ephphatha," that is, "Be opened." ³⁵And the person's ears were opened, the tongue was released, and the person spoke plainly. ³⁶And Jesus charged them to tell no one; but the more he charged them, the more zealously they proclaimed it. ³⁷And they were astonished beyond measure, saying, "Jesus has done all things well, even making those who are deaf to hear and those who are mute to speak."

8 In those days, when again a great crowd had gathered who had nothing to eat, Jesus called the disciples and said to them, ²"I have compassion on the crowd, because they have been with me now three days, and have nothing to eat; ³and if I send them away hungry to their homes, they will faint on the way; and some of them have come a long way." ⁴And Jesus' disciples answered, "How can one feed these people with bread here in the desert?" ⁵Jesus asked them, "How many loaves have you?" They said, "Seven." ⁶And Jesus commanded the crowd to sit down on the ground. Then taking the seven loaves, and having given thanks, Jesus broke them and gave them to the disciples to set before the crowd. ⁷And they had a few small fish; and having blessed them, Jesus commanded that these also should be set before them. ⁸And they ate, and were satisfied; and they took up the broken pieces left over, seven baskets full. ⁹And there were about four thousand people. ¹⁰And Jesus sent them away, and immediately, having gotten into the boat with the disciples, Jesus went to the district of Dalmanutha.

11 The Pharisees came and began to argue with Jesus, seeking a sign from heaven, to test Jesus. ¹²And sighing deeply in spirit, Jesus said, "Why does this generation seek a sign? Truly, I say to you, no sign shall be given to this generation." ¹³And Jesus left them, and getting into the boat again, departed to the other side.

14 Now they had forgotten to bring bread; and they had only one loaf with them in the boat. ¹⁵And Jesus cautioned them, saying, "Watch out, beware of the leaven of the Pharisees and the leaven of Herod." ¹⁶And they discussed it with one another, saying, "We have no bread."

¹⁷And being aware of it, Jesus said to them, "Why do you discuss the fact that you have no bread? Do you not yet perceive or understand? Are your hearts hardened? ¹⁸Having eyes do you not see, and having ears do you not hear? And do you not remember? ¹⁹When I broke the five loaves for the five thousand, how many baskets full of broken pieces did you take up?" They answered, "Twelve." ²⁰"And the seven for the four thousand, how many baskets full of broken pieces did you take up?" And they answered, "Seven." ²¹And Jesus said to them, "Do you not yet understand?"

22 And they came to Bethsaida. And some people brought a person who was blind to Jesus, and begged Jesus to touch the person. ²³And Jesus took the blind person's hand, and they walked out of the village; and after Jesus spat on the blind person's eyes and laid on hands, Jesus inquired, "Do you see anything?" ²⁴And the person who was blind looked up and said, "I see people; but they look like trees, walking." ²⁵Then again Jesus laid hands on the eyes of the blind person, who looked intently, and was restored, and saw everything clearly. ²⁶And Jesus sent the person home, saying, "Do not even enter the village."

27 And Jesus went on with the disciples, to the villages of Caesarea Philippi; and on the way he asked them, "Who do people say that I am?" ²⁸And they said, "John the Baptist; and others say, Elijah; and others one of the prophets." ²⁹And Jesus asked them, "But who do you say that I am?" Peter answered, "You are the Messiah." ³⁰And Jesus charged them to tell no one.

31 And Jesus began to teach them that the Human One must suffer many things, and be rejected by the elders and the chief priests and the scribes, and be killed, and after three days rise again. ³²And Jesus said this plainly. And Peter took Jesus, and began to rebuke him. ³³But turning and seeing the disciples, Jesus rebuked Peter, and said, "Get behind me, Satan! For you are not siding with God, but with humankind."

34 And Jesus called the crowd with the disciples, and said to them, "If any would come after me, let them deny themselves and take up their cross and follow me. ³⁵For those who would save their life will lose it; and those who lose their life for my sake and the gospel's will save it. ³⁶For what advantage is it, to gain the whole world and forfeit one's life? ³⁷For what shall one give in return for one's life? ³⁸For any who are ashamed of me and of my words in this adulterous and sinful generation, of them will the Human One also be ashamed, when the Human One comes in the glory of God with the holy angels."

9 ¹And Jesus said to them, "Truly, I say to you, there are some standing here who will not taste death before they see that the dominion of God has come with power."

2 And after six days Jesus took Peter and James and John, and led them up a high mountain apart by themselves; and Jesus was trans-

figured before them, [3]and his garments became glistening, intensely bright, as no one on earth could bleach them. [4]And Elijah with Moses appeared to them; and they were talking to Jesus. [5]And Peter said to Jesus, "Rabbi, it is well that we are here; let us make three booths, one for you and one for Moses and one for Elijah." [6]Peter did not know what to say, for they were very afraid. [7]And a cloud overshadowed them, and a voice came out of the cloud, "This is my beloved Child; to this one you shall listen." [8]And suddenly looking around they no longer saw anyone with them but Jesus only.

9 And as they were coming down the mountain, Jesus charged them to tell no one what they had seen, until the Human One should have risen from the dead. [10]So they kept the matter to themselves, questioning what the rising from the dead meant. [11]And they asked Jesus, "Why do the scribes say that first Elijah must come?" [12]And Jesus answered them, "Elijah does come first to restore all things; so how is it that the scriptures say that the Human One is to suffer many things and be treated with contempt? [13]But I say to you that Elijah has come, and they did to him whatever they pleased, as it is written of him."

14 And when they came to the disciples, they saw a great crowd about them, and scribes arguing with them. [15]And immediately, when all the crowd saw Jesus they were greatly amazed and ran up to Jesus and greeted him. [16]And Jesus asked them, "What are you discussing with them?" [17]And one of the crowd answered, "Teacher, I brought my son to you, for he has a spirit that keeps him from speaking; [18]and wherever it seizes him, it dashes him down; and he foams and grinds his teeth and becomes rigid; and I asked your disciples to cast it out, and they were not able." [19]And Jesus answered them, "O faithless generation, how long am I to be with you? How long am I to bear with you? Bring him to me." [20]And they brought the boy to Jesus; and when the spirit saw Jesus, immediately it convulsed the boy, and he fell on the ground and rolled about, foaming at the mouth. [21]And Jesus asked his father, "How long has he had this?" And his father said, "From childhood. [22]And it has often cast him into the fire and into the water, to destroy him; but if you can do anything, have pity on us and help us." [23]And Jesus said to him, "If you can! All things are possible to one who believes." [24]Immediately the father of the child cried out and said, "I believe; help my unbelief?" [25]And when Jesus saw that a crowd came running together, he rebuked the unclean spirit, saying to it, "You spirit that keeps this boy from speaking and hearing, I command you, come out of him, and never enter him again." [26]And after crying out and convulsing the boy terribly, it came out, and the boy was like a corpse; so that most of them said, "He is dead." [27]But Jesus took the boy by the hand and lifted him up, and he arose. [28]And when Jesus had entered the house, the disciples asked him privately, "Why could we not cast

it out?" ²⁹And Jesus said to them, "This kind cannot be driven out by anything but prayer."

30 They went on from there and passed through Galilee. And Jesus would not have anyone know it; ³¹for he was teaching the disciples, saying to them, "The Human One will be betrayed into human hands, and will be killed by them; and having been killed, the Human One will rise after three days." ³²But they did not understand the saying, and they were afraid to ask Jesus.

33 And they came to Capernaum; and having entered the house, Jesus asked them, "What were you discussing on the way?" ³⁴But they were silent; for on the way they had discussed with one another who was the greatest. ³⁵And Jesus sat down and called the twelve and said to them, "Anyone who would be first must be last of all and servant of all." ³⁶And Jesus took a child, and put the child in the midst of them; and taking the child in his arms, Jesus said to them, ³⁷"Whoever receives one such child in my name receives me; and whoever receives me, receives not me but the one who sent me."

38 John said to Jesus, "Teacher, we saw someone casting out demons in your name, and we forbade it, because the one who did it was not following us." ³⁹But Jesus said, "Do not forbid such a person; for no one who does a mighty work in my name will be able soon after to speak evil of me. ⁴⁰For whoever is not against us is for us. ⁴¹For truly, I say to you, whoever gives you a cup of water to drink because you bear the name of Christ will by no means go unrewarded.

42 "Whoever causes one of these little ones who believe in me to sin, it would be better to have a great millstone hung around their neck and to be thrown into the sea. ⁴³And if your hand causes you to sin, cut it off; it is better for you to enter life maimed than with two hands to go to hell, to the unquenchable fire.* ⁴⁵And if your foot causes you to sin, cut it off; it is better for you to enter life lame than with two feet to be thrown into hell.* ⁴⁷And if your eye causes you to sin, pluck it out; it is better for you to enter the dominion of God with one eye than with two eyes to be thrown into hell, ⁴⁸where their worm does not die, and the fire is not quenched. ⁴⁹For everyone will be salted with fire. ⁵⁰Salt is good; but if the salt has lost its saltness, how will you season it? Have salt in yourselves, and be at peace with one another."

10 And Jesus left there and went to the region of Judea and beyond the Jordan, and crowds gathered around again; and again, as was his custom, Jesus taught them.

---

* Verses 44 and 46 (which are identical with verse 48) are omitted by the best ancient authorities.

2 And Pharisees came up and in order to test Jesus asked, "Is it lawful for a husband to divorce his wife?" ³Jesus answered them, "What did Moses command you?" ⁴They said, "Moses allowed a husband to write a certificate of divorce, and to put her away." ⁵But Jesus said to them, "For your hardness of heart Moses wrote you this commandment. ⁶But from the beginning of creation, 'God made them male and female.' ⁷For this reason a man shall leave his father and mother and be joined to his wife, ⁸and the two shall become one flesh.' So they are no longer two but one flesh. ⁹What therefore God has joined together, let no one separate."

10 And in the house the disciples asked Jesus again about this matter. ¹¹And Jesus said to them, "Whoever divorces his wife and marries another, commits adultery against her; ¹²and if she divorces her husband and marries another, she commits adultery."

13 And they were bringing children to Jesus, that he might touch them; and the disciples rebuked them. ¹⁴But when Jesus saw it he was indignant, and said to them, "Let the children come to me, do not hinder them; for to such belongs the dominion of God. ¹⁵Truly, I say to you, whoever does not receive the dominion of God like a child shall not enter it." ¹⁶And Jesus took the children in his arms and blessed them, laying his hands upon them.

17 And as Jesus was setting out on a journey, someone ran up and knelt before him, and asked, "Good Teacher, what must I do to inherit eternal life?" ¹⁸And Jesus said, "Why do you call me good? No one is good but God alone. ¹⁹You know the commandments: 'Do not kill, Do not commit adultery, Do not steal, Do not bear false witness, Do not defraud, Honor your father and mother.'" ²⁰And the questioner said to Jesus, "Teacher, all these I have observed from my youth." ²¹And Jesus looked upon the questioner with love and said, "You lack one thing; go, sell what you have, and give to the poor, and you will have treasure in heaven; and come, follow me." ²²Dismayed by this word, the person went away sorrowful because of having great possessions.

23 And Jesus looked around and said to the disciples, "How hard it will be for those who have riches to enter the dominion of God!" ²⁴And the disciples were amazed at Jesus' words. But Jesus said to them again, "Children, how hard it is to enter the dominion of God! ²⁵It is easier for a camel to go through the eye of a needle than for a rich person to enter the dominion of God." ²⁶And they were astonished, and said to Jesus, "Then who can be saved?" ²⁷Jesus looked at the disciples and said, "With human beings it is impossible, but not with God; for all things are possible with God." ²⁸Peter began to say to Jesus, "Indeed, we have left everything and followed you." ²⁹Jesus said, "Truly, I say to you, there is no one who has left house or brothers or sisters or mother or father or children or lands, for my sake and for the gospel, ³⁰who will not receive a hundredfold now in this time, houses and brothers and sisters

and mothers and children and lands, with persecutions, and in the age to come eternal life. ³¹But many that are first will be last, and the last first."

32 And they were on the road, going up to Jerusalem, and Jesus was walking ahead of them; and they were amazed, and those who followed were afraid. And taking the twelve again, Jesus began to tell them what was to happen to him, ³³saying, "Look, we are going up to Jerusalem; and the Human One will be delivered to the chief priests and the scribes, and will be condemned to death, and delivered to the Gentiles; ³⁴and the Human One will be mocked by the Gentiles, and spat upon, and scourged, and killed; and after three days the Human One will rise."

35 And James and John, the sons of Zebedee, came forward to Jesus, and said, "Teacher, we want you to do for us whatever we ask of you." ³⁶And Jesus said to them, "What do you want me to do for you?" ³⁷And they said, "Grant us to sit, one at your right hand and one at your left, in your glory." ³⁸But Jesus said to them, "You do not know what you are asking. Are you able to drink the cup that I drink, or to be baptized with the baptism with which I am baptized?" ³⁹And they said to Jesus, "We are able." And Jesus said to them, "The cup that I drink you will drink; and with the baptism with which I am baptized, you will be baptized; ⁴⁰but to sit at my right hand or at my left is not mine to grant, but it is for those for whom it has been prepared." ⁴¹And when the ten heard it, they began to be indignant at James and John. ⁴²And Jesus called them to him and said, "You know that those who are supposed to rule over the Gentiles lord it over them, and their great leaders exercise authority over them. ⁴³But it shall not be so among you; but whoever would be great among you must be your servant, ⁴⁴and whoever would be first among you must be slave of all. ⁴⁵For the Human One also came not to be served but to serve, and to give up life as a ransom for many."

46 And they came to Jericho; and as Jesus was leaving Jericho with the disciples and a great crowd, Bartimaeus, a blind beggar, the son of Timaeus, was sitting by the roadside. ⁴⁷And hearing that it was Jesus of Nazareth, Bartimaeus began to cry out and say, "Jesus, Child of David, have mercy on me!" ⁴⁸And many rebuked Bartimaeus, telling him to be silent; but he cried out all the more, "Child of David, have mercy on me!" ⁴⁹And Jesus stopped and said, "Call him." And they called him, saying, "Take heart; rise, Jesus is calling you." ⁵⁰And throwing off his mantle, Bartimaeus sprang up and came to Jesus. ⁵¹And Jesus said to him, "What do you want me to do for you?" And he replied, "Teacher, let me receive my sight." ⁵²And Jesus said, "Go your way; your faith has made you well." And immediately Bartimaeus received his sight and followed Jesus on the way.

11 And when they drew near to Jerusalem, to Bethphage and Bethany, at the Mount of Olives, Jesus sent two of the disciples, ²and said to them, "Go into the village opposite you, and immediately as you enter it you will find a colt tied, on which no one has ever sat; untie it and bring it. ³If anyone says to you, 'Why are you doing this?' say, 'The Lord has need of it and will send it back here immediately.' " ⁴And they went away, and found a colt tied at the door out in the open street; and they untied it. ⁵And those who stood there said to them, "What are you doing, untying the colt?" ⁶And the disciples told them what Jesus had said; and they let the disciples go. ⁷And the disciples brought the colt to Jesus, and threw their garments on it; and Jesus sat upon it. ⁸And many spread their garments on the road, and others spread leafy branches which they had cut from the fields. ⁹And those who went before and those who followed cried out, "Hosanna! Blessed is the one who comes in the name of the Lord! ¹⁰Blessed is the dominion of our ancestor David! Hosanna in the highest!"

11 And Jesus entered Jerusalem, and went into the temple; and having looked around at everything, since it was already late, he went out to Bethany with the twelve.

12 On the following day, when they came from Bethany, Jesus was hungry. ¹³And seeing in the distance a fig tree in leaf, Jesus went to see if he could find anything on it. And coming near it, Jesus found nothing but leaves, for it was not the season for figs. ¹⁴And Jesus said to it, "May no one ever eat fruit from you again." And the disciples heard it.

15 They came to Jerusalem. And Jesus entered the temple and began to drive out those who sold and those who bought in the temple, and overturned the tables of the money changers and the seats of those who sold pigeons; ¹⁶and Jesus would not allow anyone to carry anything through the temple. ¹⁷And Jesus taught, and said to them, "Is it not written, 'My house shall be called a house of prayer for all the nations'? But you have made it a den of robbers." ¹⁸And the chief priests and the scribes heard it and sought a way to destroy Jesus; for they feared him, because Jesus' teaching astonished the whole crowd. ¹⁹And when evening came they went out of the city.

20 As the disciples passed by in the morning, they saw the fig tree withered away to its roots. ²¹And Peter remembered and said to Jesus, "Rabbi, look! The fig tree which you cursed has withered." ²²And Jesus answered them, "Have faith in God. ²³Truly, I say to you, if you say to this mountain, 'Be taken up and cast into the sea,' and if you do not doubt in your heart, but believe that what you say will come to pass, it will be done for you. ²⁴Therefore I tell you, whatever you ask in prayer, believe that you have received it, and it will be yours. ²⁵And whenever you stand praying, forgive, if you have anything against anyone, so that

God your Father and Mother who is in heaven also may forgive you your trespasses."*

27 They came again to Jerusalem. And as Jesus was walking in the temple, the chief priests and the scribes and the elders came up ²⁸and asked, "By what authority are you doing these things, or who gave you this authority to do them?" ²⁹Jesus said to them, "I will ask you a question; answer me, and I will tell you by what authority I do these things. ³⁰Was John's baptism of divine or human origin? Answer me." ³¹And they argued with one another, "If we say, 'Divine,' Jesus will say, 'Why then did you not believe him?" ³²But shall we say, 'It was of human origin'?"—they were afraid of the people, for all held that John was a real prophet. ³³So they answered Jesus, "We do not know." And Jesus said to them, "Neither will I tell you by what authority I do these things."

12 Jesus began to speak to them in parables. "There was a person who planted a vineyard, and set a hedge around it, and dug a pit for the wine press, and built a tower, and let it out to tenants, and went into another country. ²When the time came, that owner sent a servant to the tenants to get from them some of the fruit of the vineyard. ³And they took the servant and beat him, and sent him away empty-handed. ⁴Again the owner sent them another servant, whom they wounded in the head and treated shamefully. ⁵And the owner sent another, whom they killed; and so with many others, some they beat and some they killed. ⁶The owner had still one other, a beloved child; and finally sent that child to them, saying, 'They will respect my offspring.' ⁷But those tenants said to one another, 'This is the heir; come, let us kill the heir, and the inheritance will be ours.' ⁸And they seized and killed the heir, and cast the body out of the vineyard. ⁹Therefore the owner of the vineyard will come and destroy the tenants, and give the vineyard to others. ¹⁰Have you not read this scripture:

'The very stone which the builders rejected
has become the head of the corner;
¹¹this was the Lord's doing,
and it is marvelous in our eyes'?"

12 Perceiving that Jesus had told the parable against them, they tried to arrest him, but, fearing the crowd, they left Jesus and went away.

13 And they sent Jesus some of the Pharisees and some of the Herodians, to entrap him while talking. ¹⁴And they came and said, "Teacher, we know that you are true, and treat no one in a special way; for you do

* Other ancient authorities add verse 26, *"But if you do not forgive, neither will your Father and Mother who is in heaven forgive your trespasses."*

not regard a person's status, but truly teach the way of God. Is it lawful to pay taxes to Caesar, or not? ¹⁵Should we pay them, or should we not?" But knowing their hypocrisy, Jesus said to them, "Why put me to the test? Bring me a coin, and let me look at it." ¹⁶And they brought one. And Jesus said to them, "Whose likeness and inscription is this?" They answered, "Caesar's." ¹⁷Jesus said to them, "Render to Caesar the things that Caesar's, and to God the things that are God's." And they were amazed.

18 Some Sadducees, who say that there is no resurrection, came up and asked Jesus a question, saying, ¹⁹"Teacher, Moses wrote for us that if a man's brother dies and leaves a wife, but leaves no child, the man must take the wife, and raise up children for his brother. ²⁰There were seven brothers; the first took a wife, and when he died left no children; ²¹and the second took her, and died, leaving no children; and the third likewise; ²²and the seven left no children. Last of all the woman also died. ²³In the resurrection whose wife will she be? For the seven had her as wife."

24 Jesus said to them, "Is not this why you are wrong, that you know neither the scriptures nor the power of God? ²⁵For when they rise from the dead, they neither marry nor are given in marriage, but are like angels in heaven. ²⁶And as for the dead being raised, have you not read in the book of Moses, in the passage about the bush, how God said to him, 'I am the God of Abraham, and the God of Isaac, and the God of Jacob'? ²⁷God is not God of the dead, but of the living; you are quite wrong."

28 One of the scribes came up and heard them disputing with one another, and seeing that Jesus answered them well, asked, "Which commandment is the first of all?" ²⁹Jesus answered, "The first is, 'Hear, O Israel: The Lord our God, the Lord is one; ³⁰and you shall love the Lord your God with all your heart, and with all your soul, and with all your mind, and with all your strength.' ³¹The second is this, 'You shall love your neighbor as yourself.' There is no other commandment greater than these." ³²And the scribe said to Jesus, "You are right, Teacher; you have truly said that God is one, and there is no other but God; ³³and to love God with all the heart, and with all the understanding, and with all the strength, and to love one's neighbor as oneself, is much more than all whole burnt offerings and sacrifices." ³⁴And when Jesus saw that the scribe answered wisely, Jesus said to him, "You are not far from the dominion of God." And after that no one dared to ask Jesus any question.

35 And as Jesus taught in the temple he said, "How can the scribes say that the Messiah is David's offspring? ³⁶David himself, inspired by the Holy Spirit, declared,

'God said to my Lord,
Sit at my right hand,
till I put your enemies under your feet.'

37David himself calls the Messiah Lord; so how can the Messiah be David's offspring?" And the great crowd heard him gladly.

38 And in his teaching Jesus said, "Beware of the scribes, who like to go about in long robes, and to have salutations in the marketplaces 39and the best seats in the synagogues and the places of honor at feasts, 40who devour widows' houses and for a pretense make long prayers. They will receive the greater condemnation."

41 And Jesus sat down opposite the treasury, and watched the crowd putting money into the treasury. Many rich people put in large sums. 42And a poor widow came, and put in two copper coins, which make a penny. 43And Jesus called the disciples, and said to them, "Truly, I say to you, this poor widow has put in more than all those who are contributing to the treasury. 44For they all contributed out of their abundance; but she out of her poverty has put in everything she had, her whole living."

13 As Jesus came out of the temple, one of the disciples said to him, "Look, Teacher, what wonderful stones and what wonderful buildings!" 2And Jesus said, "Do you see these great buildings? There will not be left here one stone upon another that will not be thrown down."

3 As Jesus sat on the Mount of Olives opposite the temple, Peter and James and John and Andrew asked him privately, 4"Tell us, when will this be, and what will be the sign when these things are all to be accomplished?" 5And Jesus said to them, "Take heed that no one leads you astray. 6Many will come in my name, saying, 'I am the one!' and they will lead many astray. 7And when you hear of wars and rumors of wars, do not be alarmed; this must take place, but the end is not yet. 8For nation will rise against nation, and dominion against dominion; there will be earthquakes in various places, and there will be famines; this is but the beginning of the sufferings.

9 "But take heed to yourselves; for you will be delivered up to councils; and you will be beaten in synagogues; and you will stand before governors and rulers for my sake, to bear testimony before them. 10And the gospel must first be preached to all nations. 11When they bring you to trial and deliver you up, do not be anxious beforehand about what you are to say; but say whatever is given you in that hour, for it is not you who speak, but the Holy Spirit. 12And brothers and sisters will deliver up each other to death, and parents their children, and children will rise against parents and have them put to death; 13and you will be

hated by all for my name's sake. But the one who endures to the end will be saved.

14 "But when you see the desolating sacrilege set up where it ought not to be (let the reader understand), then let those who are in Judea flee to the mountains; ¹⁵let those who are on the housetops not go down, nor enter their houses, to take anything away; ¹⁶and let those who are in the field not turn back to take their mantles. ¹⁷And alas for those who are pregnant, and for those who are nursing their infants in those days! ¹⁸Pray that it may not happen in winter. ¹⁹For in those days there will be such tribulation as has not been from the beginning of the creation which God created until now, and never will be. ²⁰And if the Lord had not shortened the days, no human being would be saved; but for the sake of the elect, whom God chose, God shortened the days. ²¹Then if anyone says to you, 'Look, here is the Messiah!' or 'Look, there is the Messiah!' do not believe it. ²²False Messiahs and false prophets will arise and show signs and wonders, to lead astray, if possible, the elect. ²³But take heed; I have told you all things beforehand.

24 "But in those days, after that tribulation, the sun will be darkened, and the moon will not give its light, ²⁵and the stars will be falling from heaven, and the powers in the heavens will be shaken. ²⁶And then they will see the Human One coming in clouds with great power and glory. ²⁷Then the Human One will send out the angels, and gather the elect from the four winds, from the ends of the earth to the ends of heaven.

28 "From the fig tree learn its lesson: as soon as its branch becomes tender and puts forth its leaves, you know that summer is near. ²⁹So also, when you see these things taking place, you know that the Human One is near, at the very gates. ³⁰Truly, I say to you, this generation will not pass away before all these things take place. ³¹Heaven and earth will pass away, but my words will not pass away.

32 "But of that day or that hour no one knows, not even the angels in heaven, nor the Child, but only God. ³³Take heed, watch; for you do not know when the time will come. ³⁴It is like someone going on a journey, who, upon leaving home, puts the servants in charge, each with a particular task, and commands the doorkeeper to be on the watch. ³⁵Watch therefore—for you do not know when the owner of the house will come, in the evening, or at midnight, or soon after midnight, or in the morning—³⁶lest the owner come suddenly and find you asleep. ³⁷And what I say to you I say to all: Watch."

14 It was now two days before the Passover and the feast of Unleavened Bread. And the chief priests and the scribes were seeking how to arrest Jesus by stealth, and kill him; ²for they said, "Not during the feast, lest there be a great turmoil among the people."

3 And while Jesus was at Bethany sitting at table in the house of Simon—a man who had leprosy—a woman came with an alabaster flask of ointment of pure nard, very costly, and she broke the flask and poured it over Jesus' head. 4But there were some who said to themselves indignantly, "Why was the ointment wasted in this way? 5For this ointment might have been sold for thousands of dollars, and given to the poor." And they reproached her. 6But Jesus said, "Let her alone; why do you trouble her? She has done a beautiful thing to me. 7For you always have the poor with you, and whenever you will, you can do good to them; but you will not always have me. 8She has done what she could; she has anointed my body beforehand for burying. 9And truly, I say to you, wherever the gospel is preached in the whole world, what she has done will be told in memory of her."

10 Then Judas Iscariot, who was one of the twelve, went to the chief priests in order to betray Jesus to them. 11And when they heard it they were glad, and promised to give Judas money. And Judas sought an opportunity to betray Jesus.

12 And on the first day of Unleavened Bread, when they sacrificed the passover lamb, the disciples said to Jesus, "Where will you have us go and prepare for you to eat the passover?" 13And Jesus sent two of the disciples, and said to them, "Go into the city, and a man carrying a jar of water will meet you; follow him, 14and wherever he enters, say to the householder, 'The Teacher says, Where is my guest room, where I am to eat the passover with my disciples?' 15And the householder will show you a large upper room furnished and ready; there prepare for us." 16So the disciples set out and went to the city, and found it as Jesus had told them; and they prepared the passover.

17 And when it was evening Jesus came with the twelve. 18And as they were at table eating, Jesus said, "Truly, I say to you, one of you will betray me, one who is eating with me." 19They began to be sorrowful, and to say to Jesus one after another, "Is it I?" 20Jesus said to them, "It is one of the twelve, the one who is dipping bread into the dish with me. 21For the Human One goes as it is written, but woe to that person by whom the Human One is betrayed! It would have been better for that person not to have been born."

22 And as they were eating, Jesus took bread, and blessed, and broke it, and gave it to them, and said, "Take; this is my body." 23And Jesus took a cup, and after giving thanks, gave it to them, and they all drank of it. 24And Jesus said to them, "This is my blood of the covenant, which is poured out for many. 25Truly, I say to you, I shall not drink again of the fruit of the vine until that day when I drink it new in the dominion of God."

26 And when they had sung a hymn, they went out to the Mount of Olives. 27And Jesus said to them, "You will all fall away; for it is written,

'I will strike the shepherd, and the sheep will be scattered.' ²⁸But after I am raised up, I will go before you to Galilee." ²⁹Peter said to Jesus, "Even though they all fall away, I will not." ³⁰And Jesus said to Peter, "Truly, I say to you, this very night, before the cock crows twice, you will deny me three times." ³¹But Peter said vehemently, "If I must die with you, I will not deny you." And they all said the same.

32 And they went to a place which was called Gethsemane; and Jesus said to the disciples, "Sit here, while I pray." ³³And taking Peter and James and John, Jesus began to be greatly distressed and troubled, ³⁴and said to them, "My soul is very sorrowful, even to death; remain here, and watch." ³⁵And going a little farther, Jesus fell on the ground and prayed that, if it were possible, the hour might pass from him. ³⁶And Jesus said, "God, my Mother and Father, all things are possible to you; remove this cup from me; yet not what I will, but what you will." ³⁷And Jesus came and found them sleeping, and said to Peter, "Simon, are you asleep? Could you not watch one hour? ³⁸Watch and pray that you may not enter into temptation; the spirit indeed is willing, but the flesh is weak." ³⁹And again Jesus went away and prayed, saying the same words. ⁴⁰And again Jesus came and found them sleeping, for their eyes were very heavy; and they did not know what to answer. ⁴¹And Jesus came the third time, and said to them, "Are you still sleeping and taking your rest? It is enough; the hour has come; the Human One is betrayed into the hands of sinners. ⁴²Rise, let us be going; see, my betrayer is at hand."

43 And immediately, while Jesus was still speaking, Judas came, one of the twelve, and with him a crowd with swords and clubs, from the chief priests and the scribes and the elders. ⁴⁴Now the betrayer had given them a sign, saying, "The one I will kiss is the man; seize him and lead him away under guard." ⁴⁵And when Judas came, he went up to Jesus at once, and said, "Rabbi!" And Judas kissed Jesus. ⁴⁶And they laid hands on Jesus and seized him. ⁴⁷One of those who stood by drew a sword, and struck the slave of the high priest and cut off his ear. ⁴⁸And Jesus said to them, "Have you come out as against a robber, with swords and clubs to capture me? ⁴⁹Day after day I was with you in the temple teaching, and you did not seize me. But let the scriptures be fulfilled." ⁵⁰And they all forsook Jesus, and fled.

51 And a young man followed Jesus, with nothing but a linen cloth about his body; and they seized him, ⁵²but he left the linen cloth and ran away naked.

53 And they led Jesus to the high priest; and all the chief priests and the elders and the scribes were assembled. ⁵⁴And Peter had followed Jesus at a distance, right into the courtyard of the high priest, and was sitting with the guards, warming himself at the fire. ⁵⁵Now the chief priests and the whole council sought testimony against Jesus to put him

to death; but they found none. ⁵⁶For many bore false witness against Jesus, and their witness did not agree. ⁵⁷And some stood up and bore false witness, saying, ⁵⁸"We heard Jesus say, 'I will destroy this temple that is made with hands, and in three days I will build another, not made with hands.'" ⁵⁹Yet not even so did their testimony agree. ⁶⁰And the high priest stood up in the midst, and asked Jesus, "Have you no answer to make? What is it that these witnesses testify against you?" ⁶¹But Jesus was silent and made no answer. Again the high priest asked Jesus, "Are you the Messiah, the Child of the Blessed?" ⁶²And Jesus said, "I am; and you will see the Human One seated at the right hand of Power, and coming with the clouds of heaven." ⁶³And the high priest tore the priestly garments, and said, "Why do we still need witnesses? ⁶⁴You have heard his blasphemy. What is your decision?" And they all condemned Jesus as deserving death. ⁶⁵And some began to spit on Jesus, and to cover his face, and to strike him, saying, "Prophesy!" And the guards received Jesus with blows.

66 And as Peter was below in the courtyard, one of the maids of the high priest came; ⁶⁷and seeing Peter warming himself, she looked at him, and said, "You also were with the Nazarene, Jesus." ⁶⁸But Peter denied it, saying, "I neither know nor understand what you mean." And he went out into the gateway. ⁶⁹And the maid saw him, and began again to say to the bystanders, "This is one of them." ⁷⁰But again Peter denied it. And after a little while again the bystanders said to Peter, "Certainly you are one of them; for you are a Galilean." ⁷¹But Peter began to invoke a curse on himself and to swear, "I do not know this one of whom you speak." ⁷²And immediately the cock crowed a second time. And Peter remembered how Jesus had said, "Before the cock crows twice, you will deny me three times." And Peter broke down and wept.

15 And as soon as it was morning the chief priests, with the elders and scribes, and the whole council held a consultation; and they bound Jesus and led him away and delivered him to Pilate. ²And Pilate asked Jesus, "Are you the King of the Jews?" And Jesus answered, "You have said so." ³And the chief priests accused Jesus of many things. ⁴And Pilate again asked Jesus, "Have you no answer to make? See how many charges they bring against you." ⁵But Jesus made no further answer, so that Pilate wondered.

6 Now at the feast Pilate used to release for them one prisoner for whom they asked. ⁷And among the rebels in prison, who had committed murder in the insurrection, there was a man called Barabbas. ⁸And the crowd came up and began to ask Pilate to do what he used to do for them. ⁹And Pilate answered them, "Do you want me to release for you the King of the Jews?" ¹⁰For Pilate perceived that it was out of envy that the chief priests had delivered up Jesus. ¹¹But the chief priests stirred up

the crowd to have Pilate release for them Barabbas instead. [12]And Pilate again said to them, "Then what shall I do with the one whom you call the King of the Jews?" [13]And they cried out again, "Crucify him." [14]And Pilate said to them, "Why, what evil has he done?" But they shouted all the more, "Crucify him." [15]So Pilate, wishing to satisfy the crowd, released for them Barabbas; and having scourged Jesus, Pilate delivered him to be crucified.

16 And the soldiers led Jesus away inside the palace (that is, the praetorium); and they called together the whole battalion. [17]And they clothed Jesus in a purple cloak, and plaiting a crown of thorns they put it on him. [18]And they began to salute Jesus, "Hail, King of the Jews!" [19]And they struck Jesus' head with a reed, and spat upon him, and they knelt down in homage to him. [20]And when they had mocked Jesus, they stripped him of the purple cloak, and put his own clothes on him. And they led Jesus out to be crucified.

21 And they compelled a passer-by, Simon of Cyrene, who was coming in from the country, the father of Alexander and Rufus, to carry Jesus' cross. [22]And they brought Jesus to the place called Golgotha (which means the place of a skull). [23]And they offered Jesus wine mingled with myrrh; but he did not take it. [24]And they crucified Jesus, and divided his garments among them, casting lots for them, to decide what each should take. [25]And it was nine o'clock in the morning when they crucified Jesus. [26]And the inscription of the charge against him read, "The King of the Jews." [27]And with Jesus they crucified two robbers, one on the right and one on the left.* [29]And those who passed by derided Jesus, wagging their heads, and saying, "Aha! You who would destroy the temple and build it in three days, [30]save yourself, and come down from the cross!" [31]So also the chief priests, together with the scribes, mocked Jesus, saying to one another, "He saved others, but cannot save himself. [32]Let the Messiah, the Ruler of Israel, come down now from the cross, that we may see and believe." Those who were crucified with Jesus also reviled him.

33 And when noon had come, there was darkness over the whole land until three o'clock. [34]And at three o'clock Jesus cried with a loud voice, "Eloi, Eloi, lama sabachthani?" which means, "My God, my God, why have your forsaken me?" [35]And some of the bystanders hearing it said, "Look, Jesus is calling Elijah." [36]And one ran and, filling a sponge full of vinegar, put it on a reed and gave it to Jesus to drink, saying, "Wait, let us see whether Elijah will come to take Jesus down." [37]And Jesus uttered a loud cry, and died. [38]And the curtain of the temple was torn in two, from top to bottom. [39]And when the centurion, who stood

* Other ancient authorities add verse 28, *And the scripture was fulfilled, which says, "He was reckoned with the transgressors."*

facing Jesus, saw that Jesus died in this way, he said, "Truly this was the Child of God!"

40 There were also women looking on from afar, among whom were Mary Magdalene, and Mary the mother of James the younger and of Joses, and Salome, ⁴¹who, when Jesus was in Galilee, followed him, and ministered to him; and also many other women who came up with Jesus to Jerusalem.

42 And when the evening had come, since it was the day of Preparation, that is, the day before the sabbath, ⁴³Joseph of Arimathea, a respected member of the council, who was also looking for the dominion of God, took courage and went to Pilate, and asked for the body of Jesus. ⁴⁴And Pilate wondered if Jesus were already dead; and summoning the centurion, Pilate asked him whether Jesus had died much earlier. ⁴⁵And on learning from the centurion that Jesus was dead, Pilate granted the body to Joseph. ⁴⁶And Joseph bought a linen shroud, and taking him down, wrapped him in the linen shroud, and laid him in a tomb which had been hewn out of the rock; and Joseph rolled a stone against the door of the tomb. ⁴⁷Mary Magdalene and Mary the mother of Joses saw where Jesus was laid.

16 And when the sabbath was past, Mary Magdalene, and Mary the mother of James, and Salome, bought spices, so that they might go and anoint Jesus. ²And very early on the first day of the week they went to the tomb when the sun had risen. ³And they were saying to one another, "Who will roll away the stone for us from the door of the tomb?" ⁴And looking up, they saw that the stone was rolled back—it was very large. ⁵And entering the tomb, they saw a youth sitting on the right side, dressed in a white robe; and they were amazed. ⁶And the youth said to them, "Do not be amazed; you seek Jesus of Nazareth, who was crucified. Jesus has risen and is not here; see the place where they laid the body. ⁷But go, tell the disciples and Peter that Jesus is going before you to Galilee; there you will see Jesus, as he told you." ⁸And they went out and fled from the tomb; for trembling and astonishment had come upon them; and they said nothing to anyone, for they were afraid.

9 Now having risen early on the first day of the week, Jesus appeared first to Mary Magdalene, from whom Jesus had cast out seven demons. ¹⁰She went and told those who had been with Jesus, as they mourned and wept. ¹¹But when they heard that Jesus was alive and had been seen by her, they would not believe it.

12 After this Jesus appeared in another form to two of them, as they were walking into the country. ¹³And they went back and told the rest, but they did not believe them.

14 Afterward Jesus appeared to the eleven themselves as they sat at table, and upbraided them for their unbelief and hardness of heart, because they had not believed those who saw Jesus after Jesus had risen. [15]And Jesus said to them, "Go into all the world and preach the gospel to the whole creation. [16]Whoever believes and is baptized will be saved; but whoever does not believe will be condemned." [17]And these signs will accompany those who believe: in my name they will cast out demons; they will speak in new tongues; [18]they will pick up serpents, and if they drink any deadly thing, it will not hurt them; they will lay their hands on the sick, and they will recover."

19 So then the Lord Jesus, after speaking to them, was taken up into heaven, and sat down at the right hand of God. [20]And they went forth and preached everywhere, while the Lord worked with them and confirmed the message by the signs that attended it. Amen.

Luke

1 Inasmuch as many have undertaken to compile a narrative of the things which have been accomplished among us, ²just as they were delivered to us by those who from the beginning were eyewitnesses and ministers of the word, ³it seemed good to me also, having followed all things closely for some time past, to write an orderly account for you, most excellent Theophilus, ⁴that you may know the truth concerning the things of which you have been informed.

5 In the days of Herod, king of Judea, there was a priest named Zechariah, of the division of Abijah; and he had a wife of the daughters of Aaron, whose name was Elizabeth. ⁶And they were both righteous before God, walking in all the commandments and ordinances of God blameless. ⁷But they had no child, because Elizabeth was barren, and both were advanced in years.

8 Now while Zechariah was serving as priest before God when his division was on duty, ⁹according to the custom of the priesthood, it fell to him by lot to enter God's temple and burn incense. ¹⁰And the whole crowd of people were praying outside at the hour of incense. ¹¹And there appeared to him an angel of God standing on the right side of the altar of incense. ¹²And Zechariah was troubled when he saw the angel, and fear fell upon him. ¹³But the angel said to him, "Do not be afraid, Zechariah, for your prayer is heard, and your wife Elizabeth will bear you a son, and you will call his name John.

¹⁴And you will have joy and gladness,
   and many will rejoice at his birth;
¹⁵for he will be great before God,
   and he will drink no wine or strong drink,

and will be filled with the Holy Spirit,
even from his mother's womb.
¹⁶And he will turn many of the children of Israel to the Lord
their God,
¹⁷and he will go before God in the spirit and power of Elijah,
to turn the hearts of the parents to the children,
and the disobedient to the wisdom of the just,
to make ready for God a people prepared."

¹⁸And Zechariah said to the angel, "How shall I know this? For I am an old man, and my wife is advanced in years." ¹⁹And the angel answered him, "I am Gabriel, who stand in the presence of God; and I was sent to speak to you, and to bring you this good news. ²⁰And indeed, you will be silent and unable to speak until the day that these things happen, because you did not believe my words, which will be fulfilled in their time. ²¹And the people were waiting for Zechariah, and they wondered at his delay in the temple. ²²And when he came out, he could not speak to them, and they perceived that he had seen a vision in the temple; and he made signs to them and remained unable to speak. ²³And when his time of service was ended, he went home.

24 After these days Zechariah's wife Elizabeth conceived, and for five months she hid herself, saying, ²⁵"Thus God has done to me in the days when God looked on me, to take away my reproach."

26 In the sixth month the angel Gabriel was sent from God to a city of Galilee named Nazareth, ²⁷to a virgin betrothed to a man whose name was Joseph, of the house of David; and her name was Mary. ²⁸And the angel came to her and said, "Hail, O favored one, God is with you!" ²⁹But she was greatly troubled at the saying, and considered in her mind what sort of greeting this might be. ³⁰And the angel said to her, "Do not be afraid, Mary, for you have found favor with God. ³¹You will conceive in your womb and bear a child, whose name you shall call Jesus.

³²This one will be great, and will be called the Child of the Most
High;
and the Lord God will give to that Child the throne of David,
the ancestor of the Child,
³³to reign over the house of Jacob forever;
and of that reign there will be no end."

34 And Mary said to the angel, "How shall this be, since I have no husband?" ³⁵And the angel said to her,

"The Holy Spirit will come upon you,
and the power of the Most High will overshadow you;
therefore the child to be born will be called holy,
the Child of God.

³⁶And your kinswoman Elizabeth in her old age has also conceived a child; and this is the sixth month with her who was called barren. ³⁷For with God nothing will be impossible." ³⁸And Mary said, "I am the servant of God; let it be to me according to your word." And the angel departed from her.

39 In those days Mary arose and went with haste into the hill country, to a city of Judah, ⁴⁰and she entered the house of Zechariah and greeted Elizabeth. ⁴¹And when Elizabeth heard the greeting of Mary, the baby leaped in her womb; and Elizabeth was filled with the Holy Spirit ⁴²and she exclaimed with a loud cry, "Blessed are you among women, and blessed is the fruit of your womb! ⁴³And why is this granted me, that the mother of my Lord should come to me? ⁴⁴For when the voice of your greeting came to my ears, the baby in my womb leaped for joy. ⁴⁵And blessed is she who believed that there would be a fulfillment of what was spoken to her from God." ⁴⁶And Mary said,

"My soul magnifies the Lord,
⁴⁷and my spirit rejoices in God my Savior, *this*
⁴⁸who has regarded the low estate of ~~God~~'s servant.
For henceforth all generations will call me blessed;
⁴⁹for the one who is mighty has done great things for me,
and holy is God's name.
⁵⁰And God's mercy is on those who fear God
from generation to generation.
⁵¹God has shown strength with God's arm,
and has scattered the proud in the imagination of their hearts,
⁵²God has put down the mighty from their thrones,
and exalted those of low degree;
⁵³God has filled the hungry with good things,
and has sent the rich empty away.
⁵⁴God has helped God's servant Israel,
in remembrance of God's mercy,
⁵⁵as God spoke to our ancestors,
to Abraham and Sarah and to their posterity forever."

⁵⁶And Mary remained with Elizabeth about three months, and returned to her home.

57 Now the time came for Elizabeth to be delivered, and she gave birth to a son. ⁵⁸And her neighbors and relatives heard that God had shown great mercy to her, and they rejoiced with her. ⁵⁹And on the eighth day they came to circumcise the child; and they wanted to name him Zechariah after his father, ⁶⁰but his mother said, "No; he will be called John." ⁶¹And they said to her, "None of your relatives is called by this name." ⁶²And they made signs to Zechariah, inquiring what he wanted the child called. ⁶³And he asked for a writing tablet, and

to everyone's surprise, wrote, "His name is John." ⁶⁴And immediately Zechariah's mouth was opened and his tongue loosed, and he spoke, blessing God. ⁶⁵And fear came on all their neighbors. And all these things were talked about through all the hill country of Judea; ⁶⁶and all who heard them laid them up in their hearts, saying, "What then will this child be?" For the hand of God was with him.

67 And the child's father, Zechariah, was filled with the Holy Spirit, and prophesied, saying,

⁶⁸"Blessed be the Lord God of Israel,
who has visited and redeemed God's people,
⁶⁹and has raised up a horn of salvation for us
in the house of God's servant David,
⁷⁰as God spoke by the mouth of the holy prophets from of old,
⁷¹that we should be saved from our enemies,
and from the hand of all who hate us;
⁷²to perform the mercy promised to our ancestors,
and to remember God's holy covenant,
⁷³the oath which God swore to our ancestor Abraham, ⁷⁴to grant
us
that we, being delivered from the hand of our enemies,
might serve God without fear,
⁷⁵in holiness and righteousness before God all the days of our life.
⁷⁶And you, my child, will be called the prophet of the Most High;
for you will go before God to prepare God's ways,
⁷⁷to give knowledge of salvation to God's people
in the forgiveness of their sins,
⁷⁸through the tender mercy of our God,
when the day shall dawn upon us from on high
⁷⁹to give light to those who sit in darkness and in the shadow of
death,
to guide our feet into the way of peace."

⁸⁰And the child grew and became strong in spirit, and he was in the wilderness till the day of his manifestation to Israel.

2 In those days a decree went out from Caesar Augustus that all the world should be enrolled. ²This was the first enrollment, when Quirinius was governor of Syria. ³And all went to be enrolled, each to their own city. ⁴And Joseph also went up from Galilee, from the city of Nazareth, to Judea, to the city of David, which is called Bethlehem, because he was of the house and lineage of David, ⁵to be enrolled with Mary, his betrothed who was with child. ⁶And while they were there, the time came for her to be delivered. ⁷And she gave birth to her first-

born son, whom she wrapped in swaddling clothes and laid in a manger, because there was no place for them in the inn.

8 And in that region there were shepherds out in the field, keeping watch over their flock by night. [9]And an angel of God appeared to them, and the glory of God shone around them, and they were filled with fear. [10]And the angel said to them, "Be not afraid; for I bring you good news of a great joy which will come to all the people; [11]for to you is born this day in the city of David a Savior, who is the Messiah, the Lord. [12]And this will be a sign for you: you will find a baby wrapped in swaddling clothes and lying in a manger." [13]And suddenly there was with the angel a multitude of the heavenly host praising God and saying,

[14]"Glory to God in the highest,
 and on earth peace among those with whom God is pleased!"

15 When the angels went away from them into heaven, the shepherds said to one another, "Let us go over to Bethlehem and see this thing that has happened, which God has made known to us." [16]And they went with haste, and found Mary and Joseph, and the baby lying in a manger. [17]And when they saw it they made known the saying which had been told them concerning this child; [18]and all who heard it wondered at what the shepherds told them. [19]But Mary kept all these things, pondering them in her heart. [20]And the shepherds returned, glorifying and praising God for all they had heard and seen, as it had been told them.

21 And at the end of eight days, the child was circumcised and was called Jesus, the name given by the angel before the child was conceived in the womb.

22 And when the time came for their purification according to the law of Moses, they brought the child Jesus up to Jerusalem to be presented to God, [23](as it is written in God's law, "Every male that opens the womb will be called holy to God"), [24]and to offer a sacrifice according to what is said in God's law, "a pair of turtledoves, or two young pigeons." [25]Now there was a man in Jerusalem, whose name was Simeon, who was righteous and devout, looking for the consolation of Israel, and the Holy Spirit was upon him. [26]And it had been revealed to Simeon by the Holy Spirit that he should not see death before he had seen God's Messiah. [27]And inspired by the Spirit, Simeon came into the temple; and when the parents brought in the child Jesus, to do for him according to the custom of the law, [28]Simeon took the child in his arms and blessed God and said,

[29]"God, now let your servant depart in peace,
 according to your word;
[30]for my eyes have seen your salvation
[31]which you have prepared in the presence of all people,

³²a light for revelation to the Gentiles,
and for glory to your people Israel."

33 And the father and mother of Jesus marveled at what was said
about their child; ³⁴and Simeon blessed them and said to Mary, Jesus'
mother,

"This child is set for the fall and rising of many in Israel,
and for a sign that is spoken against
³⁵(and a sword will pierce through your own soul also),
that thoughts out of many hearts may be revealed."

36 And there was a prophet, Anna, the daughter of Phanuel, of the
tribe of Asher; she was very old, having lived with her husband seven
years, ³⁷and as a widow till she was eighty-four. She did not depart from
the temple, worshiping with fasting and prayer night and day. ³⁸And
coming up at that very hour she gave thanks to God, and spoke about
the child to all who were looking for the redemption of Jerusalem.

39 And when Mary and Joseph had performed everything according to God's law, they returned into Galilee, to their own city, Nazareth.
⁴⁰And the child grew and became strong, filled with wisdom; and the
favor of God was upon the child.

41 Now Jesus' parents went to Jerusalem every year at the feast of
the Passover. ⁴²And when he was twelve years old, they went up according to custom; ⁴³and when the feast was ended, as they were returning,
the boy Jesus stayed behind in Jerusalem. His parents did not know it,
⁴⁴but supposing him to be in their group they went a day's journey, and
they sought him among their relatives and friends; ⁴⁵and when they did
not find him, they returned to Jerusalem, seeking him. ⁴⁶After three days
they found Jesus in the temple, sitting among the teachers, listening to
them and asking them questions; ⁴⁷and all who heard him were amazed
at his understanding and his answers. ⁴⁸And when they saw him they
were astonished; and his mother said, "Son, why have you treated us
so? Your father and I have been looking for you anxiously." ⁴⁹And Jesus
said to them, "How is it that you sought me? Did you not know that I
must be in the house of God my Father and Mother?" ⁵⁰And they did
not understand the saying which Jesus spoke to them. ⁵¹And he went
down with them and came to Nazareth, and was obedient to them; and
his mother kept all these things in her heart.

52 And Jesus increased in wisdom and in stature, and in favor with
God and humankind.

3 In the fifteenth year of the reign of Tiberius Caesar, Pontius Pilate
being governor of Judea, and Herod being tetrarch of Galilee, and
his brother Philip tetrarch of the region of Ituraea and Trachonitis, and

Lysanias tetrarch of Abilene, ²in the high-priesthood of Annas and Caiaphas, the word of God came to John, the son of Zechariah and Elizabeth, in the wilderness; ³and John went into all the region about the Jordan, preaching a baptism of repentance for the forgiveness of sins. ⁴As it is written in the book of the words of Isaiah the prophet,

"The voice of one crying in the wilderness:
Prepare the way of the Lord,
make the paths of the Lord straight.
⁵Every valley shall be filled,
and every mountain and hill shall be brought low,
and the crooked shall be made straight
and the rough ways shall be made smooth;
⁶and all flesh shall see the salvation of God."

7 John the Baptist said therefore to the crowds that came out to be baptized by him, "You brood of vipers! Who warned you to flee from the wrath to come? ⁸Bear fruits that befit repentance, and do not begin to say to yourselves, 'We have Abraham as our father'; for I tell you, God is able from these stones to raise up children to Abraham. ⁹Even now the axe is laid to the root of the trees; every tree therefore that does not bear good fruit is cut down and thrown into the fire."

10 And the crowds asked John, "What then shall we do?" ¹¹And he answered them, "Let anyone who has two coats share with a person who has none; and let anyone who has food do likewise." ¹²Tax collectors also came to be baptized. and said to John, "Teacher, what shall we do?" ¹³And he said to them, "Collect no more than is appointed you." ¹⁴Soldiers also asked him, "And we, what shall we do?" And John said to them, "Rob no one by violence or by false accusation, and be content with your wages."

15 As the people were in expectation, all of them questioning in their hearts concerning John, whether perhaps he were the Messiah, ¹⁶John answered them all, "I baptize you with water; but the one who is mightier than I is coming, the thong of whose sandals I am not worthy to untie; that one will baptize you with the Holy Spirit and with fire. ¹⁷With winnowing fork in hand, that one will clear the threshing floor, and gather the wheat into the granary, but will burn the chaff with unquenchable fire."

18 So, with many other exhortations, John preached good news to the people. ¹⁹But Herod the tetrarch, who had been reproved by John for Herodias, his brother's wife, and for all the evil things that Herod had done, ²⁰added this to them all, that he shut up John in prison.

21 Now when all the people were baptized, and when Jesus also had been baptized and was praying, the heaven was opened, ²²and the Holy

Spirit descended upon Jesus in bodily form, as a dove, and a voice came from heaven, "You are my beloved Child; with you I am well pleased."

23 When Jesus began his ministry he was about thirty years old, being the son (as was supposed) of Joseph, the son of Heli, 24the son of Matthat, the son of Levi, the son of Melchi, the son of Jannai, the son of Joseph, 25the son of Mattathias, the son of Amos, the son of Nahum, the son of Esli, the son of Naggai, 26the son of Maath, the son of Mattathias, the son of Semein, the son of Josech, the son of Joda, 27the son of Joanan, the son of Rhesa, the son of Zerubbabel, the son of Shealtiel, the son of Neri, 28the son of Melchi, the son of Addi, the son of Cosam, the son of Elmadam, the son of Er, 29the son of Joshua, the son of Eliezer, the son of Jorim, the son of Matthat, the son of Levi, 30the son of Simeon, the son of Judah, the son of Joseph, the son of Jonam, the son of Eliakim, 31the son of Melea, the son of Menna, the son of Mattatha, the son of Nathan, the son of David, 32the son of Jesse, the son of Obed, the son of Boaz, the son of Sala, the son of Nahshon, 33the son of Amminadab, the son of Admin, the son of Arni, the son of Hezron, the son of Perez, the son of Judah, 34the son of Jacob, the son of Isaac, the son of Abraham, the son of Terah, the son of Nahor, 35the son of Serug, the son of Reu, the son of Peleg, the son of Eber, the son of Shelah, 36the son of Cainan, the son of Arphaxad, the son of Shem, the son of Noah, the son of Lamech, 37the son of Methuselah, the son of Enoch, the son of Jared, the son of Mahalaleel, the son of Cainan, 38the son of Enos, the son of Seth, the son of Adam, the son of God.

4 And Jesus, full of the Holy Spirit, returned from the Jordan, and was led by the Spirit 2for forty days in the wilderness, tempted by the devil. And Jesus ate nothing in those days; and when they were ended, he was hungry. 3The devil said to Jesus, "If you are the Child of God, command this stone to become bread." 4And Jesus answered, "It is written, 'One shall not live by bread alone.'" 5And the devil took Jesus up, and showed him all the nations of the world in a moment of time, 6and said, "To you I will give all this authority and their glory; for it has been delivered to me, and I give it to whom I will. 7If you, then, will worship me, it shall all be yours." 8And Jesus answered, "It is written,

'You shall worship the Lord your God,
    and God only shall you serve.'"

9And the devil took Jesus to Jerusalem, and set him on the pinnacle of the temple, and said, "If you are the Child of God, throw yourself down from here; 10for it is written,

'God will give the angels charge of you, to guard you,'

¹¹and

> 'On their hands they will bear you up,
> lest you strike your foot against a stone.' "

¹²And Jesus replied, "It is said, 'You shall not tempt the Lord your God.' " ¹³And the devil, having ended every temptation, departed from Jesus until an opportune time.

14 And Jesus returned in the power of the Spirit into Galilee, and a report concerning him went out through all the surrounding country. ¹⁵And he taught in their synagogues, being glorified by all.

16 And Jesus came to Nazareth, where he had been brought up, and went to the synagogue, as his custom was, on the sabbath day. And he stood up to read; ¹⁷and being given the book of the prophet Isaiah, Jesus opened the book and found the place where it was written,

> ¹⁸"The Spirit of God is upon me,
> because God has anointed me to preach good news to the poor,
> and has sent me to proclaim release to the captives
> and recovering of sight to those who are blind,
> to set at liberty those who are oppressed,
> ¹⁹to proclaim the acceptable year of God."

²⁰And Jesus closed the book, and gave it back to the attendant, and sat down; and the eyes of all in the synagogue were fixed on Jesus, ²¹who began to say to them, "Today this scripture has been fulfilled in your hearing." ²²And all spoke well of him, and wondered at the gracious words which proceeded out of his mouth; and they said, "Is not this Joseph's son?" ²³And Jesus said to them, "Doubtless you will quote to me this proverb, 'Physician, heal yourself; what we have heard you did at Capernaum, do here also in your own country.' " ²⁴And Jesus said, "Truly, I say to you, no prophet is acceptable in the prophet's own country. ²⁵But in truth, I tell you, there were many widows in Israel in the days of Elijah, when the heaven was shut up three years and six months, when there came a great famine over all the land; ²⁶and Elijah was sent to none of them but only to Zarephath, in the land of Sidon, to a woman who was a widow. ²⁷And there were many people with leprosy in Israel in the time of the prophet Elisha; and none of them was cleansed, but only Naaman the Syrian." ²⁸When they heard this, all in the synagogue were filled with anger. ²⁹And they rose up and put Jesus out of the city, and led him to the brow of the hill on which their city was built, that they might throw him down headlong. ³⁰But passing through the midst of them Jesus went away.

31 Jesus went down to Capernaum, a city of Galilee, and was teaching on the sabbath. ³²And people were astonished at Jesus' teaching,

for his word was with authority. ³³And there was a person in the synagogue who had the spirit of an unclean demon, who cried out with a loud voice, ³⁴"Oh! What have you to do with us, Jesus of Nazareth? Have you come to destroy us? I know who you are, the Holy One of God." ³⁵But Jesus rebuked the demon, saying, "Be silent, and come out!" And when the demon had thrown the person down, the demon came out, having done the person no harm. ³⁶And all the people were amazed and said to one another, "What is this word? For with authority and power Jesus commands the unclean spirits, and they come out." ³⁷And reports of Jesus went out into every place in the surrounding region.

38 And Jesus arose and left the synagogue, and entered Simon's house. Now Simon's mother-in-law was ill with a high fever, and Jesus was asked to help her. ³⁹And Jesus stood over her and rebuked the fever, and it left her; and immediately she rose and served them.

40 Now when the sun was setting, all those who knew people who were sick with various diseases brought them to Jesus, who laid hands on every one of them and healed them. ⁴¹And demons also came out of many, crying, "You are the holy Child of God!" But Jesus rebuked them, and would not allow them to speak, because they knew that Jesus was the Messiah.

42 And when daylight came Jesus departed and went into a lonely place. And the people sought him and came to him, and tried to keep him from leaving them; ⁴³but Jesus said to them, "I must preach the good news of the dominion of God to the other cities also; for I was sent for this purpose." ⁴⁴And Jesus was preaching in the synagogues of Judea.

5 While the people pressed upon him to hear the word of God, Jesus was standing by the lake of Gennesaret. ²And he saw two boats by the lake; but those who were fishing had gone out of them and were washing their nets. ³Getting into one of the boats, which was Simon's, Jesus asked Simon to put out a little from the land. And Jesus sat down and taught the people from the boat. ⁴And when he had ceased speaking, he said to Simon, "Put out into the deep and let down your nets for a catch." ⁵And Simon answered, "Teacher, we worked hard all night and took nothing! But at your word I will let down the nets." ⁶And when they had done this, they enclosed a great shoal of fish; and as their nets were breaking, ⁷they beckoned to their partners in the other boat to come and help them. And they came and filled both the boats, so that they began to sink. ⁸But when Simon Peter saw it, he fell down at Jesus' knees, saying, "Depart from me, O Lord, for I am a sinful person." ⁹For Simon was astonished, and all who were with him, at the catch of fish which they had taken; ¹⁰and so also were James and John, sons of Zebedee, who were partners with Simon. And Jesus said to Simon, "Do not be afraid;

henceforth you will be catching human beings." ¹¹And when they had brought their boats to land, they left everything and followed Jesus.

12 While Jesus was in one of the cities, a person full of leprosy saw Jesus, fell down before him, and begged, "Lord, if you will, you can make me clean." ¹³And Jesus stretched out his hand, and touched the person with the leprosy, saying, "I will; be clean." And immediately the leprosy was gone. ¹⁴And Jesus charged the person not to tell anyone; but "go and show yourself to the priest, and make an offering for your cleansing, as Moses commanded, for a proof to the people." ¹⁵But now more than ever the report went abroad concerning Jesus; and great crowds gathered to hear and to be healed of their infirmities. ¹⁶But Jesus withdrew to the wilderness and prayed.

17 One of those days, as Jesus was teaching, Pharisees and teachers of the law were sitting there, who had come from every village of Galilee and Judea, and from Jerusalem; and the power of God was with Jesus to heal. ¹⁸And some people were carrying on a bed a person who was paralyzed, and they tried to bring the person in, and lay the person before Jesus; ¹⁹but finding no way to get in, because of the crowd, they went up on the roof and let the person down, with the bed, through the tiles, into the midst before Jesus. ²⁰And seeing their faith, Jesus said to the person, "Your sins are forgiven." ²¹And the scribes and the Pharisees began to question, saying, "Who is this who speaks blasphemies? Who can forgive sins but God only?" ²²Perceiving their questioning, Jesus answered, "Why do you question in your hearts? ²³Which is easier, to say, 'Your sins are forgiven you,' or to say, 'Rise and walk'? ²⁴But that you may know that the Human One has authority on earth to forgive sins"—he said to the person who was paralyzed—"I say to you, rise, take up your bed and go home." ²⁵And immediately the person rose before them, and took up the bed, and went home, glorifying God. ²⁶And amazement seized them all, and they glorified God and were filled with awe, saying, "We have seen strange things today."

27 After this Jesus went out and saw a tax collector named Levi, sitting at the tax office; and Jesus said to him, "Follow me." ²⁸And the tax collector left everything, and rose, and followed Jesus.

29 And Levi made Jesus a great feast in his house; and a large company of tax collectors and others were sitting at table with them. ³⁰And the Pharisees and their scribes murmured against the disciples, saying, "Why do you eat and drink with tax collectors and sinners?" ³¹And Jesus answered them, "Those who are well have no need of a physician, but those who are sick; ³²I have not come to call the righteous, but sinners to repentance."

33 Some people said to Jesus, "The disciples of John fast often and offer prayers, and so do the disciples of the Pharisees, but yours eat and drink." ³⁴Jesus said to them, "Can you make wedding guests fast

while the bridegroom is with them? [35]The days will come when the bridegroom is taken away from them, and then they will fast in those days." [36]He told them a parable also: "People do not tear a piece from a new garment and put it on an old garment; if they do, they will tear the new, and the piece from the new will not match the old. [37]And people do not put new wine into old wineskins; if they do, the new wine will burst the skins and it will be spilled, and the skins will be destroyed. [38]But new wine must be put into fresh wineskins. [39]And after drinking old wine, people do not desire new; for they say, 'The old is good.' "

6 One sabbath, while Jesus was going through the grainfields, the disciples plucked and ate some heads of grain, rubbing them in their hands. [2]But some of the Pharisees asked, "Why are you doing what is not lawful to do on the sabbath?" [3]And Jesus answered, "Have you not read what David did when he was hungry, he and those who were with him: [4]how he entered the house of God, and took and ate the bread of the Presence, which it is not lawful for any but the priests to eat, and also gave it to those with him?" [5]And Jesus said to them, "The Human One is lord of the sabbath."

6 On another sabbath, when Jesus entered the synagogue and taught, a person was there whose right hand was withered. [7]And the scribes and the Pharisees watched Jesus, to see whether he would heal on the sabbath, so that they might find something to accuse him of. [8]But Jesus knew their thoughts, and said to the person who had the withered hand, "Come and stand here." And the person rose and stood there. [9]And Jesus said to them, "I ask you, is it lawful on the sabbath to do good or to do harm, so save life or to destroy it?" [10]And Jesus looked around on them all, and said to the person, "Stretch out your hand." And the person did it, and the hand was restored. [11]But they were filled with fury and discussed with one another what they might do to Jesus.

12 In these days Jesus went out to the mountain to pray; and all night he continued in prayer to God. [13]And when it was day, Jesus called to himself the disciples, and chose from them twelve, who were named apostles: [14]Simon, whom Jesus named Peter, and Andrew his brother, and James and John, and Philip, and Bartholomew, [15]and Matthew, and Thomas, and James the son of Alphaeus, and Simon who was called the Zealot, [16]and Judas the son of James, and Judas Iscariot, who became a traitor.

17 And Jesus came down with them and stood on a level place, with a great crowd of the disciples and a great crowd of people from all Judea and Jerusalem and the seacoast of Tyre and Sidon, who came to hear Jesus and to be healed of their diseases; [18]and those who were troubled

with unclean spirits were cured. [19]And all the crowd sought to touch Jesus, for power came forth from him and healed them all.

20 And Jesus lifted up his eyes on the disciples, and said: "Blessed are you poor, for yours is the dominion of God.

21 "Blessed are you that hunger now, for you shall be satisfied. "Blessed are you that weep now, for you shall laugh.

22 "Blessed are you when people hate you, and when they exclude you and revile you, and cast out your name as evil, on account of the Human One! [23]Rejoice in that day, and leap for joy, for your reward is great in heaven; for so their ancestors did to the prophets.

24 "But woe to you that are rich, for you have received your consolation.

25 "Woe to you that are full now, for you shall hunger. "Woe to you that laugh now, for you shall mourn and weep.

26 "Woe to you, when all speak well of you, for so their ancestors did to the false prophets."

27 "But I say to you that hear, Love your enemies, do good to those who hate you, [28]bless those who curse you, pray for those who abuse you. [29]To a person who strikes you on the cheek, offer the other also; and from a person who takes away your coat, do not withhold even your shirt. [30]Give to everyone who begs from you; and of anyone who takes away your goods do not ask for them again. [31]And as you wish that people would do to you, do so to them.

32 "If you love those who love you, what credit is that to you? For even sinners love those who love them. [33]And if you do good to those who do good to you, what credit is that to you? For even sinners do the same. [34]And if you lend to those from whom you hope to receive, what credit is that to you? Even sinners lend to sinners, to receive as much again. [35]But love your enemies, and do good, and lend, expecting nothing in return; and your reward will be great, and you will be children of the Most High; for God is kind to the ungrateful and the selfish. [36]Be merciful, even as God your Father and Mother is merciful.

37 "Judge not, and you will not be judged; condemn not, and you will not be condemned; forgive, and you will be forgiven; [38]give, and it will be given to you; good measure, pressed down, shaken together, running over, will be put into your lap. For the measure you give will be the measure you get back."

39 Jesus also told them a parable: "Can one who is blind lead another blind person? Will they not both fall into a pit? [40]A disciple is not above a teacher, but everyone when fully taught will be like the teacher. [41]Why do you see the speck that is in your neighbor's eye, but do not notice the log that is in your own eye? [42]Or how can you say to your neighbor, 'Friend, let me take out the speck that is in your eye,' when you yourself do not see the log that is in your own eye? You hypocrite, first take the

log out of your own eye, and then you will see clearly to take out the speck that is in your neighbor's eye.

43 "For no good tree bears bad fruit, nor again does a bad tree bear good fruit; ⁴⁴for each tree is known by its own fruit. And figs are not gathered from thorns, nor are grapes picked from a bramble bush. ⁴⁵The good person out of the good treasure of the heart produces good, and the evil person out of evil treasure produces evil; for such a one speaks out of the abundance of the heart.

46 "Why do you call me 'Lord, Lord,' and not do what I tell you? ⁴⁷All who come to me and hear my words and do them, I will show you what they are like: ⁴⁸they are like a person building a house, who dug deep, and laid the foundation upon rock; and when a flood arose, the stream broke against that house, and could not shake it, because it had been well built. ⁴⁹But whoever hears and does not do them is like a person who built a house on the ground without a foundation, against which the stream broke, and immediately it fell, and the ruin of that house was great."

7 After Jesus had ended all his sayings in the hearing of the people, he entered Capernaum. ²Now a centurion had a slave who was dear to him, who was sick and at the point of death. ³After hearing about Jesus, the centurion sent elders of the Jews to ask Jesus to come and heal his slave. ⁴And when they came to Jesus, they begged earnestly, saying, "The centurion is worthy to have you do this for him, ⁵for he loves our nation and built us our synagogue." ⁶And Jesus went with them. When he was not far from the house, the centurion sent friends to him, saying, "Lord, do not trouble yourself, for I am not worthy to have you come under my roof; ⁷therefore I did not presume to come to you. But say the word, and let my servant be healed. ⁸For I am a man set under authority, with soldiers under me: and I say to one, 'Go,' and he goes; and to another, 'Come,' and he comes; and to my slave, 'Do this,' and the slave does it." ⁹When Jesus heard this he marveled at the centurion, and turned and said to the crowd that followed, "I tell you, not even in Israel have I found such faith." ¹⁰And when those who had been sent returned to the house, they found the slave well.

11 Soon afterward Jesus went to a city called Nain, and the disciples and a great crowd went with him. ¹²As he drew near to the gate of the city, a man who had died was being carried out, the only son of his mother, and she was a widow; and a large crowd from the city was with her. ¹³And when the Lord saw her, he had compassion on her and said to her, "Do not weep." ¹⁴And Jesus came and touched the bier, and the bearers stood still. And he said, "Young man, I say to you, arise." ¹⁵And the dead man sat up, and began to speak. And Jesus gave him to his mother. ¹⁶Fear seized them all; and they glorified God, saying, "A

great prophet has arisen among us!" and "God has visited God's people!" [17]And this report concerning Jesus spread through the whole of Judea and all the surrounding country.

18 John's disciples told him of all these things. [19]And calling to him two of his disciples, John sent them to the Lord, saying, "Are you the one who is to come, or shall we look for another?" [20]And when the people had come to Jesus, they said, "John the Baptist has sent us to you, saying, 'Are you the one who is to come, or shall we look for another?'" [21]In that hour Jesus cured many from their diseases and plagues and evil spirits, and on many who were blind Jesus bestowed sight. [22]And Jesus answered them, "Go and tell John what you have seen and heard: those who are blind receive their sight, those who are lame walk, those who are leprous are cleansed, and those who are deaf hear, the dead are raised up, the poor have good news preached to them. [23]And blessed is the one who takes no offense at me."

24 When John's messengers had gone, Jesus began to speak to the crowds concerning John: "What did you go out into the wilderness to behold? A reed shaken by the wind? [25]What then did you go out to see? A man clothed in soft clothing? Look here, those who are gorgeously appareled and live in luxury are in kings' courts. [26]What then did you go out to see? A prophet? Yes, I tell you, and more than a prophet. [27]This is the one of whom it is written,

> 'See, I send my messenger before your face,
> who shall prepare your way before you.'

[28]I tell you, among those born of women none is greater than John; yet the one who is least in the dominion of God is greater than he." [29](When they heard this all the people and the tax collectors justified God, having been baptized with the baptism of John; [30]but the Pharisees and the lawyers rejected the purpose of God for themselves, not having been baptized by him.)

31 "To what then shall I compare the people of this generation, and what are they like? [32]They are like children sitting in the market place and calling to one another,

> 'We piped to you, and you did not dance;
> we wailed, and you did not weep.'

[33]For John the Baptist has come eating no bread and drinking no wine; and you say, 'He has a demon.' [34]The Human One has come eating and drinking; and you say, 'See, a glutton and a drunkard, a friend of tax collectors and sinners!' [35]Yet wisdom is justified by all its children."

36 One of the Pharisees asked Jesus to eat with him, and he went into the Pharisee's house, and sat at table. [37]And a woman of the city, who was a sinner, when she learned that Jesus was sitting at table in the

Pharisee's house, brought an alabaster flask of ointment, ³⁸and stand-ing behind Jesus at his feet, weeping, she began to wet his feet with her tears, and wiped them with the hair of her head, and kissed his feet, and anointed them with the ointment. ³⁹Now when the Pharisee who had invited Jesus saw it, he said to himself, "If this person were a pro-phet, he would have known who and what sort of woman this is who is touching him, for she is a sinner." ⁴⁰And Jesus answering said to him, "Si-mon, I have something to say to you." And Simon answered, "What is it, Teacher?" ⁴¹"A certain creditor had two debtors; one owed five hundred coins, and the other fifty. ⁴²When they could not pay, the creditor forgave them both. Now which of them will love the creditor more?" ⁴³Simon an-swered, "The one, I suppose, to whom the creditor forgave more." And Jesus said to Simon, "You have judged rightly." ⁴⁴Then turning toward the woman, he said to Simon, "Do you see this woman? When I entered your house, you gave me no water for my feet, but she has wet my feet with her tears and wiped them with her hair. ⁴⁵You gave me no kiss, but from the time I came in she has not ceased to kiss my feet. ⁴⁶You did not anoint my head with oil, but she has anointed my feet with ointment. ⁴⁷Therefore I tell you, her sins, which are many, are forgiven, for she loved much; but whoever is forgiven little, loves little." ⁴⁸And Jesus said to her, "Your sins are forgiven." ⁴⁹Then those who were at table with him began to say among themselves, "Who is this, who even forgives sins?" ⁵⁰And Jesus said to the woman, "Your faith has saved you; go in peace."

8 Soon afterward Jesus went on through cities and villages, preaching and bringing the good news of the dominion of God. And the twelve were with him, ²and also some women who had been healed of evil spir-its and infirmities: Mary, called Magdalene, from whom seven demons had gone out, ³and Joanna, the wife of Chuza, Herod's steward, and Susanna, and many others, who provided for them out of their means.

4 And when a great crowd came together and people from town after town came to Jesus, he said in a parable: ⁵"A sower went out to sow seed; and as the seeds were being scattered, some of what was sown fell along the path, and was trampled under foot, and the birds of the air devoured it. ⁶And some fell on the rock; and as it grew up, it withered away, because it had no moisture. ⁷And some fell among thorns; and the thorns grew with it and choked it. ⁸And some fell into good soil and grew, and yielded a hundredfold." And having said this, Jesus called out, "Let whoever has ears to hear, hear."

9 And when Jesus' disciples asked what this parable meant, ¹⁰Jesus said, "To you it has been given to know the secrets of the dominion of God; but for others those secrets are in parables, so that seeing they may not see, and hearing they may not understand. ¹¹Now the parable is this:

The seed is the word of God. ¹²The ones along the path are those who have heard; then the devil comes and takes away the word from their hearts, that they may not believe and be saved. ¹³And the ones on the rock are those who, when they hear the word, receive it with joy; but they have no root, they believe for a while and in time of temptation fall away. ¹⁴And as for what fell among the thorns, they are the ones who hear, but as they go on their way they are choked by the cares and riches and pleasures of life, and their fruit does not mature. ¹⁵And as for that in the good soil, they are the ones who, hearing the word, hold it fast in an honest and good heart, and bring forth fruit with patience.

16 "No one after lighting a lamp covers it with something, or puts it under a bed, but puts it on a stand, that those who enter may see the light. ¹⁷For nothing is hidden that will not be made manifest, nor anything secret that will not be known and come to light. ¹⁸Take heed then how you hear; for to the one who has will more be given, and from the one who has not, even what one thinks one has will be taken away."

19 Then Jesus' mother and brothers came to Jesus, but they could not reach him for the crowd. ²⁰And someone said to Jesus, "Your mother and your brothers are standing outside, desiring to see you." ²¹But Jesus answered, "My mother and my brothers are those who hear the word of God and do it."

22 One day Jesus got into a boat with the disciples, and said to them, "Let us go across to the other side of the lake." So they set out, ²³and as they sailed Jesus fell asleep. A storm of wind then came down on the lake, and they were filling with water, and were in danger. ²⁴And they went and woke Jesus, saying, "Teacher, Teacher, we are perishing!" And Jesus awoke and rebuked the wind and the raging waves; and they ceased, and there was a calm. ²⁵Jesus said to them, "Where is your faith?" And they were afraid, and they marveled, saying to one another, "Who then is this, who commands even the wind and the water, and they obey?"

26 Then they arrived at the country of the Gerasenes, which is opposite Galilee. ²⁷And as Jesus stepped out on land, a man from the city, who had demons, met him. For a long time he had worn no clothes, and instead of living in a house, had lived among the tombs. ²⁸When he saw Jesus, he cried out and fell down before Jesus, and said with a loud voice, "What have you to do with me, Jesus, Child of the Most High God? I beseech you, do not torment me." ²⁹For Jesus had commanded the unclean spirit to come out of the man. (For many times it had seized him. He was kept under guard, and bound with chains and shackles, but he broke the bonds and was driven by the demon into the desert.) ³⁰Jesus then asked him, "What is your name?" And he replied, "Legion"; for many demons had entered him. ³¹And they begged Jesus not to command them to depart into the abyss. ³²Now a large herd of swine was

feeding there on the hillside; and they begged Jesus to let them enter these. So Jesus gave them permission. ³³Then the demons came out of the man and entered the swine, and the herd rushed down the steep bank into the lake and were drowned.

34 When the swineherds saw what had happened, they fled, and told it in the city and in the country. ³⁵Then people went out to see what had taken place, and they came to Jesus, and found the man from whom the demons had gone, sitting at Jesus' feet, clothed and in his right mind; and they were afraid. ³⁶And those who had seen it told how the one who had been possessed with demons was healed. ³⁷Then all the people of the surrounding country of the Gerasenes asked Jesus to depart from them; for they were seized with great fear; so Jesus got into the boat and returned. ³⁸The man from whom the demons had gone out begged that he might be with Jesus; but Jesus sent him away, saying, ³⁹"Return to your home, and declare how much God has done for you." So the man went away, proclaiming throughout the whole city how much Jesus had done for him.

40 Now when Jesus returned, the crowd welcomed him, for they were all waiting for him. ⁴¹And a man named Jairus, a ruler of the synagogue, came to Jesus; and falling at Jesus' feet he begged Jesus to come to his house, ⁴²for he had an only daughter, about twelve years old, and she was dying.

And as Jesus went, the people pressed around. ⁴³And a woman who had had a flow of blood for twelve years and could not be healed by anyone, ⁴⁴came up behind, and touched the fringe of Jesus' garment; and immediately her flow of blood ceased. ⁴⁵And Jesus asked, "Who was it that touched me?" When all denied it, Peter said, "Teacher, the crowds surround you and press upon you!" ⁴⁶But Jesus answered, "Someone touched me; for I perceive that power has gone out from me." ⁴⁷And when the woman saw that she was not hidden, she came trembling, and falling down before Jesus declared in the presence of all the people why she had touched Jesus, and how she had been immediately healed. ⁴⁸And Jesus said to her, "Daughter, your faith has made you well; go in peace."

49 While Jesus was still speaking, someone from the ruler's house came and said, "Your daughter is dead; do not trouble the Teacher any more." ⁵⁰But on hearing this, Jesus answered, "Do not fear; only believe, and she will be well." ⁵¹And coming to the house, Jesus permitted no one to enter with him, except Peter and John and James, and the father and mother of the child. ⁵²And all were weeping and mourning over her; but Jesus said, "Stop weeping; for she is not dead, but is sleeping." ⁵³And they began to laugh at Jesus, knowing that she was dead. ⁵⁴But taking her by the hand Jesus called out, saying, "Child, arise." ⁵⁵And her spirit returned, and she got up at once; and Jesus directed that something be

given her to eat. ⁵⁶Her parents were amazed; but Jesus charged them to tell no one what had happened.

9 Jesus called the twelve together and gave them power and authority over all demons, and to cure diseases, ²and sent them out to preach the dominion of God and to heal. ³And Jesus said to them, "Take nothing for your journey, no staff, nor knapsack, nor bread, nor money; and do not have two tunics. ⁴And stay in whatever house you enter, and from there depart. ⁵And wherever they do not receive you, when you leave that town shake off the dust from your feet as a testimony against them." ⁶And they departed and went through the villages, preaching the gospel and healing everywhere.

7 Now Herod the tetrarch heard of all the things that had happened, and he was perplexed, because it was said by some that John had been raised from the dead, ⁸by some that Elijah had appeared, and by others that one of the old prophets had risen. ⁹Herod said, "John I beheaded; but who is this about whom I hear such things?" And he sought to see Jesus.

10 On their return the apostles told Jesus what they had done. And Jesus took them and withdrew apart to a city called Bethsaida. ¹¹When the crowds learned it, they followed Jesus; and Jesus welcomed them and spoke to them of the dominion of God, and cured those who had need of healing. ¹²Now the day began to decline; and the twelve came and said to Jesus, "Send the crowd away, to go into the villages and country round about, to lodge and get provisions; for we are here in a lonely place." ¹³But Jesus said to them, "You give them something to eat." They said, "We have no more than five loaves and two fish— unless we are to go and buy food for all these people." ¹⁴For about five thousand people were there. Jesus said to the disciples, "Make them sit down in companies, about fifty each." ¹⁵And they did so, and made them all sit down. ¹⁶And taking the five loaves and the two fish, Jesus looked up to heaven, blessed and broke them, and gave them to the disciples to set before the crowd. ¹⁷And all ate and were satisfied. What was left over was taken up, twelve baskets of broken pieces.

18 Now it happened that as Jesus was praying alone the disciples were with him; and Jesus asked them, "Who do the people say that I am?" ¹⁹And they answered, "John the Baptist; but others say, Elijah; and others, that one of the old prophets has risen." ²⁰And Jesus said to them, "But who do you say that I am?" And Peter answered, "God's Messiah." ²¹But Jesus charged and commanded them to tell this to no one, ²²saying, "The Human One must suffer many things, and be rejected by the elders and chief priests and scribes, and be killed, and on the third day be raised."

23 And Jesus said to all, "If any would come after me, let them deny themselves and take up their cross daily and follow me. ²⁴For those who would save their life will lose it; and those who lose their life for my sake will save it. ²⁵For what does it profit people if they gain the whole world and lose or forfeit themselves? ²⁶For all who are ashamed of me and of my words, of them will the Human One be ashamed when that one comes in that one's own glory, and in the glory of God and of the holy angels. ²⁷But I tell you truly, there are some standing here who will not taste death before they see the dominion of God."

28 Now about eight days after these sayings Jesus took Peter and John and James, and went up on the mountain to pray. ²⁹And as Jesus was praying, the appearance of his countenance was altered, and his raiment became dazzlingly bright. ³⁰Then two men talked with him, Moses and Elijah, ³¹who appeared in glory and spoke of Jesus' departure, which he was to accomplish at Jerusalem. ³²Now Peter and those who were with him were heavy with sleep, and when they wakened they saw Jesus' glory and the two men who stood with him. ³³And as the two were parting from Jesus, Peter said to him, "Teacher, it is well that we are here; let us make three booths, one for you and one for Moses and one for Elijah"—not knowing what he said. ³⁴As Peter said this, a cloud came and overshadowed them; and they were afraid as they entered the cloud. ³⁵And a voice came out of the cloud, saying, "This is my Child, my Chosen; to this one you shall listen!" ³⁶And when the voice had spoken, Jesus was found alone. And they kept silent and told no one in those days anything of what they had seen.

37 On the next day, when they had come down from the mountain, a great crowd met them. ³⁸And then a man from the crowd called out, "Teacher, I beg you to look upon my son, for he is my only child; ³⁹and see, a spirit seizes him, and he suddenly cries out; it convulses him till he foams, and shatters him, and will hardly leave him. ⁴⁰I begged your disciples to cast it out, but they could not." ⁴¹Jesus answered, "O faithless and perverse generation, how long am I to be with you and bear with you? Bring your son here." ⁴²While the boy was coming, the demon tore him and convulsed him. But Jesus rebuked the unclean spirit, and healed the boy, and gave him back to his father. ⁴³And all were astonished at the majesty of God.

But while they were marveling at everything Jesus did, he said to the disciples, ⁴⁴"Let these words sink into your ears; for the Human One is to be betrayed into human hands." ⁴⁵But they did not understand this saying, and it was concealed from them, that they should not perceive it; and they were afraid to ask Jesus about this saying.

46 An argument arose among them as to which of them was the greatest. ⁴⁷And perceiving the thought of their hearts, Jesus took a child and put it by his side, ⁴⁸and said to them, "Whoever receives this child in

my name receives me, and whoever receives me receives the one who sent me; for the one who is least among you all is the one who is great."

49 John answered, "Teacher, we saw someone casting out demons in your name, and we forbade it, because the one who was doing it does not follow with us." ⁵⁰But Jesus said to John, "Do not forbid such a person; for whoever is not against you is for you."

51 When the days drew near for Jesus to be received up, he set his face to go to Jerusalem. ⁵²And Jesus sent messengers ahead, who went and entered a village of the Samaritans, to make ready for him, ⁵³but the people would not receive him, because his face was set toward Jerusalem. ⁵⁴And when the disciples James and John saw it, they said, "Lord, do you want us to bid fire come down from heaven and consume them?" ⁵⁵But Jesus turned and rebuked them. ⁵⁶And they went on to another village.

57 As they were going along the road, someone said to Jesus, "I will follow you wherever you go." ⁵⁸And Jesus replied, "Foxes have holes, and birds of the air have nests; but the Human One has nowhere to lie down and sleep." ⁵⁹To another Jesus said, "Follow me." But the answer came, "Lord, let me first go and bury my father." ⁶⁰But Jesus said, "Leave the dead to bury their own dead; but as for you, go and proclaim the dominion of God." ⁶¹Another said, "I will follow you, Lord; but let me first say farewell to those at my home." ⁶²Jesus replied, "No one who puts a hand to the plow and looks back is fit for the dominion of God."

10 After this the Lord appointed seventy others, and sent them on ahead, two by two, into every town and place where he himself was about to come. ²And he said to them, "The harvest is plentiful, but the laborers are few; pray therefore the Lord of the harvest to send out laborers into the harvest. ³Go your way; I send you out as lambs in the midst of wolves. ⁴Carry no purse, no bag, no sandals; and salute no one on the road. ⁵Whatever house you enter, first say, 'Peace be to this house!' ⁶And if a person of peace is there, your peace shall rest on it; but if not, it shall return to you. ⁷And remain in the same house, eating and drinking what they provide, for laborers deserve their wages; do not go from house to house. ⁸Whenever you enter a town and they receive you, eat what is set before you; ⁹heal the sick in it and say to them, 'The dominion of God has come near to you.' ¹⁰But whenever you enter a town and they do not receive you, go into its streets and say, ¹¹'Even the dust of your town that clings to our feet, we wipe off against you; nevertheless know this, that the dominion of God has come near.' ¹²I tell you, it shall be more tolerable on that day for Sodom than for that town.

13 "Woe to you, Chorazin! woe to you Bethsaida! for if the mighty works done in you had been done in Tyre and Sidon, the people would

have repented long ago, sitting in sackcloth and ashes. [14]But it shall be more tolerable in the judgment for Tyre and Sidon than for you. [15]And you, Capernaum, will you be exalted to heaven? You shall be brought down to Hades.

16 "The one who hears you hears me, and the one who rejects you rejects me, and the one who rejects me rejects the one who sent me."

17 The seventy returned with joy, saying, "Lord, even the demons are subject to us in your name!" [18]And Jesus said to them, "I saw Satan fall like lightning from heaven. [19]And now I have given you authority to tread upon serpents and scorpions, and over all the power of the enemy; and nothing shall hurt you. [20]Nevertheless do not rejoice in this, that the spirits are subject to you; but rejoice that your names are written in heaven."

21 In that same hour Jesus rejoiced in the Holy Spirit and said, "I thank you, God, Lord of heaven and earth, that you have hidden these things from the wise and understanding and revealed them to babes; yes, God, for such was your gracious will. [22]All things have been delivered to me by God my Father and Mother; and no one knows who the Child is except God, or who God is except that Child and anyone to whom the Child chooses to reveal God."

23 Then turning to the disciples Jesus said privately, "Blessed are the eyes that see what you see! [24]For I tell you that many prophets and rulers desired to see what you see, and did not see it, and to hear what you hear, and did not hear it."

25 A lawyer stood up to put Jesus to the test, saying, "Teacher, what shall I do to inherit eternal life?" [26]Jesus said to him, "What is written in the law? How do you read?" [27]And the lawyer answered, "You shall love the Lord your God with all your heart, and with all your soul, and with all your strength, and with all your mind; and your neighbor as yourself." [28]And Jesus said to the lawyer, "You have answered right; do this, and you will live."

29 But the lawyer, desiring to justify himself, said to Jesus, "And who is my neighbor?" [30]Jesus replied, "A man was going down from Jerusalem to Jericho and fell among robbers, who stripped him and beat him, and departed, leaving him half dead. [31]Now by chance a priest was going down that road; and when he saw him, the priest passed by on the other side. [32]So likewise a Levite, when he came to the place and saw him, passed by on the other side. [33]But a Samaritan, as he journeyed, came to where the man was; and when he saw the man, he had compassion, [34]and went to him and bound up his wounds, pouring on oil and wine; then the Samaritan set him on his own beast and brought him to an inn, and took care of him. [35]And the next day the Samaritan took out some money and gave it to the innkeeper, saying, 'Take care of him; and whatever more you spend, I will repay you when I come

back.' ³⁶Which of these three, do you think, proved neighbor to the man who fell among the robbers?" ³⁷The lawyer said, "The one who showed mercy on him." And Jesus replied, "Go and do likewise."

38 Now as they went on their way, Jesus entered a village; and a woman named Martha received him into her house. ³⁹And she had a sister called Mary, who sat at the Lord's feet and listened to his teaching. ⁴⁰But Martha was distracted with much serving; and she went to Jesus and said, "Lord, do you not care that my sister has left me to serve alone? Tell her then to help me." ⁴¹But the Lord answered her, "Martha, Martha, you are anxious and troubled about many things; ⁴²one thing is needful. Mary has chosen the good portion, which shall not be taken away from her."

11 Jesus was praying in a certain place, and when he ceased, one of the disciples said to him, "Lord, teach us to pray, as John taught his disciples." ²And Jesus said to them, "When you pray, say:

"O God, Father and Mother, may your name be made holy. May your dominion come. ³Give us each day the bread we need; ⁴and forgive us our sins, for we ourselves forgive everyone who is indebted to us; and do not put us to the test."

5 And Jesus said to them, "Which of you who has a friend will go to that friend at midnight and say, 'Friend, lend me three loaves; ⁶for a friend of mine has arrived on a journey, and I have nothing to serve'; ⁷and your friend will answer from within, 'Do not bother me; the door is now shut, and my children are with me in bed; I cannot get up and give you anything'? ⁸I tell you, though your friend will not get up and give you anything because of being a friend, yet because of being pressured, the friend will rise and give whatever is needed. ⁹And I tell you, Ask, and it will be given you; seek, and you will find; knock, and it will be opened to you. ¹⁰For everyone who asks receives, and the one who seeks finds, and to the one who knocks it will be opened. ¹¹What mother or father among you, if a child asks for a fish, instead of a fish will give a serpent; ¹²or if a child asks for an egg, will give a scorpion? ¹³If you then, who are evil, know how to give good gifts to your children, how much more will God the heavenly Father and Mother give the Holy Spirit to those who ask!"

14 Now Jesus was casting out a demon that was mute; and when the demon had gone out, the mute person spoke, and the people marveled. ¹⁵But some of them said, "Jesus casts out demons by Beelzebul, the ruler of demons"; ¹⁶while others, to test Jesus, sought from him a sign from heaven. ¹⁷But Jesus, knowing their thoughts, said to them, "Every dominion divided against itself is laid waste, and a divided household falls. ¹⁸And if Satan also is divided against Satan, how will Satan's dominion stand? For you say that I cast out demons by Beelzebul. ¹⁹And if

I cast out demons by Beelzebul, by whom do your offspring cast them out? Therefore they shall be your judges. ²⁰But if it is by the finger of God that I cast out demons, then the dominion of God has come upon you. ²¹When strong people, fully armed, guard their own palace, their goods are in peace; ²²but when a stronger force assails them and overcomes them, it takes away their armor in which they trusted, and divides their spoil. ²³Whoever is not with me is against me, and whoever does not gather with me scatters.

24 "When the unclean spirit has gone out of a person, it passes through waterless places seeking rest; and finding none it says, 'I will return to my house from which I came.' ²⁵And when it comes it finds the house swept and put in order. ²⁶Then it goes and brings seven other spirits, more evil than itself, and they enter and dwell there; and the last state of that person becomes worse than the first."

27 As Jesus said this, a woman in the crowd raised her voice and said, "Blessed is the womb that bore you, and the breasts that you sucked!" ²⁸But Jesus responded, "Blessed rather are those who hear the word of God and keep it!"

29 When the crowds were increasing, Jesus began to say, "This generation is an evil generation; it seeks a sign, but no sign will be given to it except the sign of Jonah. ³⁰For as Jonah became a sign to the people of Nineveh, so will the Human One be to this generation. ³¹The queen of the South will arise at the judgment with the people of this generation and condemn them; for she came from the ends of the earth to hear the wisdom of Solomon, and I tell you, something greater than Solomon is here. ³²The people of Nineveh will arise at the judgment with this generation and condemn it; for they repented at the preaching of Jonah, and indeed, something greater than Jonah is here.

33 "No one after lighting a lamp puts it in a cellar or under a bushel, but on a stand, that those who enter may see the light. ³⁴Your eye is the lamp of your body; when your eye is sound, your whole body is full of light; but when it is not sound, your body is full of darkness. ³⁵Therefore be careful lest the light in you be darkness. ³⁶If then your whole body is full of light, having no part dark, it will be wholly bright, as when a lamp with its rays gives you light."

37 While Jesus was speaking, a Pharisee asked him to dine with him; so Jesus went in and sat at table. ³⁸The Pharisee was astonished to see that Jesus did not first wash before dinner. ³⁹And the Lord said to him, "Now you Pharisees cleanse the outside of the cup and of the dish, but inside you are full of extortion and wickedness. ⁴⁰You fools! Did not the one who made the outside make the inside also? ⁴¹But give for alms those things which are within; and see, everything is clean for you.

42 "But woe to you Pharisees! for you tithe mint and rue and every herb, and neglect justice and the love of God; these you ought to have

done, without neglecting the others. ⁴³Woe to you Pharisees! for you love the best seat in the synagogues and salutations in the market places. ⁴⁴Woe to you! for you are like graves which are not seen, and people walk over them without knowing it."

45 One of the lawyers answered Jesus, "Teacher, in saying this you insult us also." ⁴⁶And Jesus said, "Woe to you lawyers also! for you load people with burdens hard to bear, and you yourselves do not touch the burdens with one of your fingers. ⁴⁷Woe to you! for you build the tombs of the prophets whom your ancestors killed. ⁴⁸So you are witnesses and consent to the deeds of your ancestors; for they killed them, and you build their tombs. ⁴⁹Therefore also the Wisdom of God said, 'I will send them prophets and apostles, some of whom they will kill and persecute,' ⁵⁰that the blood of all the prophets, shed from the foundation of the world, may be required of this generation, ⁵¹from the blood of Abel to the blood of Zechariah, who perished between the altar and the sanctuary. Yes, I tell you, it shall be required of this generation. ⁵²Woe to you lawyers! for you have taken away the key of knowledge; you did not enter yourselves, and you hindered those who were entering."

53 As Jesus went away from there, the scribes and the Pharisees began to press him hard, and to provoke him to speak of many things, ⁵⁴lying in wait to catch Jesus at something he might say.

12 In the meantime, when so many thousands of people had gathered together that they were trampling on one another, Jesus began to say to the disciples first, "Beware of the leaven of the Pharisees, which is hypocrisy. ²Nothing is covered up that will not be revealed, or hidden that will not be known. ³Therefore whatever you have said in the dark will be heard in the light, and what you have whispered in private rooms will be proclaimed upon the housetops.

4 "I tell you, my friends, do no fear those who kill the body, and after that have no more that they can do. ⁵But I will warn you whom to fear: fear the one who, having killed, has power to cast into hell; yes, I tell you, fear that one! ⁶Are not five sparrows sold for two pennies? And not one of them is forgotten before God. ⁷Why, even the hairs of your head are all numbered. Fear not; you are of more value than many sparrows.

8 "And I tell you, everyone who acknowledges me before others, the Human One also will acknowledge before the angels of God; ⁹but the one who denies me before others will be denied before the angels of God. ¹⁰And everyone who speaks a word against the Human One will be forgiven; but the one who blasphemes against the Holy Spirit will not be forgiven. ¹¹And when they bring you before the synagogues and the rulers and the authorities, do not be anxious how or what you are to answer or what you are to say; ¹²for the Holy Spirit will teach you in that very hour what you ought to say."

13 Someone in the crowd said to Jesus, "Teacher, tell my brother to divide the inheritance with me." ¹⁴But Jesus replied, "Who made me a judge or divider over you?" ¹⁵And he said to them, "Take heed, and beware of all covetousness; for one's life does not consist in the abundance of possessions." ¹⁶And Jesus told them a parable, saying, "The land of a rich man brought forth plentifully; ¹⁷and he thought to himself, 'What shall I do, for I have nowhere to store my crops?' ¹⁸And he said, 'I will do this: I will pull down my barns, and build larger ones; and there I will store all my grain and my goods. ¹⁹And I will say to myself, Self, you have lots of good things laid up for many years; take your ease, eat, drink, be merry.' ²⁰But God said to him, 'Fool! This night your life is required of you; and the things you have prepared, whose will they be?' ²¹So are those who lay up treasure for themselves, and are not rich toward God."

22 And Jesus said to the disciples, "Therefore I tell you, do not be anxious about your life, what you will eat, nor about your body, what you will put on. ²³For life is more than food, and the body more than clothing. ²⁴Consider the ravens: they neither sow nor reap, they have neither storehouse nor barn, and yet God feeds them. Of how much more value are you than the birds! ²⁵And which of you by being anxious can add a cubit to your span of life. ²⁶If then you are not able to do as small a thing as that, why are you anxious about the rest? ²⁷Consider the lilies, how they grow; they neither toil nor spin; yet I tell you, even Solomon in all his glory was not arrayed like one of these. ²⁸But if God so clothes the grass which is alive in the field today, and tomorrow is thrown into the oven, how much more will God clothe you, O you of little faith! ²⁹And do not seek what you are to eat and what you are to drink, nor be of anxious mind. ³⁰For all the nations of the world seek these things; and God knows that you need them. ³¹Instead, seek God's dominion, and these things will be yours as well.

32 "Fear not, little flock, for it is God's' good pleasure to give you the dominion. ³³Sell your possessions, and give alms; provide yourselves with purses that do not grow old, with a treasure in the heavens that does not fail, where no thief approaches and no moth destroys. ³⁴For where your treasure is, there will your heart be also.

35 "Let your loins be girded and your lamps burning, ³⁶and be like those who are waiting for their master to come home from the marriage feast, so that they may open the door at once when the master comes and knocks. ³⁷Blessed are those servants who are then found awake; truly, I say to you, the master will be girded and have them sit at table, and will come and serve them. ³⁸If the master comes at midnight, or just before dawn, and finds them so, blessed are those servants! ³⁹But know this, that if the householder had known at what hour the thief was coming, that householder would not have left the house to be bro-

ken into. ⁴⁰You also must be ready; for the Human One is coming at an unexpected hour."

41 Peter said, "Lord, are you telling this parable for us or for all?" ⁴²And the Lord said, "Who then is the faithful and wise steward, whose master will set over the household, to give them their portion of food at the proper time? ⁴³Blessed is that servant whose master finds working when he arrives. ⁴⁴Truly, I say to you, the master will set the steward over everything. ⁴⁵But if that servant thinks, 'My master is delayed in coming,' and begins to beat the servants, both men and women, and to eat and drink and get drunk, ⁴⁶the master of that servant will come on a day that the servant does not expect and at an hour that the servant does not know, and will punish the servant, who will then be assigned with the unfaithful. ⁴⁷And that servant who knew the master's will, but did not make ready or act according to the master's will, will receive a severe beating. ⁴⁸But the one who did not know, and did what deserved a beating, will receive a light beating. Everyone to whom much is given, of that one much will be required; and from the one to whom much has been committed, even more will be demanded.

49 "I came to cast fire upon the earth; and would that it were already kindled! ⁵⁰I have a baptism to be baptized with; and how I am constrained until it is accomplished! ⁵¹Do you think that I have come to give peace on earth? No, I tell you, but rather division; ⁵²for henceforth in one house there will be five divided, three against two and two against three; ⁵³they will be divided, father against son and son against father, mother against daughter and daughter against mother, mother-in-law against daughter-in-law and daughter-in-law against mother-in-law."

54 Jesus also said to the crowds, "When you see a cloud rising in the west, you say at once, 'A shower is coming'; and so it happens. ⁵⁵And when you see the south wind blowing, you say, 'There will be scorching heat'; and it happens. ⁵⁶You hypocrites! You know how to interpret the appearance of earth and sky; but why do you not know how to interpret the present time?

57 "And why do you not judge for yourselves what is right? ⁵⁸As you go with your accuser before the magistrate, make an effort to make a settlement on the way, lest your accuser drag you to the judge, and the judge hand you over to the officer, and the officer put you in prison. ⁵⁹I tell you, you will never get out till you have paid the very last cent."

13 There were some present at that very time who told Jesus of the Galileans whose blood Pilate had mingled with their sacrifices. ²Jesus asked them, "Do you think that these Galileans were worse sinners than all the other Galileans, because they suffered thus? ³I tell you, No; but unless you repent you will all likewise perish. ⁴Or those eighteen upon whom the tower in Siloam fell and killed them, do you think that

they were worse offenders than all the others who lived in Jerusalem? ⁵I tell you, No; but unless you repent you will all likewise perish."

6 And Jesus told this parable: "A man who had a fig tree planted in a vineyard came seeking fruit on it, and finding none, ⁷said to the vinedresser, 'These three years I have come seeking fruit on this fig tree, and I find none. Cut it down; why should it waste the soil?' ⁸And the vinedresser answered, 'Let it alone, sir, this year also, till I dig around it and put on manure. ⁹And if it bears fruit next year, well and good; but if not, you can cut it down.'"

10 Now Jesus was teaching in one of the synagogues on the sabbath. ¹¹And there was a woman who had had a spirit of infirmity for eighteen years; she was bent over and could not fully straighten herself ¹²And when Jesus saw her, he called her and said, "Woman, you are freed from your infirmity." ¹³And Jesus laid his hands upon her, and immediately she was made straight, and she praised God. ¹⁴But the ruler of the synagogue, indignant because Jesus had healed on the sabbath, said to the people, "There are six days on which work ought to be done; come on those days and be healed, and not on the sabbath day." ¹⁵Then the Lord answered, "You hypocrites! Does not each of you on the sabbath untie your ox or your donkey from the manger, and lead it away to water it? ¹⁶And ought not this woman, a daughter of Abraham and Sarah whom Satan bound for eighteen years, be loosed from this bond on the sabbath day?" ¹⁷As Jesus said this, all his adversaries were put to shame; and all the people rejoiced at all the wonderful things that Jesus did.

18 Jesus said therefore, "What is the dominion of God like? And to what shall I compare it? ¹⁹It is like a grain of mustard seed which a man took and sowed in his garden; and it grew and became a tree, and the birds of the air made nests in its branches."

20 And again Jesus said, "To what shall I compare the dominion of God? ²¹It is like leaven which a woman took and hid in three measures of flour, till it was all leavened."

22 Jesus went on his way through towns and villages, teaching, and journeying toward Jerusalem. ²³And someone said to him, "Lord, will those who are saved be few?" And Jesus said to them, ²⁴"Strive to enter by the narrow door; for many, I tell you, will seek to enter and will not be able. ²⁵When once the householder has risen up and shut the door, you will begin to stand outside and to knock at the door, saying, 'Lord, open to us.' You will be answered, 'I do not know where you come from.' ²⁶Then you will begin to say, 'We ate and drank in your presence, and you taught in our streets.' ²⁷But you will be told, 'I tell you, I do not know where you come from; depart from me, all you workers of iniquity!' ²⁸There you will weep and gnash your teeth, when you see Abraham and Isaac and Jacob and all the prophets in the dominion of God and you yourselves thrown out. ²⁹And people will come from east

and west, and from north and south, and sit at table in the dominion of God. ³⁰And some are last who will be first, and some are first who will be last."

31 At that very hour some Pharisees came, and said to Jesus, "Get away from here, for Herod wants to kill you." ³²And Jesus said to them, "Go and tell that fox, 'I cast out demons and perform cures today and tomorrow, and the third day I finish my course. ³³Nevertheless I must go on my way today and tomorrow and the day following; for it cannot be that a prophet should perish away from Jerusalem.' ³⁴O Jerusalem, Jerusalem, killing the prophets and stoning those who are sent to you! How often would I have gathered your children together as a hen gathers her brood under her wings, and you would not! ³⁵And now your house is forsaken. And I tell you, you will not see me until you say, 'Blessed is the one who comes in the name of the Lord!' "

14 One sabbath when Jesus went to dine at the house of a ruler who belonged to the Pharisees, they were watching him.

2 And it happened that there was a person before Jesus who had dropsy. ³And Jesus spoke to the lawyers and Pharisees, saying, "Is it lawful to heal on the sabbath, or not?" ⁴But they were silent. Then Jesus, having taken and healed the person, let the person go. ⁵And Jesus said to them, "Which of you, having a child or an ox that has fallen into a well, will not immediately pull it out on a sabbath day?" ⁶And they could not reply to this.

7 Noticing how they chose the places of honor, Jesus told a parable to those who were invited, saying to them, ⁸"When you are invited by anyone to a marriage feast, do not sit down in a place of honor, lest a more eminent person than you be invited; ⁹and the one who invited you both will come and say to you, 'Give place to this person,' and then you will begin with shame to take the lowest place. ¹⁰But when you are invited, go and sit in the lowest place, so that your host, having come, may say to you, 'Friend, go up higher'; then you will be honored in the presence of all who sit at table with you. ¹¹For all who exalt themselves will be humbled, and all who humble themselves will be exalted."

12 Jesus said also to the person who had invited him, "When you give a dinner or a banquet, do not invite your friends or your brothers and sisters or your relatives or rich neighbors, lest they also invite you in return, and you be repaid. ¹³But when you give a feast, invite those who are poor and maimed and lame and blind, ¹⁴and you will be blessed, because they cannot repay you. You will be repaid at the resurrection of the righteous."

15 One of those who sat at table, on hearing this, said to Jesus, "Blessed is whoever will eat bread in the dominion of God!" ¹⁶But Jesus

answered, "A person once gave a great banquet, and invited many; ¹⁷and at the time for the banquet the host sent a servant to say to those who had been invited, 'Come; for all is now ready.' ¹⁸But they all alike began to make excuses. The first said, 'I have bought a field, and I must go out and see it; please have me excused.' ¹⁹And another said, 'I have bought five yoke of oxen, and I go to examine them; please have me excused.' ²⁰And another said, 'I have just been married, and therefore I cannot come.' ²¹So the servant came and reported this to the householder. Then the householder in anger said to the servant, 'Go out quickly to the streets and lanes of the city, and bring in the people who are poor and maimed and blind and lame.' ²²And the servant said, 'What you commanded has been done, and still there is room.' ²³And the householder said to the servant, 'Go out to the highways and streets, and compel people to come in, that my house may be filled. ²⁴For I tell you, none of those who were invited shall taste my banquet.' "

25 Now great crowds accompanied Jesus; and he turned and said to them, ²⁶"Whoever comes to me and does not hate father and mother and wife and husband and children and brothers and sisters, yes, and even life itself, cannot be my disciple. ²⁷Whoever does not bear their own cross and come after me, cannot be my disciple. ²⁸For which of you, desiring to build a tower, does not first sit down and count the cost, whether there is enough to complete it? ²⁹Otherwise, when the foundation is laid and the tower cannot be finished, all who see it begin to mock, ³⁰saying, 'This person began to build, and was not able to finish.' ³¹Or what king, going to encounter another king in war, will not sit down first and take counsel whether he is able with ten thousand to meet the one who comes against him with twenty thousand? ³²And if not, while the other is still far away, he sends an embassy and asks terms of peace. ³³So therefore, whoever of you does not renounce all possessions cannot be my disciple.

34 "Salt is good; but if salt has lost its taste, how will its saltness be restored? ³⁵It is fit neither for the land nor for the dunghill; it is thrown away. Those who have ears to hear, let them hear."

15 Now the tax collectors and sinners were all drawing near to hear Jesus. ²And the Pharisees and the scribes murmured, saying, "This man receives sinners and eats with them."

3 So Jesus told them this parable: ⁴"Which one of you, having a hundred sheep, if he has lost one of them, does not leave the ninety-nine in the wilderness and go after the one which is lost, until he finds it? ⁵And having found it, he lays it on his shoulders, rejoicing. ⁶And when he comes home, he calls together his friends and neighbors, saying to them, 'Rejoice with me, for I have found my sheep which was lost.' ⁷Just so, I tell you, there will be more joy in heaven over one sinner who repents than over ninety-nine righteous people who need no repentance.

8 "Or what woman, having ten silver coins, if she loses one coin, does not light a lamp and sweep the house and seek diligently until she finds it? ⁹And when she has found it, she calls together her friends and neighbors, saying, 'Rejoice with me, for I have found the coin which I had lost.' ¹⁰Just so, I tell you, there is joy before the angels of God over one sinner who repents."

11 And Jesus said, "There was a man who had two sons; ¹²and the younger of them said to his father, 'Father, give me the share of property that falls to me.' And he divided his living between them. ¹³Not many days later, the younger son gathered all he had and took his journey into a far country, and there squandered his property in loose living. ¹⁴And when he had spent everything, a great famine arose in that country, and he began to be in want. ¹⁵So he went and joined himself to one of the citizens of that country, who sent him into his fields to feed swine. ¹⁶And he would gladly have fed on the pods that the swine ate; and no one gave him anything. ¹⁷But when he came to himself he said, 'How many of my father's hired servants have bread enough and to spare, but I perish here with hunger! ¹⁸I will arise and go to my father, and I will say to him, "Father, I have sinned against heaven and before you; ¹⁹I am no longer worthy to be called your son; treat me as one of your hired servants."' ²⁰And he arose and came to his father. But while he was yet at a distance, his father saw him and had compassion, and ran and embraced him and kissed him. ²¹And the son said to him, 'Father, I have sinned against heaven and before you; I am no longer worthy to be called your son.' ²²But the father said to the servants, 'Bring quickly the best robe, and put it on him; and put a ring on his hand, and shoes on his feet; ²³and bring the fatted calf and kill it, and let us eat and make merry; ²⁴for this my son was dead and is alive again, was lost and is found.' And they began to make merry.

25 "Now his elder son was in the field; and as he came and drew near to the house, he heard music and dancing. ²⁶And he called one of the servants and asked what this meant. ²⁷And the servant said to him, 'Your brother has come, and your father has killed the fatted calf, because he has received him safe and sound.' ²⁸But the elder son was angry and refused to go in. His father came out and entreated him, ²⁹but he answered his father, 'These many years I have served you, and I never disobeyed your command; yet you never gave me a kid, that I might make merry with my friends. ³⁰But when this son of yours came, who has devoured your living with harlots, you killed for him the fatted calf!' ³¹And he said to him, 'Son, you are always with me, and all that is mine is yours. ³²It was fitting to make merry and be glad, for this your brother was dead, and is alive; he was lost, and is found.'"

16 Jesus also said to the disciples, "There was a rich man who had a steward accused of wasting his goods. ²And the rich man called the steward and said, 'What is this that I hear about you? Turn in the account of your stewardship, for you can no longer be steward.' ³And the steward thought, 'What shall I do, since my master is taking the stewardship away from me? I am not strong enough to dig, and I am ashamed to beg. ⁴I have decided what to do, so that people may receive me into their houses when I am put out of the stewardship.' ⁵So, summoning the master's debtors one by one, the steward said to the first, 'How much do you owe my master?' ⁶The answer came, 'A hundred bottles of olive oil.' And the steward said, 'Take your bill, and sit down quickly and write fifty.' ⁷Then the steward said to another, 'And how much do you owe?' The answer came, 'A hundred bushels of wheat.' The steward said, 'Take your bill, and write eighty.' ⁸The master commended the dishonest steward for acting shrewdly; for the children of this world are more shrewd in dealing with their own generation than the children of light. ⁹And I tell you, make friends for yourselves by means of unrighteous mammon, so that when it fails they may receive you into the eternal habitations.

10 "One who is faithful in a very little is faithful also in much; and one who is dishonest in a very little is dishonest also in much. ¹¹If then you have not been faithful in the unrighteous mammon, who will entrust to you the true riches? ¹²And if you have not been faithful in that which is another's, who will give you that which is your own? ¹³No servant can serve two masters; for the servant will either hate the one and love the other, or be devoted to the one and despise the other. You cannot serve God and mammon."

14 The Pharisees, who were lovers of money, heard all this, and they scoffed at Jesus. ¹⁵But Jesus said to them, "You are those who justify yourselves before human beings, but God knows your hearts; for what is exalted among us is an abomination in the sight of God.

16 "The law and the prophets were until John; since then the good news of the dominion of God is preached, and everyone enters it violently. ¹⁷But it is easier for heaven and earth to pass away, than for one dot of the law to become void.

18 "Everyone who divorces his wife and marries another commits adultery, and he who marries a woman divorced from her husband commits adultery.

19 "There was a rich person, clothed in purple and fine linen, who feasted sumptuously every day. ²⁰And at the gate lay a poor man named Lazarus, full of sores, ²¹who desired to be fed with what fell from the rich person's table; moreover the dogs came and licked his sores. ²²The poor man died and was carried by the angels to Abraham's bosom. The rich person also died and was buried; ²³and being in torment in Hades, looked up, and saw Abraham far off and Lazarus in his bosom. ²⁴And the

rich person called out, 'Father Abraham, have mercy on me, and send Lazarus to dip the end of his finger in water and cool my tongue; for I am in anguish in this flame.' 25But Abraham said, 'My child, remember that you in your lifetime received your good things, and Lazarus in like manner evil things; but now he is comforted here, and you are in anguish. 26And besides all this, between us and you a great chasm has been fixed, in order that those who would pass from here to you may not be able, and none may cross from there to us.' 27And the rich person said, 'Then I beg you, father, to send Lazarus to my parents' house, 28for I have five brothers, so that he may warn them, lest they also come into this place of torment.' 29But Abraham said, 'They have Moses and the prophets; let them hear them.' 30And the rich person said, 'No, father Abraham; but if someone goes to them from the dead, they will repent.' 31Abraham answered, 'If they do not hear Moses and the prophets, neither will they be convinced if someone should rise from the dead.' "

17 Jesus said to the disciples, "Temptations to sin are sure to come; but woe to those by whom they come! 2It would be better for them if a millstone were hung around their neck and they were cast into the sea, than that they should cause one of these little ones to sin. 3Take heed to yourselves; if a member of the church sins, rebuke that member, and if that one repents, forgive; 4and if that member sins against you seven times in the day, and turns to you seven times, and says, 'I repent,' you must forgive."

5 The apostles said to the Lord, "Increase our faith!" 6And the Lord said, "If you had faith as a grain of mustard seed, you could say to this mulberry tree, 'Be rooted up, and be planted in the sea,' and it would obey you.

7 "Will any one of you, who has servants plowing or keeping sheep, say to them when they have come in from the field, 'Come at once and sit down at table'? 8Will you not rather say to them, 'Prepare supper for me, and put on your apron and wait on me, till I eat and drink; and afterward you will eat and drink'? 9Do you thank the servants because they did what was commanded? 10So you also, when you have done all that is commanded you, say, 'We are unworthy servants; we have only done what was our duty.' "

11 On the way to Jerusalem Jesus was passing along between Samaria and Galilee. 12And entering a village, he was met by ten people with leprosy, who stood at a distance 13and lifted up their voices and said, "Jesus, Teacher, have mercy on us." 14And seeing them., Jesus said, "Go and show yourselves to the priests." And as they went they were cleansed. 15Then one of them, seeing that he was healed, turned back, praising God with a loud voice; 16and he fell down at Jesus' feet, giving him thanks. Now that one was a Samaritan. 17Then Jesus said, "Were not

ten cleansed? Where are the nine? [18]Was no one found to return and give praise to God except this foreigner?" [19]And Jesus said to him, "Rise and go your way; your faith has made you well."

20 Being asked by the Pharisees when the dominion of God was coming, Jesus answered them, "The dominion of God is not coming with signs to be observed; [21]nor will people say, 'Lo, here it is!' or 'There!' for look, the dominion of God is in the midst of you."

22 And Jesus said to the disciples, "The days are coming when you will desire to see one of the days of the Human One, and you will not see it. [23]And people will say to you, 'Lo, there!' or 'Lo, here!' Do not go, do not follow them. [24]For as the lightning flashes and lights up the sky from one side to the other, so will the Human One be in that day. [25]But first the Human One must suffer many things and be rejected by this generation. [26]As it was in the days of Noah, so will it be in the days of the Human One. [27]People ate, they drank, they married, they were given in marriage, until the day when Noah entered the ark, and the flood came and destroyed them all. [28]Likewise as it was in the days of Lot—people ate, they drank, they bought, they sold, they planted, they built, [29]but on the day when Lot went out from Sodom, fire and sulphur rained from heaven and destroyed them all—[30]so will it be on the day when the Human One is revealed. [31]On that day, let anyone who is on the housetop, with goods in the house, not come down to take them away; and likewise let anyone who is in the field not turn back. [32]Remember Lot's wife. [33]Those who seek to gain their life will lose it, but those who lose their life will preserve it. [34]I tell you, in that night there will be two in one bed; one will be taken and the other left. [35]There will be two women grinding together; one will be taken and the other left."* [37]And they said to Jesus, "Where, Lord?" Jesus said to them, "Where the corpse is, there the vultures will be gathered together."

18 And Jesus told them a parable, to the effect that they ought always to pray and not lose heart. [2]He said, "In a certain city there was a judge who neither feared God nor respected people; [3]and there was a widow in that city who kept coming to the judge and saying, 'Vindicate me against my adversary.' [4]For a while the judge refused, but afterward thought, 'Though I neither fear God nor respect people, [5]yet because this widow bothers me, I will vindicate her, or she will wear me out by her continual coming.'" [6]And the Lord said, "Hear what the unrighteous judge says. [7]And will not God vindicate the elect, who cry to God day and night? Will God delay long over them? [8]I tell you, God will

---

* Other ancient authorities add verse 36, *"Two men will be in the field; one will be taken and the other left."*

vindicate them speedily. Nevertheless, when the Human One comes, will the Human One find faith on earth?"

9 Jesus told this parable to some who trusted in themselves that they were righteous and despised others: ¹⁰"Two people went up into the temple to pray, one a Pharisee and the other a tax collector. ¹¹The Pharisee stood and prayed thus with himself, 'God, I thank you that I am not like other people, extortioners, unjust, adulterers, or even like this tax collector. ¹²I fast twice a week, I give tithes of all that I get.' ¹³But the tax collector, standing far off, would not even look up to heaven, but beat his breast and said, 'God, be merciful to me a sinner!' ¹⁴I tell you, this one went home justified rather than the other; for all who exalt themselves will be humbled, but those who humble themselves will be exalted."

15 Now people were bringing even infants to Jesus so that Jesus would touch them; and when the disciples saw it, they rebuked the people. ¹⁶But Jesus called them to him, saying, "Let the children come to me, and do not hinder them; for to such belongs the dominion of God. ¹⁷Truly, I say to you, whoever does not receive the dominion of God like a child will not enter it."

18 And a ruler asked Jesus, "Good Teacher, what shall I do to inherit eternal life?" ¹⁹Jesus answered, "Why do you call me good? No one is good but God alone. ²⁰You know the commandments: 'Do not commit adultery, Do not kill, Do not steal, Do not bear false witness, Honor your father and mother.' " ²¹And the ruler said, "All these I have observed since I was young." ²²And hearing it Jesus said, "One thing you still lack. Sell all that you have and distribute to the poor, and you will have treasure in heaven; and come, follow me." ²³But on hearing this, the ruler, being very rich, became sad. ²⁴And observing this Jesus said, "How hard it is for those who have riches to enter the dominion of God! ²⁵For it is easier for a camel to go through the eye of a needle than for a rich person to enter the dominion of God." ²⁶Those who heard it said, "Then who can be saved?" ²⁷But Jesus said, "What is impossible with human beings is possible with God." ²⁸And Peter said, "Look, we have left our homes and followed you." ²⁹And Jesus said to them, "Truly, I say to you, there is no one who has left house or husband or wife or brothers or sisters or parents or children, for the sake of the dominion of God, ³⁰who will not receive many times more in this time, and in the age to come eternal life."

31 And taking the twelve, Jesus said to them, "See, we are going up to Jerusalem, and everything that is written of the Human One by the prophets will be accomplished. ³²For the Human One will be delivered to the Gentiles, and will be mocked and shamefully treated and spit upon, ³³and scourged and killed, and on the third day will rise." ³⁴But they understood none of these things; this saying was hidden from them, and they did not grasp what was said.

35 As Jesus drew near to Jericho, a blind man was sitting by the roadside begging; 36and hearing a crowd going by, he inquired what this meant. 37They told him, "Jesus of Nazareth is passing by." 38And he cried, "Jesus, Child of David, have mercy on me!" 39And those who were in front rebuked him, telling him to be silent; but he cried out all the more, "Child of David, have mercy on me!" 40And Jesus stopped, and commanded the blind man to be brought to him; and when he came near, Jesus asked him, 41"What do you want me to do for you?" He said, "Lord, let me receive my sight." 42And Jesus said to him, "Receive your sight; your faith has made you well." 43And immediately he received his sight and followed Jesus, glorifying God; and all the people, when they saw it, gave praise to God.

19 Jesus entered Jericho and was passing through. 2And there was a man named Zacchaeus, who was a chief tax collector, and rich. 3And he sought to see who Jesus was, but could not, on account of the crowd, because he was short in stature. 4So he ran on ahead and climbed up into a sycamore tree to see Jesus, who was to pass that way. 5And when Jesus came to the place, he looked up and said to him, "Zacchaeus, hurry and come down; for I must stay at your house today." 6So he hurried and came down, and received Jesus joyfully. 7And when they saw it they all murmured, "He has gone in to be the guest of a man who is a sinner." 8And Zacchaeus stood and said to the Lord, "Half of my goods I give to the poor; and if I have defrauded anyone of anything, I restore it fourfold." 9And Jesus said to him, "Today salvation has come to this house, since Zacchaeus also is a descendant of Abraham. 10For the Human One came to seek and to save the lost."

11 As they heard these things, Jesus proceeded to tell a parable, because he was near Jerusalem, and because they supposed that the dominion of God was to appear immediately. 12Jesus said therefore, "A person of noble birth went into a far country to receive royal power and then return. 13Calling ten servants, this person gave them ten pounds, and said to them, 'Trade with these till I come.' 14But the citizens hated the noble person and sent an embassy, saying, 'We do not want this person to rule over us.' 15Returning, having received royal power, the noble person commanded these servants to whom the money had been given to be called in, so as to find out what they had gained by trading. 16The first came up, saying, 'Lord, your pound has made ten pounds more.' 17The noble person said, 'Well done, good servant! Because you have been faithful in a very little, you will have authority over ten cities.' 18And the second came, saying, 'Lord, your pound has made five pounds.' 19And Jesus responded, 'And you are to be over five cities.' 20Then another came, saying 'Lord, here is your pound, which I kept laid away in a napkin; 21for I was afraid of you, because you are a severe

person; you take up what you did not lay down, and reap what you did not sow.' ²²Jesus answered, 'I will condemn you out of your own mouth, you wicked servant! You knew that I was severe, taking up what I did not lay down and reaping what I did not sow? ²³Why then did you not put my money into the bank, and at my coming I would have collected it with interest?' ²⁴And Jesus said to those who stood by, 'Take the pound from that person and give it to the one who has the ten pounds.' ²⁵(And they said to Jesus, 'Lord, that person has ten pounds!') ²⁶'I tell you, that to those who have will more be given; but from those who have not, even what they have will be taken away. ²⁷But as for these enemies of mine, who did not want me to rule over them, bring them here and slaughter them before me.'"

28 And having said this, Jesus went on ahead, going up to Jerusalem. ²⁹When he drew near to Bethphage and Bethany, at the mount that is called Olivet, he sent two of the disciples, ³⁰saying, "Go into the village opposite, where on entering you will find a colt tied, on which no one has ever yet sat; untie it and bring it here. ³¹If anyone asks you, 'Why are you untying it?' you will say this, 'The Lord has need of it.'" ³²So those who were sent went away and found it as Jesus had told them. ³³And as they were untying the colt, its owners said to them, "Why are you untying the colt?" ³⁴And they said, "The Lord has need of it." ³⁵And they brought it to Jesus, and throwing their garments on the colt they set him upon it. ³⁶And as Jesus rode along, they spread their garments on the road. ³⁷As he was already coming near to the slope that comes down from the Mount of Olives, the whole crowd of the disciples began to rejoice and praise God with a loud voice for all the mighty works that they had seen, ³⁸saying, "Blessed is the King who comes in the name of the Lord! Peace in heaven and glory in the highest!" ³⁹And some of the Pharisees in the crowd said to Jesus, "Teacher, rebuke your disciples." ⁴⁰He answered, "I tell you, if these were silent, the very stones would cry out."

41 And Jesus, drawing near and seeing the city, wept over it, ⁴²saying, "Would that even today you knew the things that make for peace! But now they are hidden from your eyes. ⁴³For the days will come upon you, when your enemies will raise up ramparts around you and surround you, and hem you in on every side, ⁴⁴and dash you to the ground, you and your children within you, and they will not leave one stone upon another within you; because you did not know the time of your visitation."

45 And Jesus entered the temple and began to drive out those who sold, ⁴⁶saying to them, "It is written, 'My house will be a house of prayer'; but you have made it a den of robbers."

47 And Jesus was teaching daily in the temple. The chief priests and the scribes and the leaders of the people sought to destroy him; ⁴⁸but

they did not find anything they could do, for all the people hung upon Jesus' words.

20 One day, as Jesus was teaching the people in the temple and preaching the gospel, the chief priests and the scribes with the elders came up ²and said, "Tell us by what authority you do these things, or who it is that gave you this authority." ³Jesus answered them, "I also will ask you a question; now tell me, ⁴Was the baptism of John from heaven, or was it of human origin?" ⁵And they discussed it with one another, saying, "If we answer, 'From heaven,' Jesus will say, 'Why did you not believe him?' ⁶But if we answer, 'Of human origin,' all the people will stone us; for they are convinced that John was a prophet." ⁷So they answered that they did not know what its source was. ⁸And Jesus said to them, "Neither will I tell you by what authority I do these things."

9 And Jesus began to tell the people this parable: "A man planted a vineyard, and let it out to tenants, and went into another country for a long while. ¹⁰When the time came, he sent a servant to the tenants, to be given some of the fruit of the vineyard; but the servant was beaten by the tenants, and sent away empty-handed. ¹¹And the owner sent another servant, whom the tenants also beat and treated shamefully, and sent away empty-handed. ¹²And he sent yet a third; this one they wounded and cast out. ¹³Then the owner of the vineyard said, 'What shall I do? I will send my beloved heir, my very own child, whom perhaps they will respect.' ¹⁴But when the tenants saw the heir, they said to themselves, 'This is the heir; let us kill this person too, that the inheritance may be ours.' ¹⁵And they cast out and killed the heir. What then will the owner of the vineyard do to them? ¹⁶He will come and destroy those tenants, and give the vineyard to others." When the people heard this, they said, "God forbid!" ¹⁷But Jesus looked at them and said, "What then is this that is written:

'The very stone which the builders rejected
has become the head of the corner'?

¹⁸Everyone who falls on that stone will be broken to pieces; but anyone on whom it falls will be crushed."

19 The scribes and the chief priests tried to lay hands on Jesus at that very hour, but they feared the people; for they perceived that Jesus had told this parable against them. ²⁰So they watched Jesus, and sent spies, who pretended to be sincere, that they might take hold of what Jesus said, so as to deliver him up to the authority and jurisdiction of the governor. ²¹They asked Jesus, "Teacher, we know that you speak and teach rightly, and show no partiality, but truly teach the way of God. ²²Is it lawful for us to give tribute to Caesar, or not?" ²³But Jesus perceived their craftiness, and said to them, ²⁴"Show me a coin. Whose

likeness and inscription has it?" They said, "Caesar's." ²⁵Jesus said to them, "Then render to Caesar the things that are Caesar's, and to God the things that are God's." ²⁶And they were not able in the presence of the people to catch Jesus by what he said; but marveling at his answer they were silent.

27 Some Sadducees came to Jesus, those who say that there is no resurrection, ²⁸and they asked a question, saying, "Teacher, Moses wrote for us that if a man's brother dies, having a wife but no children, the man must take the wife and raise up children for his brother. ²⁹Now there were seven brothers; the first took a wife, and died without children; ³⁰and the second ³¹and the third took her, and likewise all seven left no children, and died. ³²Afterward the woman also died. ³³In the resurrection, therefore, whose wife will the woman be? For the seven had her as wife."

34 And Jesus said to them, "The daughters and sons of this age marry and are given in marriage; ³⁵but those who are accounted worthy to attain to that age and to the resurrection from the dead neither marry nor are given in marriage, ³⁶for they cannot die anymore, because they are equal to angels and are children of God, being children of the resurrection. ³⁷But that the dead are raised, even Moses showed, in the passage about the bush, where he calls the Lord the God of Abraham and the God of Isaac and the God of Jacob. ³⁸Now God is not God of the dead, but of the living; for all live to God." ³⁹And some of the scribes answered, "Teacher, you have spoken well." ⁴⁰For they no longer dared to ask him any question.

41 But Jesus said to them, "How can people say that the Messiah is David's offspring? ⁴²For David himself says in the Book of Psalms,

'God said to my Lord,
Sit at my right hand,
⁴³till I make your enemies a stool for your feet.'

⁴⁴David thus calls the Messiah Lord; so how can the Messiah be David's offspring?"

45 And in the hearing of all the people Jesus said to the disciples, ⁴⁶"Beware of the scribes, who like to go about in long robes, and love salutations in the market places and the best seats in the synagogues and the places of honor at feasts, ⁴⁷who devour widows' houses and for a pretense make long prayers. They will receive the greater condemnation."

21 Jesus looked up and saw the rich putting their gifts into the treasury; ²and he saw a poor widow put in two copper coins. ³And Jesus said, "Truly I tell you, this poor widow has put in more than all

of them; ⁴for they all contributed out of their abundance, but she out of her poverty put in all she had to live on."

5 And as some spoke of the temple, how it was adorned with noble stones and offerings, Jesus said, ⁶"As for these things which you see, the days will come when there will not be left here one stone upon another that will not be thrown down." ⁷And they asked, "Teacher, when will this be, and what will be the sign when this is about to take place?" ⁸And Jesus said, "Take heed that you are not led astray; for many will come in my name, saying, 'I am the one!' and, 'The time is at hand!' Do not go after them. ⁹And when you hear of wars and tumults, do not be terrified; for this must first take place, but the end will not be at once."

10 Then Jesus said to them, "Nation will rise against nation, and kingdom against kingdom; ¹¹there will be great earthquakes, and in various places famines and pestilences; and there will be terrors and great signs from heaven. ¹²But before all this they will lay their hands on you and persecute you, delivering you up to the synagogues and prisons, and you will be brought before rulers and governors for my name's sake. ¹³This will be a time for you to bear testimony. ¹⁴Settle it therefore in your minds, not to meditate beforehand how to answer; ¹⁵for I will give you a mouth and wisdom, which none of your adversaries will be able to withstand or contradict. ¹⁶You will be delivered up even by parents and brothers and sisters and relatives and friends, and some of you they will put to death; ¹⁷you will be hated by all for my name's sake. ¹⁸But not a hair of your head will perish. ¹⁹By your endurance you will gain your lives.

20 "But when you see Jerusalem surrounded by armies, then know that its desolation has come near. ²¹Then let those who are in Judea flee to the mountains, and let those who are inside the city depart, and let not those who are out in the country enter it; ²²for these are days of vengeance, to fulfill all that is written. ²³Alas for those who are with child and for those who are nursing infants in those days! For great distress will be upon the earth and wrath upon this people; ²⁴they will fall by the edge of the sword, and be led captive among all nations; and Jerusalem will be trampled down by Gentiles, until the times of the Gentiles are fulfilled.

25 "And there will be signs in sun and moon and stars, and upon the earth distress of nations in perplexity at the roaring of the sea and the waves, ²⁶people fainting with fear and with foreboding of what is coming on the world; for the powers of the heavens will be shaken. ²⁷And then they will see the Human One coming in a cloud with power and great glory. ²⁸Now when these things begin to take place, look up and raise your heads, because your redemption is drawing near."

29 And Jesus told them a parable: "Look at the fig tree, and all the trees; ³⁰as soon as they come out in leaf, you see for yourselves and know

that the summer is already near. ³¹So also, when you see these things taking place, you know that the dominion of God is near. ³²Truly, I say to you, this generation will not pass away till all has taken place. ³³Heaven and earth will pass away, but my words will not pass away.

34 "But take heed to yourselves lest your hearts be weighed down with dissipation and drunkenness and cares of this life, and that day come upon you suddenly like a snare; ³⁵for it will come upon all who dwell upon the face of the whole earth. ³⁶But watch at all times, praying that you may have strength to escape all these things that will take place, and to stand before the Human One."

37 And every day Jesus was teaching in the temple, but at night he went out and lodged on the mount called Olivet. ³⁸And early in the morning all the people came to Jesus in the temple to hear him.

22 Now the feast of Unleavened Bread drew near, which is called the Passover. ²And the chief priests and the scribes were seeking how to put Jesus to death; for they feared the people.

3 Then Satan entered into Judas called Iscariot, who was one of the twelve; ⁴he went away and conferred with the chief priests and officers about how he might betray Jesus to them. ⁵And they were glad, and agreed to give Judas money. ⁶So he consented, and sought an opportunity to betray Jesus to them when the crowd was not present.

7 Then came the day of Unleavened Bread, on which the passover lamb had to be sacrificed. ⁸So Jesus sent Peter and John, saying, "Go and prepare the passover for us, that we may eat it." ⁹They said to him, "Where will you have us prepare it?" ¹⁰Jesus said to them, "When you have entered the city, a man carrying a jar of water will meet you; follow him into the house which he enters, ¹¹and tell the householder, 'The Teacher says to you, Where is the guest room, where I am to eat the passover with my disciples?' ¹²And the householder will show you a large upper room furnished; there make ready." ¹³And they went, and found it as Jesus had told them; and they prepared the passover.

14 And when the hour came, Jesus sat at table, and the apostles with him. ¹⁵And Jesus said to them, "I have earnestly desired to eat this passover with you before I suffer; ¹⁶for I tell you I shall not eat it until it is fulfilled in the dominion of God." ¹⁷And Jesus took a cup, and, having given thanks, said, "Take this, and divide it among yourselves; ¹⁸for I tell you that from now on I shall not drink of the fruit of the vine until the dominion of God comes." ¹⁹And Jesus took bread, and, having given thanks, broke it and gave it to them, saying, "This is my body which is given for you. Do this in remembrance of me." ²⁰And likewise the cup after supper, saying, "This cup which is poured out for you is the new covenant in my blood. ²¹But the hand of the one who betrays me is with

me on the table. ²²For the Human One goes as it has been determined; but woe to that person by whom the Human One is betrayed!" ²³And they began to question one another, which of them it was that would do this.

24 A dispute also arose among them, which of them was to be regarded as the greatest. ²⁵And Jesus said to them, "The rulers of the Gentiles lord it over them; and those in authority over them are called benefactors. ²⁶But not so with you; rather let the greatest among you become as the youngest, and the leader as one who serves. ²⁷For which is the greater, one who sits at table, or one who serves? Is it not the one who sits at table? But I am among you as one who serves.

28 "You are those who have continued with me in my trials; ²⁹and I assign a dominion to you, as God my Father and Mother assigned one to me, ³⁰that you may eat and drink at my table in my dominion, and sit on thrones judging the twelve tribes of Israel.

31 "Simon, Simon: Satan demanded to have you, in order to sift you like wheat, ³²but I have prayed for you that your faith may not fail; and when you have turned again, strengthen your brothers and sisters." ³³And Simon said to Jesus, "Lord, I am ready to go with you to prison and to death." ³⁴Jesus said, "I tell you, Peter, the cock will not crow this day, until you deny three times that you know me."

35 And Jesus said to them, "When I sent you out with no purse or bag or sandals, did you lack anything?" They said, "Nothing." ³⁶He said to them, "But now, whoever has a purse, take it, and likewise a bag. And whoever has no sword, sell your mantle and buy one. ³⁷For I tell you that this scripture must be fulfilled in me, 'And he was reckoned with transgressors'; for what is written about me has its fulfillment." ³⁸And they said, "Look, Lord, here are two swords." And Jesus said to them, "It is enough."

39 And Jesus came out, and went, as was his custom, to the Mount of Olives; and the disciples followed him. ⁴⁰And having come to the place, he said to them, "Pray that you may not enter into temptation." ⁴¹And Jesus withdrew from them about a stone's throw, and knelt down and prayed, ⁴²"God, my Father and Mother, if you are willing, remove this cup from me; nevertheless not my will, but yours, be done." ⁴³And an angel from heaven appeared to him, strengthening him. ⁴⁴And being in anguish he prayed more fervently; and his sweat became like great drops of blood falling down upon the ground. ⁴⁵And when Jesus rose from prayer, he came to the disciples and found them sleeping from sorrow, ⁴⁶and said to them, "Why do you sleep? Rise and pray that you may not enter into temptation."

47 While Jesus was still speaking, a crowd came, and the man called Judas, one of the twelve, was leading them. Judas drew near to Jesus to kiss him; ⁴⁸but Jesus said, "Judas, would you betray the Human One

with a kiss?" ⁴⁹And when those who were standing nearby saw what would follow, they said, "Lord, shall we strike with the sword?" ⁵⁰And one of them struck the slave of the high priest and cut off his right ear. ⁵¹But Jesus said, "No more of this!" And Jesus touched the ear of the slave and healed him. ⁵²Then Jesus said to the chief priests and officers of the temple and elders, who had come out against him, "Have you come out as against a robber, with swords and clubs? ⁵³When I was with you day after day in the temple, you did not lay hands on me. But this is your hour, and the power of evil."

54 Then they seized Jesus and led him away, bringing him into the high priest's house. Peter followed at a distance; ⁵⁵and when they had kindled a fire in the middle of the courtyard and sat down together, Peter sat among them. ⁵⁶Then a womanservant, seeing him as he sat in the light and gazing at him, said, "This man also was with him." ⁵⁷But Peter denied it, saying, "Woman, I do not know him." ⁵⁸And a little later someone else saw Peter, and said, "You also are one of them." But Peter said, "No, I am not." ⁵⁹And after an interval of about an hour still another insisted, saying, "Certainly this man also was with him; for he is a Galilean." ⁶⁰But Peter said, "I do not know what you are saying." And immediately, while Peter was still speaking, the cock crowed. ⁶¹And the Lord turned and looked at Peter. And Peter remembered the word which the Lord had said to him, "Before the cock crows today, you will deny me three times." ⁶²And Peter went out and wept bitterly.

63 Now the men who were holding Jesus mocked him and beat him; ⁶⁴they also blindfolded him and asked, "Prophesy! Who is it that struck you?" ⁶⁵And they spoke many other words against Jesus, reviling him.

66 When day came, the assembly of the elders of the people gathered together, both chief priests and scribes; and they led him away to their council, and they said, ⁶⁷"If you are the Messiah, tell us." But Jesus said to them, "If I tell you, you will not believe; ⁶⁸and if I ask you, you will not answer. ⁶⁹But from now on the Human One will be seated at the right hand of the power of God." ⁷⁰And they all said, "Are you the Child of God, then?" And Jesus said to them, "You say that I am." ⁷¹And they said, "What further testimony do we need? We have heard it ourselves from his own lips."

23 Then the whole company of them arose, and brought Jesus before Pilate. ²And they began to accuse him, saying, "We found this man perverting our nation, and forbidding us to give tribute to Caesar, and saying that he himself is the Messiah, a king." ³And Pilate asked Jesus, "Are you the King of the Jews?" And Jesus answered Pilate, "You have said so." ⁴And Pilate said to the chief priests and the crowds, "I find no crime in this man." ⁵But they were urgent, saying, "He stirs up the people, teaching throughout all Judea, from Galilee even to this place."

6 When Pilate heard this, he asked whether the man was a Galilean. 7And when he learned that Jesus belonged to Herod's jurisdiction, Pilate sent Jesus over to Herod, who was himself in Jerusalem at that time. 8When Herod saw Jesus, he was very glad, for he had long desired to see him, because he had heard about Jesus, and was hoping to see some sign done by him. 9So Herod questioned Jesus at some length; but he made no answer. 10The chief priests and the scribes stood by, vehemently accusing him. 11And Herod with his soldiers treated Jesus with contempt and mocked him; then, putting gorgeous clothes on Jesus, Herod sent him back to Pilate. 12And Herod and Pilate became friends with each other that very day, for before this they had been enemies.

13 Pilate then called together the chief priests and the rulers and the people, 14and said to them, "You brought me this man as one who was perverting the people; and after examining him before you, I did not find this man guilty of any of your charges; 15neither did Herod, for he sent him back to us. Nothing deserving death has been done by him; 16I will therefore chastise and release him."*

18 But they all cried out together, "Away with this man, and release to us Barabbas," 19who had been thrown into prison for an insurrection started in the city, and for murder. 20Pilate addressed them once more, desiring to release Jesus; 21but they shouted out, "Crucify, crucify him!" 22A third time Pilate said to them, "Why, what evil has he done? I have found in him no crime deserving death; I will therefore chastise and release him." 23But they were urgent, demanding with loud cries that Jesus should be crucified. And their voices prevailed. 24So Pilate gave sentence that their demand should be granted. 25He released the one who had been thrown into prison for insurrection and murder, whom they asked for; but Jesus he delivered up to their will.

26 And as they led Jesus away, they seized someone named Simon of Cyrene, who was coming in from the country, and laid on him the cross, to carry it behind Jesus. 27And a great crowd of the people followed him, among whom were women who bewailed and lamented him. 28But Jesus turning to them said, "Daughters of Jerusalem, do not weep for me, but weep for yourselves and for your children. 29For the days are coming when they will say, 'Blessed are the barren, and the wombs that never bore, and the breasts that never gave milk!' 30Then they will begin to say to the mountains, 'Fall on us'; and to the hills, 'Cover us.' 31For if they do this when the wood is green, what will happen when it is dry?"

32 Two others also, who were criminals, were led away to be put to death with Jesus. 33And when they came to the place which is called The Skull, there they crucified Jesus, and the criminals, one on the right

* Here, or after verse 19, other ancient authorities add verse 17, *Now he was obliged to release somebody to them at the festival.*

and one on the left. ³⁴And Jesus said, "Gracious God, forgive them; for they know not what they do." And they cast lots to divide his garments. ³⁵And the people stood by, watching; but the rulers scoffed at Jesus, saying, "He saved others; let him save himself, if he is the Messiah of God, the Chosen One!" ³⁶The soldiers also mocked Jesus, coming up and offering him vinegar, ³⁷and saying, "If you are the King of the Jews, save yourself!" ³⁸There was also an inscription over him, "This is the King of the Jews."

39 One of the criminals who were hanged railed at Jesus, saying, "Are you not the Messiah? Save yourself and us!" ⁴⁰But the other rebuked him, saying, "Do you not fear God, since you are under the same sentence of condemnation? ⁴¹And we indeed justly; for we are receiving the due reward of our deeds; but this one has done nothing wrong." ⁴²And he said, "Jesus, remember me when you come into your dominion." ⁴³And Jesus said, "Truly, I say to you, today you will be with me in Paradise."

44 It was now about noon, and there was darkness over the whole land until three o'clock, ⁴⁵while the sun's light failed; and the curtain of the temple was torn in two. ⁴⁶Then Jesus, crying with a loud voice, said, "God, my Father and Mother, into your hands I commit my spirit!" And having said this, Jesus died. ⁴⁷Now when the centurion saw what had taken place, he praised God, and said, "Certainly this man was innocent!" ⁴⁸And all the crowds who assembled to see the sight, when they saw what had taken place, returned home beating their breasts. ⁴⁹And all Jesus' acquaintances and the women who had followed him from Galilee stood at a distance and saw these things.

50 Now there was a man named Joseph from the Jewish town of Arimathea. He was a member of the council, a good and righteous person, ⁵¹who had not consented to their decision and action, and he was looking for the dominion of God. ⁵²This man went to Pilate and asked for the body of Jesus. ⁵³Then Joseph took the body down and wrapped it in linen, and laid the body in a rock-hewn tomb, where no one had ever yet been laid. ⁵⁴It was the day of Preparation, and the sabbath was beginning. ⁵⁵The women who had come with Jesus from Galilee followed, and saw the tomb, and how the body was laid; ⁵⁶then they returned, and prepared spices and ointments.

On the sabbath they rested according to the commandment.

24 On the first day of the week, at early dawn, the women went to the tomb, taking the spices which they had prepared. ²And they found the stone rolled away from the tomb, ³but when they went in they did not find the body. ⁴While they were perplexed about this, two men stood by them in dazzling clothes; ⁵and as the women were frightened and bowed their faces to the ground, the two said to them, "Why do you

seek the living among the dead? ⁶Remember how Jesus told you, while still in Galilee, ⁷that the Human One must be delivered into the hands of sinners, and be crucified, and on the third day rise." ⁸And the women remembered these words, ⁹and returning from the tomb they told all this to the eleven and to all the rest. ¹⁰Now it was Mary Magdalene and Joanna and Mary the mother of James and the other women with them who told this to the apostles; ¹¹but these words seemed to the apostles an idle tale, and they did not believe the women.*

13 That very day two of the disciples were going to a village named Emmaus, about seven miles from Jerusalem, ¹⁴and talking with each other about all these things that had happened. ¹⁵While they were talking and discussing together, Jesus drew near and went with them. ¹⁶But their eyes were kept from recognizing Jesus. ¹⁷And Jesus said to them, "What is this conversation which you are holding with each other as you walk?" And they stood still, looking sad. ¹⁸Then one of them, named Cleopas, answered, "Are you the only visitor to Jerusalem who does not know the things that have happened there in these days?" ¹⁹And Jesus said to them, "What things?" And they said, "Concerning Jesus of Nazareth, who was a prophet mighty in deed and word before God and all the people, ²⁰and how our chief priests and rulers delivered up this Jesus to be condemned to death, and crucified him. ²¹But we had hoped that Jesus was the one to redeem Israel. Yes, and besides all this, it is now the third day since this happened. ²²Moreover, some women of our group amazed us. They were at the tomb early in the morning ²³and did not find Jesus' body; and they came back saying that they had even seen a vision of angels, who said that Jesus was alive. ²⁴Some of those who were with us went to the tomb, and found it just as the women had said; but Jesus they did not see." ²⁵And Jesus said to them, "O foolish ones, and slow of heart to believe all that the prophets have spoken! ²⁶Was it not necessary that the Messiah should suffer these things and be glorified?" ²⁷And beginning with Moses and all the prophets, Jesus interpreted to them in all the scriptures the things concerning the Messiah.

28 So they drew near to the village to which they were going. Jesus appeared to be going further, ²⁹but they urged against it, saying, "Stay with us, for it is toward evening and the day is already about over." So Jesus went in to stay with them. ³⁰While at table with them, Jesus took the bread and blessed, and broke it, and gave it to them. ³¹And their eyes were opened and they recognized Jesus, who then vanished out of their sight. ³²They said to each other, "Did not our hearts burn within us while Jesus talked to us on the road, and opened to us the scriptures?" ³³And they rose that same hour and returned to Jerusalem; and they found the

---

* Other ancient authorities add verse 12, *But Peter rose and ran to the tomb; stooping and looking in, he saw the linen cloths by themselves; and he went home wondering at what had happened.*

eleven gathered together and those who were with them, ³⁴who said, "The Lord has risen indeed, and has appeared to Simon!" ³⁵Then they told what had happened on the road, and how Jesus was known to them in the breaking of the bread.

36 As they were saying this, that very Jesus stood among them. ³⁷But they were startled and frightened, and supposed that they saw a spirit. ³⁸And Jesus said to them, "Why are you troubled, and why do questionings rise in your hearts? ³⁹See my hands and my feet, that it is I myself; handle me, and see; for a spirit has not flesh and bones as you see that I have."* ⁴¹And while they still disbelieved for joy, and wondered, Jesus said to them, "Have you anything here to eat?" ⁴²They gave Jesus a piece of broiled fish, ⁴³and Jesus took it and ate before them.

44 Then Jesus said to them, "These are my words which I spoke to you, while I was still with you, that everything written about me in the law of Moses and the prophets and the psalms must be fulfilled." ⁴⁵Then Jesus opened their minds to understand the scriptures, ⁴⁶and said to them, "Thus it is written, that the Messiah should suffer and on the third day rise from the dead, ⁴⁷and that repentance and forgiveness of sins should be preached in the Messiah's name to all nations, beginning from Jerusalem. ⁴⁸You are witnesses of these things. ⁴⁹And I am sending the promise of God my Father and Mother upon you; but stay in the city until you are clothed with power from on high."

50 Jesus led them out as far as Bethany, and with uplifted hands blessed them. ⁵¹While blessing them, Jesus parted from them, and was carried up into heaven. ⁵²And they returned to Jerusalem with great joy, ⁵³and were continually in the temple blessing God.

* Other ancient authorities add verse 40, *And having said this, Jesus showed them the hands and the feet.*

John

1 In the beginning was the Word, and the Word was with God, and the Word was God. [2]The Word was in the beginning with God; [3]all things were made through the Word, and without the Word was not anything made that was made. [4]In the Word was life, and the life was the light of all. [5]The light shines in the deepest night, and the night has not overcome it.

6 There was a man sent from God, whose name was John. [7]John came for testimony, to bear witness to the light, that all might believe through him. [8]John was not the light, but came to bear witness to the light.

9 The true light that enlightens everyone was coming into the world. [10]The Word was in the world, and the world was made through the Word, yet the world did not know the Word. [11]The Word came to the Word's own home, but those to whom the Word came did not receive the Word. [12]But to all who received the Word, who believed in the name of the Word, power was given to become children of God; [13]who were born, not of blood nor of the will of the flesh nor of human will, but of God.

14 And the Word became flesh and dwelt among us, full of grace and truth; we have beheld the Word's glory, glory as of the only Child from God the Father and Mother. [15](John bore witness to the Child, and cried, "This was the person of whom I said, 'The one who comes after me ranks before me, for that one was before me.'") [16]And from the fullness of the Child have we all received, grace upon grace. [17]For the law was given through Moses; grace and truth came through Jesus Christ. [18]No one has ever seen God; the only Child, who is in the bosom of God the Mother and Father, that one has made God known.

19 And this is the testimony of John, when the Jews sent priests and Levites from Jerusalem to ask him, "Who are you?" ²⁰John confessed, he did not deny, but confessed, "I am not the Messiah." ²¹And they asked, "What then? Are you Elijah?" John said, "I am not." "Are you the prophet?" And he answered, "No." ²²They said then, "Who are you? Let us have an answer for those who sent us. What do you say about yourself?" ²³John said, "I am the voice of one crying in the wilderness, 'Make straight the way of the Lord,' as the prophet Isaiah said."

24 Now people had been sent from the Pharisees. ²⁵They asked John, "Then why are you baptizing, if you are neither the Messiah, nor Elijah, nor the prophet?" ²⁶John answered them, "I baptize with water; but among you stands one whom you do not know, ²⁷even the one who comes after me, the thong of whose sandal I am not worthy to untie." ²⁸This took place in Bethany beyond the Jordan, where John was baptizing.

29 John saw Jesus approaching, and said, "Here is the Lamb of God, who takes away the sin of the world! ³⁰This is the one of whom I said, 'After me comes a person who ranks before me, for that one was before me. ³¹I myself did not know who it was; but for this I came baptizing with water, that the one who was to come might be revealed to Israel." ³²And John bore witness, "I saw the Spirit descend as a dove from heaven, and it remained on Jesus. ³³I myself did not know who it was; but the one who sent me to baptize with water said to me, 'The person on whom you see the Spirit descend and remain, this is the one who baptizes with the Holy Spirit.' ³⁴And I have seen and have borne witness that this is the Child of God."

35 The next day again John was standing with two of his disciples, ³⁶and looking at Jesus walking by, he said, "Here is the Lamb of God!" ³⁷The two disciples heard John say this, and they followed Jesus. ³⁸Jesus turned, and saw them following, and said to them, "What do you seek?" And they said, "Rabbi" (which means Teacher), "where are you staying?" ³⁹Jesus said to them, "Come and see." They came and saw where Jesus was staying; and they stayed with him that day, for it was about four o'clock in the afternoon. ⁴⁰One of the two who heard John speak, and followed Jesus, was Andrew, Simon Peter's brother. ⁴¹Andrew first found his brother Simon, and said to him, "We have found the Messiah" (which is translated Christ). ⁴²Andrew brought Simon to Jesus. Jesus looked at him, and said, "So you are Simon the son of John? You shall be called Cephas" (which is translated Peter).

43 The next day Jesus decided to go to Galilee. And he found Philip and said to him, "Follow me." ⁴⁴Now Philip was from Bethsaida, the city of Andrew and Peter. ⁴⁵Philip found Nathanael and said to him, "We have found the one of whom Moses in the law and also the prophets wrote, Jesus of Nazareth, the son of Joseph." ⁴⁶Nathanael said to Philip,

"Can anything good come out of Nazareth?" Philip answered, "Come and see." [47]Jesus saw Nathanael coming, and said of him, "Here is an Israelite indeed, in whom there is no guile!" [48]Nathanael asked, "How do you know me?" Jesus answered, "Before Philip called you, when you were under the fig tree, I saw you." [49]Nathanael said to Jesus, "Rabbi, you are the Child of God! You are the Ruler of Israel!" [50]Jesus replied, "Because I said to you, I saw you under the fig tree, do you believe? You shall see greater things than these." [51]And Jesus said to Nathanael, "Truly, truly, I say to you, you will see heaven opened, and the angels of God ascending and descending upon the Human One."

2 On the third day there was a marriage at Cana in Galilee, and the mother of Jesus was there; [2]Jesus also was invited to the marriage, with the disciples. [3]When the wine gave out, the mother of Jesus said to him, "They have no wine." [4]And Jesus said to her, "O woman, what have you to do with me? My hour has not yet come." [5]His mother said to the servants, "Do whatever he tells you." [6]Now six stone jars for the Jewish rites of purification were standing there, each holding twenty or thirty gallons. [7]Jesus said to the servants, "Fill the jars with water." And they filled them up to the brim. [8]He said to them, "Now draw some out, and take it to the steward of the feast." So they took it. [9]When the steward of the feast tasted the water now become wine, and did not know where it came from (though the servants who had drawn the water knew), the steward of the feast called the bridegroom [10]and said to him, "Everyone serves the good wine first; and when people have drunk freely, then the poor wine; but you have kept the good wine until now." [11]This, the first of his signs, Jesus did at Cana in Galilee, and manifested his glory; and the disciples believed in Jesus.

12 After this Jesus went down to Capernaum, with his mother and brothers and disciples; and there they stayed for a few days.

13 The Passover was at hand, and Jesus went up to Jerusalem. [14]In the temple he found those who were selling oxen and sheep and pigeons, and the money-changers at their business. [15]And making a whip of cords, Jesus drove them all, with the sheep and oxen, out of the temple, pouring out the coins of the money-changers and overturning their tables. [16]And Jesus told those who sold the pigeons, "Take these things away; you shall not make God's house a house of trade." [17]The disciples remembered that it was written, "Zeal for your house will consume me." [18]The religious authorities then said to Jesus, "What sign have you to show us for doing this?" [19]Jesus answered them, "Destroy this temple, and in three days I will raise it up." [20]Then the authorities said, "It has taken forty-six years to build this temple, and will you raise it up in three days?" [21]But Jesus spoke of the temple of his body. [22]When therefore Jesus was raised from the dead, the disciples remembered that Jesus

had said this; and they believed the scripture and the word which Jesus had spoken.

23 Now when Jesus was in Jerusalem at the Passover feast, many believed in Jesus' name when they saw the signs which Jesus did; 24but Jesus did not trust himself to them, 25because Jesus knew all human beings and needed no one to bear witness about anybody; for Jesus truly knew what was in everyone.

3 Now there was a man of the Pharisees, named Nicodemus, a ruler of the Jews. 2Nicodemus came to Jesus by night and said, "Rabbi, we know that you are a teacher come from God; for no one can do these signs that you do, except by the power of God." 3Jesus answered Nicodemus, "Truly, truly, I say to you, unless one is born anew, one cannot see the dominion of God." 4Nicodemus replied, "How can someone be born who is old? Can anyone enter the womb of one's mother a second time and be born?" 5Jesus answered, "Truly, truly, I say to you, unless one is born of water and the Spirit, one cannot enter the dominion of God. 6That which is born of the flesh is flesh, and that which is born of the Spirit is spirit. 7Do not marvel that I said to you, 'You must be born anew.' 8The wind blows where it wills, and you hear the sound of it, but you do not know where it comes from or where it goes; so it is with everyone who is born of the Spirit." 9Nicodemus said to Jesus, "How can this be?" 10Jesus answered, "Are you a teacher of Israel, and yet you do not understand this? 11Truly, truly, I say to you, we speak of what we know, and bear witness to what we have seen; but you do not receive our testimony. 12If I have told you earthly things and you do not believe, how can you believe if I tell you heavenly things? 13No one has ascended into heaven but the one who descended from heaven, the Human One. 14And as Moses lifted up the serpent in the wilderness, so must the Human One be lifted up, 15that whoever believes in that one may have eternal life."

16 For God so loved the world that God gave God's only Child, that whoever believes in that Child should not perish but have eternal life. 17For God sent that Child into the world, not to condemn the world, but that through the Child the world might be saved. 18Whoever believes in the Child is not condemned; whoever does not believe is condemned already, for not having believed in the name of the only Child of God. 19And this is the judgment, that the light has come into the world, and people loved the night rather than the light, because their deeds were evil. 20For all who do evil hate the light, and do not come to the light, lest their deeds should be exposed. 21But all who do what is true come to the light, that it may be clearly seen that their deeds have been accomplished in God.

22 After this Jesus and the disciples went into the land of Judea; there Jesus remained with them and baptized. 23John also was baptizing at Aenon near Salim, because there was a lot of water there; and people came and were baptized. 24For John had not yet been put in prison.

25 Now a discussion arose between John's disciples and a Jew over purifying. 26And they came to John, and said to him, "Rabbi, the one who was with you beyond the Jordan, to whom you bore witness, that one is here, baptizing, and attracting everyone." 27John answered, "No one can receive anything except what is given from heaven. 28You yourselves bear me witness that I said, I am not the Messiah, but I have been sent before the Messiah. 29The one who has the bride is the bridegroom; the friend of the bridegroom, who stands and listens, rejoices greatly at the bridegroom's voice; therefore this joy of mine is now full. 30That one must increase, but I must decrease."

31 The one who comes from above is above all; anyone who is of the earth belongs to the earth, and speaks from the earth; the one who comes from heaven is above all. 32That one's testimony is to what that one has seen and heard, but no one receives it. 33Whoever receives it confirms this, that God is true. 34For the one whom God has sent utters the words of God, for it is not by measure that the Spirit is given; 35the Father and Mother loves the Child, and has given all things into the Child's hand. 36Whoever believes in the Child has eternal life; but whoever does not obey the Child shall not see life, but is subject to the wrath of God.

4 Now when the Lord knew that the Pharisees had heard that Jesus was making and baptizing more disciples than John 2(although Jesus did not baptize, but only the disciples), 3Jesus left Judea and departed again to Galilee, 4but had to pass through Samaria. 5Jesus came to a city of Samaria, called Sychar, near the field that Jacob gave to his son Joseph. 6Jacob's well was there, and so Jesus, wearied with the journey, sat down beside the well. It was about noon.

7 There came a woman of Samaria to draw water. Jesus said to her, "Give me a drink." 8For the disciples had gone away into the city to buy food. 9The Samaritan woman said to Jesus, "How is it that you, a Jew, ask a drink of me, a woman of Samaria?" For Jews have no dealings with Samaritans. 10Jesus answered her, "If you knew the gift of God, and who it is that is saying to you, 'Give me a drink,' you would have asked that person, who would then have given you living water." 11The woman said to Jesus, "You have nothing to draw with, and the well is deep; where do you get that living water? 12Are you greater than our ancestor Jacob, who gave us the well, and drank from it, as did his children and animals?" 13Jesus said to her, "Everyone who drinks of this water will thirst again, 14but whoever drinks of the water that I shall give will never

thirst; the water that I shall give will become in the one who drinks it a spring of water welling up to eternal life." ¹⁵The woman said to Jesus, "Give me this water, that I may not thirst, nor come here to draw."

16 Jesus said to her, "Go, call your husband, and come here." ¹⁷The woman answered, "I have no husband." Jesus said to her, "You are right in saying, 'I have no husband'; ¹⁸for you have had five husbands, and he whom you now have is not your husband; this you said truly." ¹⁹The woman said to Jesus, "I perceive that you are a prophet. ²⁰Our ancestors worshiped on this mountain; and you say that in Jerusalem is the place where people ought to worship." ²¹Jesus said to her, "Woman, believe me, the hour is coming when neither on this mountain nor in Jerusalem will you worship God the Father and Mother. ²²You worship what you do not know; we worship what we know, for salvation is from the Jews. ²³But the hour is coming, and now is, when the true worshipers will worship God the Mother and Father in spirit and truth, for such are those whom God seeks as worshipers. ²⁴God is spirit, and those who worship God must worship in spirit and truth." ²⁵The woman said to Jesus, "I know that Messiah is coming (the one who is called Christ), who, having come, will show us all things." ²⁶Jesus said to her, "I who speak to you am that very one."

27 Just then the disciples came. They marveled that Jesus was talking with a woman, but none said, "What do you wish?" or, "Why are you talking with her?" ²⁸So the woman left her water jar, and went away into the city, and said to the people, ²⁹"Come, see someone who told me all that I ever did. Can this be the Messiah?" ³⁰They went out of the city and were coming to Jesus.

31 Meanwhile the disciples said to Jesus, "Rabbi, eat." ³²But Jesus said to them, "I have food to eat of which you do not know." ³³So the disciples said to one another, "Has anyone brought Jesus food?" ³⁴Jesus said to them, "My food is to do the will of God who sent me, and to accomplish God's work. ³⁵Do you not say, 'There are yet four months, then comes the harvest'? I tell you, lift up your eyes, and see how the fields are already white for harvest. ³⁶One who reaps receives wages, and gathers fruit for eternal life, so that sower and reaper may rejoice together. ³⁷For here the saying holds true, 'One sows and another reaps.' ³⁸I sent you to reap that for which you did not labor; others have labored, and you have entered into their labor."

39 Many Samaritans from that city believed in Jesus because of the woman's testimony, "This person told me all that I ever did." ⁴⁰So when the Samaritans approached, they asked Jesus to stay with them; and he stayed there two days. ⁴¹And many more believed because of Jesus' word. ⁴²They said to the woman, "It is no longer because of your words that we believe, for we have heard for ourselves, and we know that this is indeed the Savior of the world."

43 After two days Jesus departed to Galilee, ⁴⁴for he testified that prophets have no honor in their own country. ⁴⁵So when Jesus came to Galilee, the Galileans welcomed him, having seen all that Jesus had done in Jerusalem at the feast, for they too had gone to the feast.

46 So Jesus came again to Cana in Galilee, where water had been made into wine. And at Capernaum there was an official whose child was ill. ⁴⁷When the official heard that Jesus had come from Judea to Galilee, he went and begged Jesus to come down and heal his child, who was at the point of death. ⁴⁸Jesus therefore said to the official, "Unless you see signs and wonders you will not believe." ⁴⁹The official said to Jesus, "Sir, come down before my child dies." ⁵⁰Jesus responded, "Go; your child will live." The official believed the word that Jesus spoke to him and went his way. ⁵¹As he was going down, his servants met him and told him that his child was living. ⁵²So he asked them the time when the child began to mend, and they answered, "Yesterday afternoon at one o'clock the fever left." ⁵³The father knew that was the time when Jesus had said to him, "Your child will live"; and he himself believed, and all his household. ⁵⁴This was now the second sign that Jesus did when he had come from Judea to Galilee.

5 After this there was a feast of the Jews, and Jesus went up to Jerusalem.

2 Now there is in Jerusalem by the Sheep Gate a pool, in Hebrew called Bethzatha, which has five porticoes, ³in which many sick people were lying—people who were blind, or lame, or paralyzed.* ⁵One person was there who had been ill for thirty-eight years. ⁶When Jesus saw this person, who Jesus knew had been lying there a long time, Jesus said, "Do you want to be healed?" ⁷The person answered, "I have no one to put me into the pool when the water is troubled, and while I am going another steps down before me." ⁸Jesus replied, "Rise, take up your pallet, and walk." ⁹And at once the person was healed, and took up the pallet and walked.

Now that day was the sabbath. ¹⁰So the Jews said to the person who was cured, "It is the sabbath, it is not lawful for you to carry your pallet." ¹¹But the person answered them, "The one who healed me said to me, 'Take up your pallet, and walk.'" ¹²They replied, "Who said to you, 'Take up your pallet, and walk'?" ¹³Now the person who had been healed did not know who it was, for Jesus had withdrawn, as there was a crowd in the place. ¹⁴Afterward Jesus found the person in the temple, and said, "See, you are well! Sin no more, so that nothing worse will happen to you." ¹⁵The person went away and told the Jews that it was Jesus who

* Other ancient authorities insert in whole or in part: *waiting for the motion of the water;* ⁴*for an angel of the Lord went down periodically into the pool, and agitated the water; and whoever stepped in first, after the agitation of the water, was healed, no matter what the disease.*

had performed the cure. [16]And this was why the Jews persecuted Jesus, because Jesus did this on the sabbath. [17]But Jesus answered them, "My Father and Mother is working still, and I am working." [18]This was why the Jews sought all the more to kill Jesus, because Jesus not only broke the sabbath but also called God Father and Mother, thereby claiming equality with God.

19 Jesus said to them, "Truly, truly, I say to you, the Child can do nothing of its own, but only what the Child sees God the Father and Mother doing; for what God does, that the Child does also. [20]For God loves God's Child, and shows the Child all that God is doing; and greater works than these will God show, that you may marvel. [21]For as God raises the dead and gives them life, so also does the Child give life to whomever the Child wishes. [22]God judges no one, but has given all judgment to the Child, [23]that all may honor that Child, even as they honor God. Whoever does not honor the Child does not honor God who sent the Child. [24]Truly, truly, I say to you, whoever hears my word and believes the one who sent me, has eternal life, and does not come into judgment, but has passed from death to life.

25 "Truly, truly, I say to you, the hour is coming, and now is, when the dead will hear the voice of the Child of God, and those who hear will live. [26]For as God has life in God's self, so God has granted the same thing to the Child, [27]and has given the Child authority to execute judgment, because of being the Human One. [28]Do not marvel at this; for the hour is coming when all who are in the tombs will hear the voice of the Child [29]and will come forth, those who have done good, to the resurrection of life, and those who have done evil, to the resurrection of judgment.

30 "I can do nothing on my own authority; as I hear, I judge; and my judgment is just, because I seek not my own will but the will of the one who sent me. [31]If I bear witness to myself, my testimony is not true; [32]there is another who bears witness to me, and I know that the testimony which that one bears to me is true. [33]You sent to John, and he has borne witness to the truth. [34]But I do not receive the testimony of human beings; I say this that you may be saved. [35]John was a burning and shining lamp, and you were willing to rejoice for a while in his light. [36]But the testimony which I have is greater than that of John; for the works which God has granted me to accomplish, these very works which I am doing bear me witness that God has sent me. [37]And God who sent me has borne witness to me. God's voice you have never heard, God's form you have never seen; [38]and you do not have God's word abiding in you, for you do not believe the one whom God has sent. [39]You search the scriptures, because you think that in them you have eternal life; and it is they that bear witness to me; [40]yet you refuse to come to me that you may have life. [41]I do not receive glory from human beings. [42]But I know that you have not the love of God within you. [43]I have come in God's

name, and you do not receive me; if others come in their own name, you will receive them. ⁴⁴How can you believe, you who receive glory from one another and do not seek the glory that comes from the only God? ⁴⁵Do not think that I shall accuse you to God; it is Moses, on whom you set your hope, who accuses you. ⁴⁶If you believed Moses, you would believe me, for Moses wrote of me. ⁴⁷But if you do not believe the writings of Moses, how will you believe my words?"

6 After this Jesus went to the other side of the Sea of Galilee, which is the Sea of Tiberias. ²And a crowd followed, because they saw the signs which he did on those who were diseased. ³Jesus went up on the mountain, and there sat down with the disciples. ⁴Now the Passover, the Jewish feast, was at hand. ⁵Looking up, then, and seeing that a crowd was approaching, Jesus said to Philip, "How are we to buy bread, so that these people may eat?" ⁶This Jesus said to test Philip, for Jesus knew what he would do. ⁷Philip answered, "Thousands of dollars would not buy enough bread for each of them to get a little." ⁸One of the disciples, Andrew, Simon Peter's brother, said to Jesus, ⁹"There is a child here who has five barley loaves and two fish; but what are they among so many?" ¹⁰Jesus said, "Make the people sit down." Now there was a lot of grass in the place; so the people sat down, in number about five thousand. ¹¹Jesus then took the loaves, and having given thanks, distributed them to those who were seated; so also the fish, as much as they wanted. ¹²And when they had eaten their fill, Jesus told the disciples, "Gather up the fragments left over, that nothing may be lost." ¹³So they gathered them up and filled twelve baskets with fragments from the five barley loaves, left by those who had eaten. ¹⁴When the people saw the sign which Jesus had done, they said, "This is indeed the prophet who is to come into the world!"

15 Perceiving then that they were about to come and take him by force to make him king, Jesus withdrew again to the mountain alone.

16 When evening came, Jesus' disciples went down to the sea, ¹⁷got into a boat, and started across the sea to Capernaum. It was already night, and Jesus had not yet come to them. ¹⁸The sea rose because a strong wind was blowing. ¹⁹When they had rowed about three or four miles, they saw Jesus walking on the sea and drawing near to the boat. They were frightened, ²⁰but Jesus said to them, "It is I; do not be afraid." ²¹Then they were glad to take Jesus into the boat, and immediately the boat was at the land to which they were going.

22 On the next day the people who remained on the other side of the sea saw that there had been only one boat there, and that Jesus had not entered the boat with the disciples, but that the disciples had gone away alone. ²³However, boats from Tiberias came near the place where they had eaten the bread after the Lord had given thanks. ²⁴So when the

people saw that Jesus was not there, nor the disciples, they themselves got into the boats and went to Capernaum, seeking Jesus.

25 When they found Jesus on the other side of the sea, they said to him, "Rabbi, when did you come here?" ²⁶Jesus answered them, "Truly, truly, I say to you, you seek me, not because you saw signs, but because you ate your fill of the loaves. ²⁷Do not labor for the food which perishes, but for the food which endures to eternal life, which the Human One will give to you; for that one, God the Father and Mother has confirmed." ²⁸Then they said to Jesus, "What must we do to be doing the works of God?" ²⁹Jesus answered them, "This is the work of God, that you believe in the one whom God has sent." ³⁰So they said to Jesus, "Then what sign do you do, that we may see, and believe you? What work do you perform? ³¹Our ancestors ate the manna in the wilderness; as it is written, 'They were given bread from heaven to eat.' " ³²Jesus then said to them, "Truly, truly, I say to you, it was not Moses who gave you the bread from heaven; God gives you the true bread from heaven. ³³For the bread of God is that which comes down from heaven, and gives life to the world." ³⁴They said to Jesus, "Give us this bread always."

35 Jesus said to them, "I am the bread of life; whoever comes to me shall not hunger, and whoever believes in me shall never thirst." ³⁶But I said to you that you have seen me and yet do not believe. ³⁷All that God the Father and Mother gives me will come to me; and anyone who comes to me I will not cast out. ³⁸For I have come down from heaven, not to do my own will, but the will of the one who sent me; ³⁹and this is the will of the one who sent me, that I should lose nothing of all that one gave me, but raise it up at the last day. ⁴⁰For this is the will of my God, that all who see the Child and believe in the Child should have eternal life; and I will raise them up at the last day."

41 The religious authorities then murmured at Jesus for saying, "I am the bread which came down from heaven." ⁴²They said, "Is not this Jesus, the son of Joseph, whose father and mother we know? How does he now say, 'I have come down from heaven'?" ⁴³Jesus answered them, "Do not murmur among yourselves. ⁴⁴No one can come to me unless drawn by God the Father and Mother who sent me; and I will raise that one at the last day. ⁴⁵It is written in the prophets, 'And they shall all be taught by God.' Everyone who has heard and learned from God comes to me. ⁴⁶Not that anyone has seen God except the one who is from God; that one has seen God. ⁴⁷Truly, truly, I say to you, whoever believes has eternal life. ⁴⁸I am the bread of life. ⁴⁹Your ancestors ate the manna in the wilderness, and they died. ⁵⁰This is the bread which comes down from heaven, that people may eat of it and not die. ⁵¹"I am the living bread which came down from heaven; anyone who eats of this bread will live forever; and the bread which I shall give for the life of the world is my flesh."

52 The religious authorities then disputed among themselves, saying, "How can this man give us his flesh to eat?" ⁵³So Jesus said to them, "Truly, truly, I say to you, unless you eat the flesh and drink the blood of the Human One, you have no life in you; ⁵⁴those who eat my flesh and drink my blood have eternal life, and I will raise them up at the last day. ⁵⁵For my flesh is food indeed, and my blood is drink indeed. ⁵⁶Those who eat of my flesh and drink of my blood abide in me, and I in them. ⁵⁷As the living God sent me, and I live because of God, so whoever partakes of me will live because of me. ⁵⁸This is the bread which came down from heaven, not such as our ancestors ate and died; whoever eats this bread will live forever." ⁵⁹This Jesus said in the synagogue, while teaching at Capernaum.

60 Many of the disciples, when they heard it, said, "This is a hard saying; who can listen to it?" ⁶¹But Jesus, knowing that the disciples murmured at it, said to them, "Do you take offense at this? ⁶²Then what if you were to see the Human One ascending back to heaven? ⁶³It is the spirit that gives life, the flesh is of no avail; the words that I have spoken to you are spirit and life. ⁶⁴But there are some of you who do not believe." For Jesus knew from the first who those were that did not believe, and who it was that would betray him. ⁶⁵And Jesus said, "This is why I told you that no one can come to me unless it is granted by God the Father and Mother."

66 After this many of the disciples drew back and no longer went about with Jesus. ⁶⁷Jesus said to the twelve, "Do you also wish to go away?" ⁶⁸Simon Peter answered him, "Lord, to whom shall we go? You have the words of eternal life; ⁶⁹and we have believed, and have come to know, that you are the Holy One of God." ⁷⁰Jesus answered them, "Did I not choose you, the twelve, and one of you is a devil?" ⁷¹Jesus spoke of Judas the son of Simon Iscariot, for he, one of the twelve, was to betray Jesus.

7 After this Jesus went about in Galilee, and would not go about in Judea, because the religious authorities sought to kill him. ²Now the Jews' feast of Tabernacles was at hand. ³So Jesus' brothers said to him, "Leave here and go to Judea, that your disciples may see the works you are doing. ⁴For no one works in secret who seeks to be known openly. If you do these things, show yourself to the world." ⁵For even Jesus' brothers did not believe in him. ⁶Jesus said to them, "My time has not yet come, but your time is always here. ⁷The world cannot hate you, but it hates me because I testify of it that its works are evil. ⁸Go to the feast yourselves; I am not going up to this feast, for my time has not yet fully come." ⁹Saying this, Jesus remained in Galilee.

10 But after Jesus' brothers had gone up to the feast, then Jesus also went up, not publicly but in private. ¹¹The religious authorities were

looking for Jesus at the feast, and saying, "Where is he?" [12]And there was a lot of muttering about him among the people. While some said, "Jesus is a good man," others said, "No, he is leading people astray." [13]Yet for fear of the authorities no one spoke openly of him.

14 About the middle of the feast Jesus went up into the temple and taught. [15]The religious authorities marveled at it, saying, "How is it that this person who has never studied has learning?" [16]So Jesus answered them, "My teaching is not mine, but is from the one who sent me; [17]if any wish to do God's will, they will know whether the teaching is from God or whether I am speaking on my own authority. [18]All who speak on their own authority seek their own glory; but the person who seeks the glory of the one who sent that person is true, and in that person there is no falsehood. [19]Did not Moses give you the law? Yet none of you keeps the law. Why do you seek to kill me?" [20]The people answered, "You have a demon! Who is seeking to kill you?" [21]Jesus answered them, "I did one deed, and you all marvel at it. [22]Moses gave you circumcision (not that it is from Moses, but from our ancestors), and you circumcise a person on the sabbath. [23]If a person receives circumcision on the sabbath, so that the law of Moses may not be broken, are you angry with me because I made a person's whole body well on the sabbath? [24]Do not judge by appearances, but judge with right judgment."

25 Some of the people of Jerusalem therefore said, "Is not this the person whom they seek to kill? [26]And here is this person speaking openly, and they say nothing about it! Can it be that the authorities really know that this is the Messiah? [27]Yet we know where this person comes from; but when the Messiah appears, no one will know where the Messiah comes from. [28]So Jesus, teaching in the temple, proclaimed, "You know me, and you know where I come from. But I have not come of my own accord; the one who sent me is true, and that one you do not know. [29]I know that one, and from that one, who sent me, I come." [30]So they sought to arrest Jesus; but no one laid on hands, for Jesus' hour had not yet come. [31]Yet many of the people believed in Jesus; they asked, "Will the Messiah, having appeared, do more signs than this person has done?"

32 The Pharisees heard the crowd muttering in this way about Jesus, and the chief priests and Pharisees sent officers to make the arrest. [33]Jesus then said, "I will be with you a little longer, and then I go to the one who sent me; [34]you will seek me and you will not find me; where I am you cannot come." [35]The religious authorities said to one another, "Where does this person intend to go to escape us? To the Dispersion among the Greeks and teach them? [36]What does this person mean by saying, 'You will seek me and you will not find me,' and 'Where I am you cannot come'?"

37 On the last day of the feast, the great day, Jesus stood up and

proclaimed, "Let anyone who thirsts come to me and drink. [38]Whoever believes in me, as the scripture has said, 'Out of that one's heart shall flow rivers of living water.' " [39]Now this Jesus said about the Spirit, which those who believed in Jesus were to receive; for as yet the Spirit had not been given, because Jesus was not yet glorified.

40 When they heard these words, some of the people said, "This is really the prophet." [41]Others said, "This is the Messiah." But some asked, "Is the Messiah to come from Galilee? [42]Has not the scripture said that the Messiah is descended from David, and comes from Bethlehem, the village where David was?" [43]So there was a division among the people over Jesus. [44]Some of them wanted to make an arrest, but no one laid on any hands.

45 The officers then went back to the chief priests and Pharisees, who said to them, "Why did you not bring Jesus?" [46]The officers answered, "No one ever spoke like this person!" [47]The Pharisees answered them, "Are you led astray, you also? [48]Have any of the authorities or of the Pharisees believed in Jesus? [49]But the crowd, who do not know the law, are accursed." [50]Nicodemus, who had gone to Jesus before, and who was one of them, said, [51]"Does our law judge anyone without first giving a hearing and learning what has been done?" [52]They replied, "Are you from Galilee too? Search and you will see that no prophet is to rise from Galilee."

8 [53]They all went to their own house, [1]but Jesus went to the Mount of Olives. [2]Early in the morning Jesus came again to the temple; all the people came to him, and he sat down and taught them. [3]The scribes and the Pharisees brought a woman who had been caught in adultery, and placing her in the midst [4]they said, "Teacher, this woman has been caught in the act of adultery. [5]Now in the law Moses commanded us to stone such. What do you say about her?" [6]This they said to test Jesus, that they might have some charge to bring against him. Jesus bent down and wrote with his finger on the ground. [7]And as they continued to ask Jesus, he stood up and said to them, "Let the one who is without sin among you be the first to throw a stone at her." [8]And once more Jesus bent down and wrote with his finger on the ground. [9]But when they heard it, they went away, one by one, beginning with the eldest, and Jesus was left alone with the woman standing before him. [10]Jesus looked up and said to her, "Woman, where are they? Has no one condemned you? [11]She said, "No one, Lord." And Jesus said, "Neither do I condemn you; go, and do not sin again."

12 Again Jesus spoke to them, saying, "I am the light of the world; anyone who follows me will not walk in the night, but will have the light of life." [13]The Pharisees then said to Jesus, "You are bearing witness to yourself; your testimony is not true." [14]Jesus answered, "Even if I do bear

witness to myself, my testimony is true, for I know where I have come from and where I am going, but you do not know where I come from or where I am going. ¹⁵You judge according to the flesh, I judge no one. ¹⁶Yet even if I do judge, my judgment is true, for it is not I alone who judge, but I and the one who sent me. ¹⁷In your law it is written that the testimony of two people is true; ¹⁸I bear witness to myself, and God the Father and Mother who sent me bears witness to me." ¹⁹They said to Jesus therefore, "Where is your God?" Jesus answered, "You know neither me nor my God; if you knew me, you would know God also." ²⁰These words Jesus spoke in the treasury while teaching in the temple; but no one made an arrest, because Jesus' hour had not yet come.

21 Again Jesus said to them, "I go away, and you will seek me and die in your sin; where I am going, you cannot come." ²²Then the religious authorities said, "Will Jesus commit suicide, having said, 'Where I am going, you cannot come'?" ²³Jesus said to them, "You are from below, I am from above; you are of this world, I am not of this world. ²⁴I told you that you would die in your sins, for you will die in your sins unless you believe that I am the one." ²⁵They asked Jesus, "Who are you?" Jesus said to them, "Even what I have told you from the beginning. ²⁶I have much to say about you and much to judge; but the one who sent me is true, and I declare to the world what I have heard from that one." ²⁷They did not understand that Jesus spoke to them of God. ²⁸So Jesus said, "When you have lifted up the Human One, then you will know that I am the one, and that I do nothing on my own authority but speak only the things that God taught me. ²⁹The one who sent me is with me, and has not left me alone, for I always do what is pleasing to that one." ³⁰As Jesus said these things, many believed in Jesus.

31 Jesus then said to the religious leaders who had believed in him, "If you continue in my word, you are truly my disciples, ³²and you will know the truth, and the truth will make you free." ³³They answered, "We are descendants of Abraham and Sarah, and have never been in bondage to anyone. How is it that you say, 'You will be made free'?"

34 Jesus answered them, "Truly, truly, I say to you, everyone who commits sin is a slave to sin. ³⁵The slave does not continue in the house forever; the offspring continues forever. ³⁶So if the Offspring makes you free, you will be free indeed. ³⁷I know that you are descendants of Abraham and Sarah; yet you seek to kill me, because my word finds no place in you. ³⁸I speak of what I have seen with my Father and Mother, and you do what you have heard from your father and mother."

39 They answered Jesus, "Abraham is our father." Jesus said to them, "If you were Abraham's children, you would do what Abraham did, ⁴⁰but now you seek to kill me, one who has told you the truth which I heard from God; this is not what Abraham did. ⁴¹You do what your father did." They responded, "We were not born of fornication; we have

one father and mother, God alone." ⁴²Jesus said to them, "If God were your Mother and Father, you would love me, for I proceeded and came forth from God; I came not of my own accord, but God sent me. ⁴³Why do you not understand what I say? It is because you cannot bear to hear my word. ⁴⁴You are descended from the devil, and your will is to do that one's desires. The devil was a murderer from the beginning, and has nothing to do with the truth, because there is no truth in the devil. When the devil lies, the devil speaks according to the very nature of the devil, who is a liar and the parent of lies. ⁴⁵But, because I tell the truth, you do not believe me. ⁴⁶Which of you convicts me of sin? If I tell the truth, why do you not believe me? ⁴⁷Anyone born of God hears the words of God; the reason why you do not hear them is that you are not of God."

48 The religious authorities answered Jesus, "Are we not right in saying that you are a Samaritan and have a demon?" ⁴⁹Jesus answered, "I do not have a demon; but I honor my God, and you dishonor me. ⁵⁰Yet I do not seek my own glory; there is one who seeks it and that one will be the judge. ⁵¹Truly, truly, I say to you, anyone who keeps my word will never see death." ⁵²The authorities said to Jesus, "Now we know that you have a demon. Abraham died, as did the prophets; and you say, 'Anyone who keeps my word will never taste death.' ⁵³Are you greater than our father Abraham, who died? And the prophets died! Who do you claim to be?" ⁵⁴Jesus answered, "If I glorify myself, my glory is nothing; it is God my Father and Mother who glorifies me, who you say is your God. ⁵⁵But you have not known God. I know God. If I said, I do not know God, I would be a liar like you; but I do know God and I keep God's word. ⁵⁶Your father Abraham rejoiced that he was to see my day; he saw it and was glad." ⁵⁷The authorities then said to Jesus, "You are not yet fifty years old, and have you seen Abraham?" ⁵⁸Jesus said to them, "Truly, truly, I say to you, before Abraham was, I am." ⁵⁹So they took up stones to throw at Jesus; but Jesus hid, and went out of the temple.

9 As Jesus passed by, he saw a person blind from birth. ²And the disciples asked Jesus, "Rabbi, who sinned, this person or the parents, that the child was born blind?" ³Jesus answered, "It was not that this person sinned, or the parents, but that the works of God might be made manifest. ⁴We must work the works of the one who sent me, while it is day; night comes, when no one can work. ⁵As long as I am in the world, I am the light of the world." ⁶As Jesus said this, he spat on the ground and made clay of the spittle and anointed with the clay the eyes of the person who was blind, ⁷saying, "Go, wash in the pool of Siloam" (which means Sent). So the person who was blind went and washed and came back seeing. ⁸The neighbors and those who had seen that person be-

fore as a beggar said, "Is not this the one who used to sit and beg?" [9]Some said, "Yes, it is"; others said, "No, but they look alike." The one born blind said, "I am that person." [10]They said, "Then how were your eyes opened?" [11]The answer came, "The one called Jesus made clay and anointed my eyes and said to me, 'Go to Siloam and wash'; so I went and washed and received my sight." [12]They asked, "Where is he?" The one born blind said, "I do not know.

13 They brought to the Pharisees the person who had formerly been blind. [14]Now it was a sabbath day when Jesus made the clay and opened the blind one's eyes. [15]The Pharisees again asked that person how sight had been restored. And the answer came, "He put clay on my eyes, and I washed, and I see." [16]Some of the Pharisees said, "This one is not from God, for he does not keep the sabbath." But others said, "How can a person who is a sinner do such signs?" There was a division among them [17]So they again said to the person born blind, "What do you say about him, since he has opened your eyes?" The answer came, "He is a prophet."

18 The religious leaders did not believe that the person had been blind and had received sight, until they called the parents of the one who had received sight, [19]and asked them, "Is this your child, who you say was born blind? How then does this child now see?" [20]The parents answered, "We know that this is our child, who was born blind; [21]but how sight was given or how the eyes were opened we do not know. Ask our child, who is of age and will speak directly." [22]The parents said this because they feared the leaders of the synagogue, for the leaders had already agreed that anyone who confessed Jesus to be the Messiah would be put out of the synagogue. [23]Therefore the parents said, "Ask our child, who is of age."

24 So for the second time they called the one who had been blind, and said, "Give God the praise; we know that this man is a sinner." [25]The one born blind answered, "Whether he is a sinner, I do not know; one thing I know, that though I was blind, now I see." [26]They said, "What did he do to you? How did he open your eyes?" [27]The answer came, "I have told you already, and you would not listen. Why do you want to hear it again? Do you too want to become Jesus' disciples?" [28]And they reviled the one born blind, saying, "You are his disciple, but we are disciples of Moses. [29]We know that God has spoken to Moses but as for this one, we do not know where he comes from." [30]The one who had been blind answered "Why, this is a marvel! You do not know where he comes from, and yet he opened my eyes. [31]We know that God does not listen to sinners, but if anyone is a worshiper of God and does God's will, God listens. [32]Never since the world began has it been heard that anyone opened the eyes of a person born blind. [33]If this one were not from God, he could do nothing." [34]They answered, "You were born in

utter sin, and would you teach us?" And they cast out the one who had been blind.

35 Jesus found the one who he heard had been cast out and said, "Do you believe in the Human One?" [36]The one born blind answered, "And who is it, sir, so that I may believe in whoever it is?" [37]Jesus said, "You have seen who it is, and it is the very one who speaks to you." [38]The one who had been blind said, "Lord, I believe," and worshiped Jesus. [39]Jesus said, "For judgment I came into this world, that those who do not see may see, and that those who see may become blind." [40]Some of the Pharisees nearby heard this, and they said to Jesus, "Are we also blind?" [41]Jesus said to them, "If you were blind, you would have no guilt; but now that you say, 'We see,' your guilt remains."

10 "Truly, truly, I say to you, anyone who does not enter the sheep-fold by the door but climbs in by another way, is a thief and a robber; [2]but the one who enters by the door is the shepherd of the sheep. [3]To this one the gatekeeper opens; the sheep hear the voice of the shepherd who calls them by name and leads them out. [4]After bringing all of them out, the shepherd goes before them, and the sheep follow, for they know the shepherd's voice. [5]A stranger they will not follow, but they will flee away, for they do not know the voice of strangers." [6]This figure Jesus used with the disciples, but they did not understand what he was saying to them.

7 So Jesus said again, "Truly, truly, I say to you, I am the door of the sheep. [8]All who came before me are thieves and robbers; but the sheep did not heed them. [9]I am the door; whoever enters by me will be saved, and will go in and out and find pasture. [10]The thief comes only to steal and kill and destroy; I came that they may have life, and have it abundantly. [11]I am the good shepherd. The good shepherd is willing to die for the sheep. [12]A hireling who is not a shepherd, whose own the sheep are not, sees the wolf coming and leaves the sheep and flees; and the wolf snatches them and scatters them. [13]One who is a hireling flees, caring nothing for the sheep. [14]I am the good shepherd; I know my own and my own know me, [15]as God the Mother and Father knows me and I know God; and I lay down my life for the sheep. [16]And I have other sheep, that are not of this fold; I must bring them also, and they will heed my voice. So there will be one flock, one shepherd. [17]For this reason God loves me, because I lay down my life, that I may take it again. [18]No one takes it from me, but I lay it down of my own accord. I have power to lay it down, and I have power to take it again; this charge I have received from God my Father and Mother."

19 There was again a division among the religious authorities because of these words. [20]Many of them said, "Jesus has a demon, and is mad; why listen?" [21]Others said, "These are not the sayings of one

who has a demon. Can a demon open the eyes of people who are blind?"

22 It was the feast of the Dedication at Jerusalem; [23]it was winter, and Jesus was walking in the temple, in the portico of Solomon. [24]So the religious authorities gathered around Jesus and said to him, "How long will you keep us in suspense? If you are the Messiah, tell us plainly." [25]Jesus answered them, "I told you, and you do not believe. The works that I do in the name of God my Father and Mother, they bear witness to me; [26]but you do not believe, because you do not belong to my sheep. [27]My sheep hear my voice, and I know them, and they follow me; [28]and I give them eternal life, and they shall never perish, and no one shall snatch them out of my hand. [29]God, who has given them to me, is greater than all, and no one is able to snatch them out of God's hand. [30]I and God the Mother and Father are one."

31 The religious leaders took up stones again to stone Jesus. [32]But Jesus answered them, "I have shown you many good works from God; for which of these do you stone me?" [33]The leaders answered, "It is not for a good work that we stone you but for blasphemy; because you, being a human being, make yourself God." [34]Jesus responded, "Is it not written in your law, 'I said, you are gods'? [35]If those to whom the word of God came were called 'gods,' (and scripture cannot be annulled), [36]do you say of the one whom God consecrated and sent into the world, 'You are blaspheming,' because I said, 'I am the Child of God'? [37]If I am not doing the works of God, then do not believe me; [38]but if I do them, even though you do not believe me, believe the works, that you may know and understand that God is in me and I am in God." [39]Again they tried to arrest Jesus, who escaped from their hands.

40 Jesus went away across the Jordan to the place where John at first baptized, and remained there. [41]And many came to Jesus; and they said, "John did no sign, but everything that John said about this person was true." [42]And many believed in Jesus there.

11 Now a certain person was ill, Lazarus of Bethany, the village of Mary and her sister Martha. [2]It was Mary who anointed the Lord with ointment and wiped his feet with her hair, whose brother Lazarus was ill. [3]So the sisters sent to Jesus, saying, "Lord, the one you love is ill." [4]But hearing it, Jesus said, "This illness is not unto death; it is for the glory of God, so that the Child of God may be glorified by means of it.

5 Now Jesus loved Martha and her sister, Mary, and Lazarus. [6]And hearing that Lazarus was ill, Jesus stayed two days longer in the place where he was. [7]Then after this Jesus said to the disciples, "Let us go into Judea again." [8]The disciples replied, "Rabbi, the religious authorities were just now seeking to stone you, and are you going there again?" [9]Jesus answered, "Are there not twelve hours in the day? Those who

walk in the day do not stumble, because they see the light of this world. [10]But those who walk in the night stumble because the light is not in them." [11]Thus Jesus spoke to the disciples, and then added, "Our friend Lazarus has fallen asleep, but I go to awaken him out of sleep." [12]The disciples replied, "Lord, if he has fallen asleep, he will recover." [13]Now Jesus had spoken of the death of Lazarus, but they thought that he meant taking rest in sleep. [14]Then Jesus told them plainly, "Lazarus is dead; [15]and for your sake I am glad I was not there, so that you may believe. But let us go to him." [16]Thomas, called the Twin, said to the other disciples, "Let us also go, that we may die with him."

17 Now when Jesus came, he found that Lazarus had already been in the tomb four days. [18]Bethany was near Jerusalem, about two miles away, [19]and many of the Jews had come to Martha and Mary to console them concerning their brother. [20]When Martha heard that Jesus was coming, she went and met him, while Mary sat in the house. [21]Martha said to Jesus, "Lord, if you had been here, my brother would not have died. [22]And even now I know that whatever you ask from God, God will give you." [23]Jesus said to her, "Your brother will rise again." [24]Martha replied, "I know that he will rise again in the resurrection at the last day." [25]Jesus said to her, "I am the resurrection and the life; those who believe in me, though they die, yet shall they live, [26]and whoever lives and believes in me shall never die. Do you believe this?" [27]She said to Jesus, "Yes, Lord, I believe that you are the Messiah, the Child of God, the one who is coming into the world."

28 When Martha had said this, she went and called her sister Mary, saying quietly, "The Teacher is here and is calling for you." [29]And when Mary heard it, she rose quickly and went to him. [30]Now Jesus had not yet come to the village, but was still in the place where Martha had met him. [31]When the Jews who were with her in the house, consoling her, saw Mary rise quickly and go out, they followed her, supposing that she was going to the tomb to weep there. [32]Then Mary, when she came and saw Jesus, fell at his feet, and said, "Lord, if you had been here, my brother would not have died." [33]When Jesus saw her weeping, and the Jews who came with her also weeping, he was indignant in spirit and troubled, [34]and said, "Where have you laid Lazarus?" They answered, "Lord, come and see." [35]Jesus wept. [36]So the Jews said, "See how Jesus loved him!" [37]But some of them said, "Could not the one who opened the eyes of the person born blind have kept this one from dying?"

38 Then Jesus, again indignant, came to the tomb; it was a cave, and a stone lay against it. [39]Jesus said, "Take away the stone." Martha, the sister of the one who had died, said to Jesus, "Lord, by this time there will be an odor, for he has been dead four days." [40]Jesus said to her, "Did I not tell you that if you would believe you would see the glory of God?" [41]So they took away the stone. And Jesus looked up and said, "God, my

Mother and Father, I thank you that you have heard me. [42]I already knew that you hear me always, but I have said this on account of the people standing by, that they may believe that you sent me." [43]Having said this, Jesus cried with a loud voice, "Lazarus, come out." [44]The dead man came out, his hands and feet bound with bandages, and his face wrapped with a cloth. Jesus said to them, "Unbind him, and let him go."

45 Many of the Jews therefore, who had come with Mary and had seen what was done, believed in Jesus, [46]but some of them went to the Pharisees and told them what Jesus had done. [47]So the chief priests and the Pharisees gathered the council, and said, "What are we to do? For this person performs many signs. [48]If we let it continue, everyone will believe, and the Romans will come and destroy both our holy place and our nation." [49]But one of them, Caiaphas, who was high priest that year, said to them, "You know nothing at all; [50]you do not understand that it is better for you that one person should die for the people, than that the whole nation should perish." [51]Caiaphas did not say this of his own accord, but being high priest that year he prophesied that Jesus would die for the nation, [52]and not for the nation only, but to gather into one the children of God who are scattered abroad. [53]So from that day on they took counsel how to put Jesus to death.

54 Jesus therefore no longer went about openly among the Jews, but went from there to the country near the wilderness, to a town called Ephraim, staying with the disciples.

55 Now the Passover of the Jews was at hand, and many went up from the country to Jerusalem before the Passover, to purify themselves. [56]They were looking for Jesus and saying to one another as they stood in the temple, "What do you think? That Jesus will not come to the feast?" [57]Now the chief priests and the Pharisees had given orders that anyone who knew where Jesus was should let them know, so that they might arrest Jesus.

12 Six days before the Passover, Jesus came to Bethany, where Lazarus was, whom Jesus had raised from the dead. [2]There they made Jesus a supper; Martha served, and Lazarus was one of those at the table. [3]Mary took a pound of costly ointment of pure nard and anointed the feet of Jesus and wiped them with her hair; and the house was filled with the fragrance of the ointment. [4]But Judas Iscariot, one of the disciples (the one who was to betray Jesus), said, [5]"Why was this ointment not sold for thousands of dollars and given to the poor?" [6]This Judas said, not that he cared for the poor but because he was a thief, and having the money box, he used to take what was put into it. [7]Jesus said, "Let her alone, let her keep it for the day of my burial. [8]The poor you always have with you, but you do not always have me."

9 When the great crowd of the Jews learned that Jesus was there,

they came, not only on account of Jesus but also to see Lazarus, whom Jesus had raised from the dead. [10]So the chief priests planned to put Lazarus also to death, [11]because on account of him many of the Jews were going away and believing in Jesus.

12 The next day a great crowd who had come to the feast heard that Jesus was coming to Jerusalem. [13]So they took branches of palm trees and went out to meet him, crying, "Hosanna! Blessed is the one who comes in the name of the Lord, even the Ruler of Israel!" [14]And Jesus found a young donkey and sat upon it; as it is written,

> [15]"Fear not, beloved Zion;
> your ruler is coming,
> sitting on a donkey's colt!"

[16]The disciples did not understand this at first; but when Jesus was glorified, then they remembered that this had been written of Jesus and had been done to him. [17]The crowd that had been with him when he called Lazarus out of the tomb and raised him from the dead bore witness. [18]The reason why the crowd went to meet Jesus was that they heard he had done this sign. [19]The Pharisees then said to one another, "You see that you can do nothing; look, the world has gone after him."

20 Now among those who went up to worship at the feast were some Greeks. [21]So these came to Philip, who was from Bethsaida in Galilee, and said, "Sir, we wish to see Jesus." [22]Philip went and told Andrew; Andrew went with Philip and they told Jesus. [23]And Jesus answered them, "The hour has come for the Human One to be glorified. [24]Truly, truly, I say to you, unless a grain of wheat falls into the earth and dies, it remains alone; but if it dies, it bears much fruit. [25]Those who love their life lose it, and those who hate their life in this world will keep it for eternal life. [26]Anyone who serves me must follow me; and where I am, there shall my servant be also; anyone who serves me will be honored by God the Father and Mother.

27 "Now is my soul troubled. And what shall I say? 'God, save me from this hour'? No, for this purpose I have come to this hour. [28]God, glorify your name." Then a voice came from heaven, "I have glorified it, and I will glorify it again." [29]The crowd standing by heard it and said that it had thundered. Others said, "An angel has spoken to him." [30]Jesus answered, "This voice has come for your sake, not for mine. [31]Now is the judgment of this world, now shall the ruler of this world be cast out; [32]and I, when I am lifted up from the earth, will draw all people to myself." [33]Jesus said this to show by what death he was to die. [34]The crowd answered, "We have heard from the law that the Messiah remains forever. How can you say that the Human One must be lifted up? Who is this Human One?" [35]Jesus said to them, "The light is with you for a little longer. Walk while you have the light, lest the night overtake you;

those who walk in the night do not know where they are going. ³⁶While you have the light, believe in the light, that you may become children of light."

Having said this, Jesus departed and hid from them. ³⁷Though Jesus had done so many signs before the people, yet they did not believe in Jesus; ³⁸it was so that the word spoken by the prophet Isaiah might be fulfilled:

"God, who has believed our report,
and to whom has the arm of the God been revealed?"

³⁹Therefore they could not believe. For Isaiah also said,

⁴⁰"God has blinded their eyes and hardened their heart,
lest they should see with their eyes and perceive with their
heart,
and turn for me to heal them."

41 Isaiah said this because of seeing the Messiah's glory, and spoke about that one. ⁴²Nevertheless many even of the authorities believed in Jesus, but for fear of the Pharisees they did not confess it, lest they would be put out of the synagogue: ⁴³for they loved the praise of human beings more than the praise of God.

44 And Jesus cried out and said, "Everyone who believes in me, believes not in me but in the one who sent me. ⁴⁵And everyone who sees me sees the one who sent me. ⁴⁶I have come as light into the world, that whoever believes in me may not remain in the night. ⁴⁷I do not judge anyone who hears my sayings and does not keep them; for I did not come to judge the world but to save the world. ⁴⁸All who reject me and do not receive my sayings have a judge; the word that I have spoken will be their judge on the last day. ⁴⁹For I have not spoken on my own authority; God who sent me has commanded me what to say and what to speak. ⁵⁰And I know that God's commandment is eternal life. What I say, therefore, I say just as God has spoken to me."

13 Now before the feast of the Passover, when Jesus knew that the hour had come to depart out of this world to God the Father and Mother, having loved his own who were in the world, he loved them to the end. ²And during supper, when the devil had already put it into the heart of Judas Iscariot, Simon's son, to betray him, ³Jesus, knowing that God had given all things into Jesus' own hands and that he had come from God and was going to God, ⁴rose from supper, laid aside his robe, and put a towel around him. ⁵Then Jesus poured water into a basin, and began to wash the disciples' feet, and to wipe them with the towel that was around him. ⁶He came to Simon Peter; and Peter said to him, "Lord, do you wash my feet?" ⁷Jesus answered, "What I am doing you do not

know now, but afterward you will understand." ⁸Peter said to him, "You will never wash my feet." Jesus answered, "If I do not wash you, you have no part in me." ⁹Simon Peter said to Jesus, "Lord, not my feet only but also my hands and my head!" ¹⁰Jesus replied, "One who has bathed does not need to wash, except for the feet, but is clean all over; and you are clean, but not every one of you." ¹¹For he knew who was to betray him; that was why Jesus said, "You are not all clean."

12 Having washed their feet, and put on his robe, and returned to the table, Jesus said to them, "Do you know what I have done to you? ¹³You call me Teacher and Lord; and you are right, for so I am. ¹⁴If I then, your Lord and Teacher, have washed your feet, you also ought to wash one another's feet. ¹⁵For I have given you an example, that you also should do as I have done to you. ¹⁶Truly, truly, I say to you, a servant is not greater than a master; nor is one who is sent greater than the sender. ¹⁷If you know these things, blessed are you if you do them. ¹⁸I am not speaking of you all; I know whom I have chosen; it is that the scripture may be fulfilled, 'One who ate my bread has lifted the heel against me.' ¹⁹I tell you this now, before it takes place, that when it does take place you may believe that I am the one. ²⁰Truly, truly, I say to you, whoever receives anyone whom I send receives me; and whoever receives me receives the one who sent me."

21 Having spoken thus, Jesus was troubled in spirit, and testified, "Truly, truly, I say to you, one of you will betray me." ²²The disciples looked at one another, uncertain of whom he spoke. ²³One of the disciples, the one whom Jesus loved, was lying close to Jesus' breast; ²⁴so Simon Peter beckoned to that disciple and said, "Tell us who it is of whom Jesus speaks." ²⁵So lying thus, close to the breast of Jesus, the one whom Jesus loved said to him, "Lord, who is it?" ²⁶Jesus answered, "It is the one to whom I will give this piece of bread when I have dipped it." Having dipped it, he gave it to Judas, the son of Simon Iscariot. ²⁷Then after Judas received it, Satan entered into him. Jesus said to him, "What you are going to do, do quickly." ²⁸Now no one at the table knew why Jesus said this to Judas. ²⁹Some thought that, because Judas had the money box, Jesus was telling him, "Buy what we need for the feast," or that Judas should give something to the poor. ³⁰So, after receiving the piece of bread, Judas immediately went out; and it was night.

31 When Judas had gone out, Jesus said, "Now is the Human One glorified, and in that one God is glorified; ³²if God is glorified in the Human One, God will also glorify that very one in God's self, and will glorify that one immediately. ³³Little children, yet a little while I am with you. You will seek me; and as I said to the religious authorities so now I say to you, 'Where I am going you cannot come.' ³⁴A new commandment I give to you, that you love one another; even as I have loved you,

that you also love one another. 35By this all will know that you are my disciples, if you have love for one another."

36 Simon Peter said to Jesus, "Lord, where are you going?" Jesus answered, "Where I am going you cannot follow me now; but you will follow afterward." 37Peter said, "Lord, why cannot I follow you now? I will lay down my life for you." 38Jesus answered, "Will you lay down your life for me? Truly, truly, I say to you, the cock will not crow till you have denied me three times.

14 "Let not your hearts be troubled; believe in God, believe also in me. 2In the house of God my Father and Mother are many rooms; if it were not so, would I have told you that I go to prepare a place for you? 3And when I go and prepare a place for you, I will come again and will take you to myself, that where I am you may be also. 4And you know the way where I am going." 5Thomas said to Jesus, "Lord, we do not know where you are going; how can we know the way?" 6Jesus said to Thomas, "I am the way, and the truth, and the life; no one comes to God, but by me. 7If you had known me, you would have known God also; henceforth you know God and have seen God."

8 Philip said to Jesus, "Lord, show us God, and we will be satisfied." 9Jesus replied, "Have I been with you so long, and yet you do not know me, Philip? Whoever has seen me has seen God; how can you say, 'Show us God'? 10Do you not believe that I am in God and God in me? The words that I say to you I do not speak on my own authority; but God who dwells in me does God's works. 11Believe me that I am in God and God in me; or else believe me for the sake of the works themselves.

12 "Truly, truly, I say to you, all who believe in me will also do the works that I do; and greater works than these will they do, because I go to God. 13Whatever you ask in my name, I will do it, that God the Father and Mother may be glorified in God's Child; 14if you ask anything in my name, I will do it.

15 "If you love me, you will keep my commandments. 16And I will pray to God the Mother and Father, who will give you another Counselor, to be with you forever—17the Spirit of truth, whom the world cannot receive, because it neither sees nor knows this Spirit. But you know the Spirit, who dwells with you, and will be in you.

18 "I will not leave you desolate; I will come to you. 19Yet a little while, and the world will see me no more, but you will see me; because I live, you also will live. 20In that day, you will know that I am in God, and you in me, and I in you. 21Whoever has my commandments and keeps them, that is the one who loves me; and all who love me will be loved by God,and I will love them and manifest myself to them. 22Judas (not Iscariot) said to Jesus, "Lord, how is it that you will manifest yourself to us, and not to the world?" 23Jesus said, "If any love me, they will keep

my word, and God my Father and Mother will love them, and we will come to them and make our home with them. ²⁴Those who do not love me do not keep my words; and the word which you hear is not mine but God's who sent me.

25 "These things I have spoken to you, while I am still with you. ²⁶But the Counselor, the Holy Spirit, whom God will send in my name, will teach you all things, and bring to your remembrance all that I have said to you. ²⁷Peace I leave with you; my peace I give to you; not as the world gives do I give to you. Let not your hearts be troubled, neither let them be afraid. ²⁸You heard me say to you, 'I go away, and I will come to you.' If you loved me, you would have rejoiced, because I go to God; for God the Mother and Father is greater than I. ²⁹And now I have told you before it takes place, so that when it does take place, you may believe. ³⁰I will no longer talk much with you, for the ruler of this world is coming. That ruler has no power over me; ³¹but I do as God has commanded, so that the world may know that I love God. Rise, let us be going.

15 "I am the true vine, and God my Father and Mother is the vine-dresser. ²Every branch of mine that bears no fruit, God takes away, and every branch that does bear fruit God prunes, that it may bear more fruit. ³You are already made clean by the word which I have spoken to you. ⁴Abide in me, and I in you. As the branch cannot bear fruit by itself, unless it abides in the vine, neither can you, unless you abide in me. ⁵I am the vine, you are the branches. All who abide in me, and I in them, they are the ones who bear much fruit, for apart from me you can do nothing. ⁶Anyone who does not abide in me is thrown out as a branch and withers; and the branches are gathered, thrown into the fire and burned. ⁷If you abide in me, and my words abide in you, ask whatever you will, and it will be done for you. ⁸By this God is glorified, that you bear much fruit, and so prove to be my disciples. ⁹As God the Father and Mother has loved me, so have I loved you; abide in my love. ¹⁰If you keep my commandments, you will abide in my love, just as I have kept God's commandments and abide in God's love. ¹¹These things I have spoken to you, that my joy may be in you, and that your joy may be full.

12 "This is my commandment, that you love one another as I have loved you. ¹³Greater love has no one than this, that one lay down one's life for a friend. ¹⁴You are my friends if you do what I command you. ¹⁵No longer do I call you servants, for the servant does not know what the master is doing; but I have called you friends, for all that I have heard from God I have made known to you. ¹⁶You did not choose me, but I chose you and appointed you that you should go and bear fruit and that your fruit should abide; so that whatever you ask God the Father

and Mother in my name may be given to you. [17]This I command you, to love one another.

18 "If the world hates you, know that it has hated me before it hated you. [19]If you were of the world, the world would love its own; but because you are not of the world, but I chose you out of the world, therefore the world hates you. [20]Remember the word that I said to you, 'A servant is not greater than a master.' If they persecuted me, they will persecute you; if they kept my word, they will keep yours also. [21]But all this they will do to you on my account, because they do not know the one who sent me. [22]If I had not come and spoken to them, they would have no excuse for their sin. [23]Whoever hates me hates God my Father and Mother also. [24]If I had not done among them the works which no one else did, they would not have sin; but now they have seen and hated both me and God. [25]It is to fulfill the word that is written in their law, 'They hated me without a cause.' [26]But when the Counselor comes, whom I shall send to you from God—even the Spirit of truth, who proceeds from God—that one will bear witness to me, [27]and you also are witnesses, because you have been with me from the beginning.

16 "I have said all this to you to keep you from falling away. [2]They will put you out of the synagogues; indeed, the hour is coming when those who kill you will think they are offering service to God. [3]And they will do this because they have not known God, or me. [4]But I have said these things to you, that when their hour comes you may remember that I told you of them.

"I did not say these things to you from the beginning, because I was with you. [5]But now I am going to the one who sent me; yet none of you asks me, 'Where are you going?' [6]But because I have said these things to you, sorrow has filled your hearts. [7]Nevertheless I tell you the truth: it is to your advantage that I go away, for if I do not go away, the Counselor will not come to you; but if I go, I will send the Counselor to you, [8]who, having come, will convince the world of sin and of righteousness and of judgment: [9]of sin, because they do not believe in me; [10]of righteousness, because I go to God, and you will see me no more; [11]of judgment, because the ruler of this world is judged.

12 "I have yet many things to say to you, but you cannot bear them now. [13]When the Spirit of truth comes, that Spirit will guide you into all the truth; for the Spirit will not speak independently, but will speak only what the Spirit hears, and will declare to you the things that are to come. [14]The Spirit will glorify me by taking what is mine and declaring it to you. [15]All that God the Mother and Father has is mine; therefore I said that the Spirit will take what is mine and declare it to you.

16 "A little while, and you will see me no more; again a little while, and you will see me." [17]Some of the disciples said to one another, "What

is this that Jesus says to us, 'A little while, and you will not see me, and again a little while, and you will see me'; and, 'because I go to God'?" [18]They said, "What does Jesus mean by 'a little while'? We do not know what that means." [19]Jesus, knowing that they wanted to ask, said to them, "Is this what you are asking yourselves, what I meant by saying, 'A little while, and you will not see me, and again a little while, and you will see me'? [20]Truly, truly, I say to you, you will weep and lament, but the world will rejoice; you will be sorrowful, but your sorrow will turn into joy. [21]When a woman is in travail she has sorrow, because her hour has come; but when she is delivered of the child, she no longer remembers the anguish, for joy that a child is born into the world. [22]So you have sorrow now, but I will see you again and your hearts will rejoice, and no one will take your joy from you. [23]In that day you will ask nothing of me. Truly, truly, I say to you, if you ask anything of God, God will give it to you in my name. [24]Up to now you have asked nothing in my name; ask, and you will receive, that your joy may be full.

25 "I have said this to you in figures of speech; the hour is coming when I will no longer speak to you in such figures, but will tell you plainly of God. [26]In that day you will ask in my name; and I do not say to you that I will pray to God for you; [27]for God loves you, because you have loved me and have believed that I came from God. [28]I came from God and have come into the world; again, I am leaving the world and going to God."

29 Jesus' disciples said, "Oh, now you are speaking plainly, not in any figures of speech! [30]Now we know that you know all things, and need no one to question you; by this we believe that you came from God." [31]Jesus answered them, "Do you now believe? [32]The hour is coming, indeed it has come, when you will be scattered, each to your own home, and you will leave me alone; yet I am not alone, for God is with me. [33]I have said this to you, that in me you may have peace. In the world you have tribulation; but take courage, I have overcome the world."

17 Having spoken these words, Jesus looked up to heaven and said, "God my Mother and Father, the hour has come; glorify your Child, so that the Child may glorify you, [2]since you have given that Child power over all flesh, to give eternal life to all whom you have given your Child. [3]And this is eternal life, that they know you the only true God, and Jesus Christ whom you have sent. [4]I glorified you on earth, having accomplished the work which you gave me to do; [5]and now, God my Father and Mother, glorify me in your own presence with the glory which I had with you before the world was made.

6 "I have manifested your name to those whom you gave me out of the world; yours they were, and you gave them to me, and they have kept your word. [7]Now they know that everything that you have given

me is from you; ⁸for I have given them the words which you gave me, and they have received them and know in truth that I came from you; and they have believed that you sent me. ⁹I am praying for them; I am not praying for the world but for those whom you have given me, for they are yours; ¹⁰all mine are yours, and yours are mine, and I am glorified in them. ¹¹And now I am no longer in the world, but they are in the world, and I am coming to you. Holy God my Mother and Father, keep them in your name, which you have given me, that they may be one, even as we are one. ¹²While I was with them, I kept them in your name, which you have given me; I have guarded them, and none of them is lost but the one destined for destruction, that the scripture might be fulfilled. ¹³But now I am coming to you; and these things I speak in the world, that they may have my joy fulfilled in themselves. ¹⁴I have given them your word; and the world has hated them because they are not of the world, even as I am not of the world. ¹⁵I do not pray that you would take them out of the world, but that you would keep them from the evil one. ¹⁶They are not of the world, even as I am not of the world. ¹⁷Sanctify them in the truth; your word is truth. ¹⁸As you sent me into the world, so I have sent them into the world. ¹⁹And for their sake I consecrate myself, that they also may be consecrated in truth.

20 "I do not pray for these only, but also for those who believe in me through their word, ²¹that they may all be one; even as you, O God, my Mother and Father, are in me, and I in you, that they also may be in us, so that the world may believe that you have sent me. ²²The glory which you have given me I have given to them, that they may be one even as we are one, ²³I in them and you in me, that they may become perfectly one, so that the world may know that you have sent me and have loved them even as you have loved me. ²⁴O God, I desire that they also, whom you have given me, may be with me where I am, to behold my glory which you have given me in your love for me before the foundation of the world. ²⁵O righteous God, the world has not known you, but I have known you; and these know that you have sent me. ²⁶I made known to them your name, and I will make it known, that the love with which you have loved me may be in them, and I in them.

18 After praying for the disciples, Jesus went out with them across the Kidron valley, where there was a garden which they entered. ²Now Judas, who betrayed him, also knew the place; for Jesus often met there with the disciples. ³So Judas, taking a band of soldiers and some officers from the chief priests and the Pharisees, went there with lanterns and torches and weapons. ⁴Then Jesus, knowing all that was to befall him, came forward and said to them, "Whom do you seek?" ⁵They answered, "Jesus of Nazareth." Jesus said to them, "I am the one." Judas, the betrayer, was standing with them. ⁶When Jesus said to them, "I

am the one," they drew back and fell to the ground. [7]Again Jesus asked them, "Whom do you seek?" And they said, "Jesus of Nazareth." [8]Jesus answered, "I told you that I am the one; so, if you seek me, let these others go." [9]This was to fulfill the word which he had spoken, "Of those whom you gave me I lost not one." [10]Then Simon Peter, having a sword, drew it and struck the high priest's slave and cut off his right ear. The slave's name was Malchus. [11]Jesus said to Peter, "Put your sword into its sheath; shall I not drink the cup which God the Father and Mother has given me?"

12 So the band of soldiers and their captain and the officers of the religious authorities seized and bound Jesus. [13]First they led him to Annas, who was the father-in-law of Caiaphas, the high priest that year. [14]It was Caiaphas who had given counsel to the religious authorities that it was expedient that one person should die for the people.

15 Simon Peter followed Jesus, and so did another disciple, who was known to the high priest, and who entered the court of the high priest along with Jesus, [16]while Peter stood outside at the door. So the other disciple, who was known to the high priest, went out and spoke to the maid who kept the door, and brought Peter in. [17]The maid who kept the door said to Peter, "Are not you also one of this man's disciples?" Peter said, "I am not." [18]Now the servants and officers had made a charcoal fire, because it was cold, and they were standing and warming themselves; Peter also was with them, standing and warming himself.

19 The high priest then questioned Jesus about his disciples and teaching. [20]Jesus answered the high priest, "I have spoken openly to the world; I have always taught in synagogues and in the temple, where all Jews come together; I have said nothing secretly. [21]Why do you ask me? Ask those who have heard me, what I said to them; they know what I said." [22]When Jesus had said this, one of the officers standing by struck him with his hand, saying, "Is that how you answer the high priest?" [23]Jesus answered the officer, "If I have spoken wrongly, bear witness to the wrong; but if I have spoken rightly, why do you strike me?" [24]Annas then sent Jesus bound to Caiaphas the high priest.

25 Now Simon Peter was standing and warming himself. They said to him, "Are not you also one of Jesus' disciples?" He denied it and said, "I am not." [26]One of the servants of the high priest, a relative of the slave whose ear Peter had cut off, asked, "Did I not see you in the garden with him?" [27]Peter again denied it; and at once the cock crowed.

28 Then they led Jesus from the house of Caiaphas to the praetorium. It was early. They themselves did not enter the praetorium, so that they might not be defiled, but might eat the passover. [29]So Pilate went out to them and said, "What accusation do you bring against this person?" [30]They answered Pilate, "If this one were not an evildoer, we would not have handed him over." [31]Pilate said to them, "Take him your-

selves and make judgment by your own law." The religious authorities said to Pilate, "It is not lawful for us to put anyone to death." ³²This was to fulfill the word which Jesus had spoken to show by what death he was to die.

33 Pilate entered the praetorium again and called Jesus, and said, "Are you the King of the Jews?" ³⁴Jesus answered, "Do you say this of your own accord, or did others say it to you about me?" ³⁵Pilate answered, "Am I one of you? Your own nation and the chief priests have handed you over to me; what have you done?" ³⁶Jesus answered, "My dominion is not of this world; if my dominion were of this world, my servants would fight, that I might not be handed over to the religious authorities; but my dominion is not from the world." ³⁷Pilate said to Jesus, "So you are a king?" Jesus answered, "You say that I am a king. For this I was born, and for this I have come into the world, to bear witness to the truth. Everyone who is of the truth hears my voice." ³⁸Pilate said to Jesus, "What is truth?"

And having said this, Pilate went out to the religious authorities again, and told them, "I find no crime in this person. ³⁹But you have a custom that I should release someone for you at the Passover; will you have me release for you the King of the Jews?" ⁴⁰They cried out in reply, "Not Jesus, but Barabbas!" Now Barabbas was a robber.

19 Then Pilate had Jesus beaten. ²And the soldiers plaited a crown of thorns, and put it on Jesus' head, and arrayed him in a purple robe; ³they came up, saying, "Hail, King of the Jews!" and struck him with their hands. ⁴Pilate went out again, and said to them, "See, I am bringing him out to you, that you may know that I find no crime in him." ⁵So Jesus came out, wearing the crown of thorns and the purple robe. Pilate said to them, "Here he is!" ⁶When the chief priests and the officers saw Jesus, they cried out, "Crucify, crucify!" Pilate said to them, "Take him yourselves and crucify him, for I find no crime in him." ⁷The religious authorities answered Pilate, "We have a law, and by that law Jesus ought to die, having claimed to be the Child of God." ⁸Hearing these words, Pilate was the more afraid. ⁹Pilate entered the praetorium again and said to Jesus, "Where are you from?" But Jesus gave no answer. ¹⁰Pilate therefore said to him, "You will not speak to me? Do you not know that I have power to release you, and power to crucify you?" ¹¹Jesus replied, "You would have no power over me unless it had been given you from above; therefore the one who delivered me to you has the greater sin."

12 Upon this Pilate sought to release Jesus, but the religious authorities cried out, "If you release this person, you are not Caesar's friend; everyone who claims to be a king opposes Caesar." ¹³Hearing these words, Pilate brought Jesus out and sat down on the judgment seat at

a place called The Pavement, and in Hebrew, Gabbatha. [14]Now it was the day of Preparation of the Passover; it was about the sixth hour. Pilate said to the Jews, "Here is your King!" [15]They cried out, "Away, away with him, crucify him!" Pilate said to them, "Shall I crucify your King?" The chief priests answered, "We have no king but Caesar." [16]Then Pilate handed him over to them to be crucified.

17 So they took Jesus, who went out bearing his own cross, to the place called the place of a skull, which is called in Hebrew Golgotha. [18]There they crucified him, along with two others, one on either side, and Jesus between them. [19]Pilate also wrote a title and put it on the cross; it read, "Jesus of Nazareth, the King of the Jews." [20]Many of the Jews read this title, for the place where Jesus was crucified was near the city; and it was written in Hebrew, in Latin, and in Greek. [21]The chief priests of the Jews then said to Pilate, "Do not write, 'The King of the Jews,' but, 'This one said, I am King of the Jews.' [22]Pilate answered, "What I have written I have written."

23 When the soldiers had crucified Jesus they took his robe and divided it into four parts, one for each soldier; also his tunic. But the tunic was without seam, woven from top to bottom; [24]so they said to one another, "Let us not tear it, but cast lots for it to see whose it shall be." This was to fulfill the scripture,

"They parted my robe among them,
and for my clothing they cast lots."

25 So the soldiers did this. But standing by the cross of Jesus were his mother, and his mother's sister, Mary the wife of Clopas, and Mary Magdalene. [26]When Jesus saw his mother, and the disciple whom he loved standing near, he said to his mother, "Woman, here is your child!" [27]Then Jesus said to the disciple, "Here is your mother!" And from that hour the disciple took her home.

28 After this, Jesus, knowing that all was now finished, said (to fulfill the scripture), "I thirst." [29]A bowl full of vinegar stood there; so they put a sponge full of the vinegar on hyssop and held it to his mouth. [30]After receiving the vinegar, Jesus said, "It is finished," and bowed his head and gave up the spirit.

31 Since it was the day of Preparation, in order to prevent the bodies from remaining on the cross on the sabbath (for that sabbath was a high day), the religious authorities asked Pilate that their legs might be broken, and that they might be taken away. [32]So the soldiers came and broke the legs of the first, and of the other who had been crucified with Jesus; [33]but when they came to Jesus and saw that he was already dead, they did not break his legs. [34]But one of the soldiers pierced Jesus' side with a spear, and at once there came out blood and water. [35]The one who saw it has borne witness—this testimony is true, and the witness

knows that it is the truth—that you also may believe. ³⁶For these things took place that the scripture might be fulfilled, "Not a bone of him shall be broken." ³⁷And again another scripture says, "They shall look on the one whom they have pierced."

38 After this Joseph of Arimathea, who was a disciple of Jesus, but secretly, for fear of the religious authorities, asked Pilate for permission to take away the body of Jesus, and Pilate granted it. So Joseph came and took away Jesus' body. ³⁹Nicodemus also, who had at first come to Jesus by night, came bringing a mixture of myrrh and aloes, about a hundred pounds in weight. ⁴⁰They took the body of Jesus, and bound it in linen cloths with the spices, as is the burial custom of the Jews. ⁴¹Now in the place where Jesus was crucified there was a garden, and in the garden a new tomb where no one had ever been laid. ⁴²So because of the Jewish day of Preparation, as the tomb was close at hand, they laid Jesus there.

20 Now on the first day of the week Mary Magdalene came to the tomb early, while it was not yet light, and saw that the stone had been taken away from the tomb. ²So she ran, and went to Simon Peter and the other disciple, the one whom Jesus loved, and said to them, "They have taken the Lord out of the tomb, and we do not know where they have laid him." ³Peter then came out with the other disciple, and they went toward the tomb. ⁴They both ran, but the other disciple out-ran Peter, reached the tomb first, ⁵and stooping to look in, saw the linen cloths lying there, but did not go in. ⁶Then Simon Peter came, following after, and went into the tomb; Peter saw the linen cloths lying, ⁷and the napkin, which had been on Jesus' head, not lying with the linen cloths but rolled up in a place by itself. ⁸Then the other disciple, who reached the tomb first, also went in, and saw and believed; ⁹for as yet they did not know the scripture, that Jesus must rise from the dead. ¹⁰Then the disciples went back to their homes.

11 But Mary stood weeping outside the tomb, and as she wept she stooped to look into the tomb; ¹²and she saw two angels in white, sitting where the body of Jesus had lain, one at the head and one at the feet. ¹³They said to her, "Woman, why are you weeping?" She said to them, "Because they have taken away my Lord, and I do not know where they have laid him." ¹⁴Saying this, she turned round and saw Jesus standing, but she did not know that it was Jesus. ¹⁵Jesus said to her, "Woman, why are you weeping? Whom do you seek?" Supposing Jesus to be the gardener, she answered, "Sir, if you have carried Jesus away, tell me where you have laid him, and I will take him away." ¹⁶Jesus said to her, "Mary." She turned and responded in Hebrew, "Rabboni!" (which means Teacher). ¹⁷Jesus said to her, "Do not hold me, for I have not yet ascended to God; but go to my friends and say to them, I am ascending to God my Father and Mother and your Father and Mother, to

my God and your God." [18]Mary Magdalene went and said to the disciples, "I have seen the Lord"; and she told them that Jesus had said these things to her.

19 On the evening of that day, the first day of the week, the doors being shut where the disciples were, for fear of the religious authorities, Jesus came and stood among them and said to them, "Peace be with you." [20]Having said this, Jesus showed them Jesus' hands and side. Then the disciples were glad when they saw the Lord. [21]Jesus said to them again, "Peace be with you. As God the Father and Mother has sent me, even so I send you." [22]Having said this, Jesus breathed on them, and said to them, "Receive the Holy Spirit. [23]If you forgive the sins of any, they are forgiven; if you retain the sins of any, they are retained."

24 Now Thomas, one of the twelve, called the Twin, was not with them when Jesus came. [25]So the other disciples told him, "We have seen the Lord." But Thomas said to them, "Unless I see in Jesus' hands the print of the nails, and place my finger in the mark of the nails, and place my hand in Jesus' side, I will not believe."

26 Eight days later, the disciples were again in the house, and Thomas was with them. The doors were shut, but Jesus came and stood among them, and said, "Peace be with you." [27]Then Jesus said to Thomas, "Put your finger here, and see my hands; and put out your hand, and place it in my side; do not be faithless, but believing." [28]Thomas answered, "My Lord and my God!" [29]Jesus said to Thomas, "Have you believed because you have seen me? Blessed are those who have not seen and yet believe."

30 Now Jesus did many other signs in the presence of the disciples, which are not written in this book; [31]but these are written that you may believe that Jesus is the Christ, the Child of God, and that believing you may have life in Jesus' name.

21 Jesus appeared again to the disciples by the Sea of Tiberias, and appeared in this way. [2]Simon Peter, Thomas called the Twin, Nathanael of Cana in Galilee, the sons of Zebedee, and two other disciples were together. [3]Simon Peter said to them, "I am going fishing." They said to him, "We will go with you." They went out and got into the boat; but that night they caught nothing.

4 Just as the day was breaking, Jesus stood on the beach; yet the disciples did not know that it was Jesus. [5]Jesus said to them, "Children, have you any fish?" They answered, "No." [6]Jesus said to them, "Cast the net on the right side of the boat, and you will find some." So they cast it, and now they were not able to haul it in, for the quantity of fish. [7]That disciple whom Jesus loved said to Peter, "It is the Lord!" When Simon Peter heard that it was the Lord, he put on his clothes, for he was stripped for work, and sprang into the sea. [8]But the other disciples came

in the boat, dragging the net full of fish, for they were not far from the land, but about a hundred yards off.

9 When they got out on land, they saw a charcoal fire there, with fish lying on it, and bread. ¹⁰Jesus said to them, "Bring some of the fish that you have just caught. ¹¹So Simon Peter went aboard and hauled the net ashore, full of large fish, a hundred and fifty-three of them; and although there were so many, the net was not torn. ¹²Jesus said to them, "Come and have breakfast." Now none of the disciples dared ask, "Who are you?" They knew it was the Lord. ¹³Jesus came and took the bread and gave it to them, and did the same with the fish. ¹⁴This was now the third time that Jesus was revealed to the disciples after being raised from the dead.

15 When they had finished breakfast, Jesus said to Simon Peter, "Simon, son of John, do you love me more than these?" He said to Jesus, "Yes, Lord; you know that I love you." Jesus said to him, "Feed my lambs." ¹⁶A second time Jesus said to him, "Simon, son of John, do you love me?" He replied, "Yes, Lord, you know that I love you." Jesus said to him, "Tend my sheep." ¹⁷Jesus said to him the third time, "Simon, son of John, do you love me?" Peter was distressed because Jesus said to him the third time, "Do you love me?" And he said to Jesus, "Lord, you know everything; you know that I love you." Jesus said to him, "Feed my sheep. ¹⁸Truly, truly, I say to you when you were young, you readied yourself and walked where you wished; but when you grow old, you will stretch out your hands, and another will get you ready and carry you where you do not wish to go." ¹⁹(This Jesus said to show by what death Peter was to glorify God.) And after this Jesus said to him, "Follow me."

20 Peter turned and saw following them the disciple whom Jesus loved, who had lain close to Jesus' breast at the supper and had said, "Lord, who is it who is going to betray you?" ²¹When Peter saw this disciple, he said to Jesus, "Lord, what will happen to this person?" ²²Jesus answered, "If it is my will that this disciple remain until I come, what is that to you? Follow me!" ²³The saying spread abroad in the community that this disciple was not to die; yet Jesus did not say to the disciple anything about not dying, but, "If it is my will that this disciple remain until I come, what is that you?"

24 This is the disciple who is bearing witness to these things, and who has written these things; and we know that the testimony of this disciple is true.

25 But there are also many other things which Jesus did; and if every one of them were to be written down, I suppose that the world itself could not contain the books that would be written.

The Letters of Paul

Romans

1 Paul, a servant of Jesus Christ, called to be an apostle, set apart for the gospel of God ²promised by God beforehand through the prophets in the holy scriptures, ³the gospel concerning the Child of God, descended from David according to the flesh ⁴and designated Child of God in power according to the Spirit of holiness by Christ's resurrection from the dead, Jesus Christ our Lord, ⁵through whom we have received grace and apostleship to bring about the obedience of faith for the sake of Christ's name among all the nations, ⁶including yourselves who are called to belong to Jesus Christ;

7 To all God's beloved in Rome, who are called to be saints:

Grace to you and peace from God our Father and Mother and from the Lord Jesus Christ.

8 First, I thank my God through Jesus Christ for all of you, because your faith is proclaimed in all the world. ⁹For God is my witness, whom I serve with my spirit in the gospel of God's Child, that without ceasing I mention you always in my prayers, ¹⁰asking that somehow by God's will I may now at last succeed in coming to you. ¹¹For I long to see you, that I may impart to you some spiritual gift to strengthen you, ¹²that is, that we may be mutually encouraged by each other's faith, both yours and mine. ¹³I want you to know, friends, that I have often intended to come to you (but thus far have been prevented), in order that I may reap some harvest among you as well as among the rest of the Gentiles. ¹⁴I am under obligation both to Greeks and to barbarians, both to the wise and to the foolish: ¹⁵so I am eager to preach the gospel to you also who are in Rome.

16 For I am not ashamed of the gospel: it is the power of God for salvation to everyone who has faith, to the Jew first and also to the Greek.

¹⁷For in the gospel the righteousness of God is revealed through faith for faith; as it is written "Whoever through faith is righteous will live."

18 For the wrath of God is revealed from heaven against all ungodliness and wickedness of people who by their wickedness suppress the truth. ¹⁹For what can be known about God is plain to them, because God has shown it to them. ²⁰Ever since the creation of the world God's invisible nature, namely, God's eternal power and deity, has been clearly perceived in the things that have been made. So they are without excuse; ²¹for although they knew God they did not honor God as God or give thanks to God, but they became futile in their thinking and their senseless minds were deadened. ²²Claiming to be wise, they became fools, ²³ and exchanged the glory of the immortal God for images resembling mortal human beings or birds or animals or reptiles.

24 Therefore God gave them up in the lusts of their hearts to impurity, to the dishonoring of their bodies among themselves, ²⁵because they exchanged the truth about God for a lie and worshiped and served the creature rather than the Creator, who is blessed for ever! Amen.

26 For this reason God gave them up to dishonorable passions. Their women exchanged natural relations for unnatural, ²⁷and the men likewise gave up natural relations with women and were consumed with passion for one another, men committing shameless acts with men and receiving in their own persons the due penalty for their error.

28 And since they did not see fit to acknowledge God, God gave them up to a base mind and to improper conduct. ²⁹They were filled with all manner of wickedness, evil, covetousness, malice. Full of envy, murder, strife, deceit, malignity, they are gossips, ³⁰slanderers, haters of God, insolent, haughty, boastful, inventors of evil, disobedient to parents, ³¹foolish, faithless, heartless, ruthless. ³²Though they know God's decree that those who do such things deserve to die, they not only do them but approve those who practice them.

2 Therefore you have no excuse, whoever you are, when you judge another; for in passing judgment upon another you condemn yourself, because you, the judge, are doing the very same things. ²We know that the judgment of God rightly falls upon those who do such things. ³Do you suppose, whoever you are, that when you judge those who do such things and yet do them yourself, you will escape the judgment of God? ⁴Or do you presume upon the riches of God's kindness and forbearance and patience? Do you not know that God's kindness is meant to lead you to repentance? ⁵But by your hard and impenitent heart you are storing up wrath for yourself on the day of wrath when God's righteous judgment will be revealed. ⁶For God will render to all people according to their works: ⁷to those who by patience in well-doing

seek for glory and honor and immortality, there will be eternal life; [8]but for those who are factious and do not obey the truth, but obey wickedness, there will be wrath and fury. [9]There will be tribulation and distress for every human being who does evil, the Jew first and also the Greek, [10]but glory and honor and peace for everyone who does good, the Jew first and also the Greek. [11]For God shows no partiality.

12 All who have sinned without the law will also perish without the law, and all who have sinned under the law will be judged by the law. [13]For it is not the hearers of the law who are righteous before God, but the doers of the law who will be justified. [14]When Gentiles who have not the law do by nature what the law requires, they are a law to themselves, even though they do not have the law. [15]They show that what the law requires is written on their hearts, while their conscience also bears witness and their conflicting thoughts accuse or perhaps excuse them [16]on that day when, according to my gospel, God judges people's secrets by Christ Jesus.

17 But if you call yourself a Jew and rely upon the law and boast of your relation to God [18]and know God's will and approve what is excellent, because you are instructed in the law, [19]and if you are sure that you are a guide to those who are blind, a light to those who are evil, [20]a corrector of the foolish, a teacher of children, having in the law the embodiment of knowledge and truth—[21]you then who teach others, will you not teach yourself? While you preach against stealing, do you steal? [22]You who say that one must not commit adultery, do you commit adultery? You who abhor idols, do you rob temples? [23]You who boast in the law, do you dishonor God by breaking the law? [24]For, as it is written, "The name of God is blasphemed among the Gentiles because of you."

25 Circumcision indeed is of value if you obey the law; but if you break the law, your circumcision becomes uncircumcision [26]So, if those who are uncircumcised keep the precepts of the law, will not their uncircumcision be regarded as circumcision? [27]Then those who are physically uncircumcised but keep the law will condemn you who have the written code and circumcision but break the law. [28]For one is not a real Jew who is one outwardly, nor is true circumcision something external and physical. [29]One is a Jew who is one inwardly, and real circumcision is a matter of the heart, spiritual and not literal. Such a one has praise not from others but from God.

3 Then what advantage has the Jew? Or what is the value of circumcision? [2]Much in every way. To begin with, the Jews are entrusted with the oracles of God. [3]What if some were unfaithful? Does their faithlessness nullify the faithfulness of God? [4]By no means! Let God be true though every human being be a liar, as it is written,

"That you may be justified in your words,
and prevail when you are judged."

5But if our wickedness serves to show the justice of God, what will we
say? That God is unjust to inflict wrath on us? (I speak in a human
way.) 6By no means! For then how could God judge the world? 7But if
through my falsehood God's truthfulness abounds to God's glory, why
am I still being condemned as a sinner? 8And why not do evil that good
may come?—as some people slanderously charge us with saying. Their
condemnation is just.

9 What then? Are we Jews any better off? No, not at all, for I have
already charged that all people, both Jews and Greeks, are under the
power of sin, 10as it is written:

"None is righteous, no, not one;
11no one understands, no one seeks for God.
12All have turned aside, together they have gone wrong;
no one does good, not even one."
13"Their throat is an open grave,
they use their tongues to deceive."
"The venom of asps is under their lips."
14"Their mouth is full of curses and bitterness."
15"Their feet are swift to shed blood,
16in their paths are ruin and misery,
17and the way of peace they do not know."
18"There is no fear of God before their eyes."

19 Now we know that whatever the law says it speaks to those who
are under the law, so that every mouth may be stopped, and the whole
world may be held accountable to God. 20For no human being will be
justified in God's sight by works of the law, since through the law comes
knowledge of sin.

21 But now the righteousness of God has been manifested apart
from law, although the law and the prophets bear witness to it, 22the
righteousness of God through faith in Jesus Christ for all who believe.
For there is no distinction; 23since all have sinned and fall short of the
glory of God, 24they are justified by God's grace as a gift, through the redemption which is in Christ Jesus, 25whom God put forward as a blood
expiation, to be received by faith. This was to show God's righteousness,
because in divine forbearance God had passed over former sins; 26it was
to prove at the present time that God is indeed righteous and justifies
the one who has faith in Jesus.

27 Then what becomes of our boasting? It is excluded. On what principle? On the principle of works? No, but on the principle of faith. 28For
we hold that one is justified by faith apart from works of law. 29Or is

God the God of Jews only? Is God not the God of Gentiles also? Yes, of Gentiles also, [30]since God is one, and will justify the circumcised on the ground of their faith and the uncircumcised through their faith. [31]Do we then overthrow the law by this faith? By no means! On the contrary, we uphold the law.

4 What then shall we say about Abraham, our ancestor according to the flesh? [2]For if Abraham was justified by works, he has something to boast about, but not before God. [3]For what does the scripture say? "Abraham believed God, and it was reckoned to him as righteousness." [4]Now to one who works, wages are not reckoned as a gift but as the worker's due. [5]And to one who does not work but trusts God who justifies the ungodly, faith is reckoned as righteousness. [6]So also David pronounces a blessing upon the one to whom God reckons righteousness apart from works:

> [7]"Blessed are those whose iniquities are forgiven, and whose sins are covered;
> [8]blessed are those against whom the Lord will not reckon their sin."

9 Is this blessing pronounced only upon the Jews, or also upon the Gentiles? We say that faith was reckoned to Abraham as righteousness. [10]How then was it reckoned to him? Was it before or after circumcision? It was not after, but before. [11]Abraham received circumcision as a sign or seal of the righteousness which he had by faith while still uncircumcised. The purpose was to make Abraham the ancestor of all uncircumcised believers, who have righteousness reckoned to them [12]and likewise the ancestor of the circumcised believers who follow the example of the faith which our ancestor Abraham had before circumcision.

13 The promise to Abraham and Sarah and to their descendants, that they should inherit the world, did not come through the law but through the righteousness of faith. [14]If it is the adherents of the law who are to be the heirs, faith is null and the promise is void. [15]For the law brings wrath, but where there is no law there is no transgression.

16 That is why it depends on faith, in order that the promise may rest on grace and be guaranteed to all their descendants—not only to the adherents of the law but also to those who share the faith of Abraham, who with Sarah is the ancestor of us all; [17]as it is written, "I have made you the ancestor of many nations"—in the presence of the God in whom Abraham believed, who gives life to the dead and calls into existence the things that do not exist. [18]In hope Abraham believed against hope, in order to become the ancestor of many nations; as he had been told, "So shall your descendants be." [19]Abraham, being about a hundred

years old, did not weaken in faith when considering his own body to be as good as dead, or when considering the barrenness of Sarah's womb. [20]No distrust made Abraham waver concerning the promise of God, but he grew strong in faith, giving glory to God, [21]fully convinced that God was able to do what God had promised. [22]That is why Abraham's faith was "reckoned to him as righteousness." [23]But the words, "it was reckoned to him," were written not for Abraham's sake alone, [24]but for ours also. It will be reckoned to us who believe in the one who raised from the dead Jesus our Lord, [25]who was put to death for our trespasses and raised for our justification.

5 Therefore, since we are justified by faith, we have peace with God through our Lord Jesus Christ, [2]through whom we have obtained access to this grace in which we stand, and we rejoice in our hope of sharing the glory of God. [3]More than that, we rejoice in our sufferings, knowing that suffering produces endurance, [4]and endurance produces character, and character produces hope, [5]and hope does not disappoint us, because God's love has been poured into our hearts through the Holy Spirit who has been given to us.

6 While we were still weak, at the right time Christ died for the ungodly. [7]Why, one will hardly die for a righteous person—though perhaps for a good person one will dare even to die. [8]But God shows love for us in that while we were still sinners, Christ died for us. [9]Since, therefore, we are now justified by the blood of Christ, much more shall we be saved by Christ from the wrath of God. [10]For if while we were enemies we were reconciled to God by the death of God's Child, much more, now that we are reconciled, shall we be saved by Christ's life. [11]Not only so, but we also rejoice in God through our Lord Jesus Christ, through whom we have now received our reconciliation.

12 Therefore, as sin came into the world through one person and death through sin, and so death spread to all humankind because all sinned—[13]sin indeed was in the world before the law was given, but sin is not counted where there is no law. [14]Yet death reigned from Adam to Moses, even over those whose sins were not like the transgression of Adam, who was a type of the one who was to come.

15 But the free gift is not like the trespass. For if the many died through the trespass of one person, much more have the grace of God and the free gift in the grace of that one person Jesus Christ abounded for the many. [16]And the free gift is not like the effect of that one person's sin. For the judgment following one trespass brought condemnation, but the free gift following many trespasses brings justification. [17]If, because of the trespass of one person, death reigned through that one, much more will those who receive the abundance of grace and the free gift of righteousness reign in life through the one person Jesus Christ.

18 Then as the trespass of one person led to condemnation for all, so the act of righteousness of one person leads to acquittal and life for all. ¹⁹For as by the disobedience of one person the many were made sinners, so by the obedience of one person the many will be made righteous. ²⁰Law came in, to increase the trespass; but where sin increased, grace abounded all the more, ²¹so that, as sin reigned in death, grace also might reign through righteousness to eternal life through Jesus Christ our Lord.

6 What shall we say then? Are we to continue in sin that grace may abound? ²By no means! How can we who died to sin still live in it? ³Do you not know that all of us who have been baptized into Christ Jesus were baptized into Christ's death? ⁴We were buried therefore with Christ by baptism into death, so that as Christ was raised from the dead by the glory of God the Father and Mother, we too might walk in newness of life.

5 For if we have been united with Christ in a death like that of Christ, we shall certainly be united with Christ in a resurrection like that of Christ. ⁶We know that our old self was crucified with Christ so that the sinful body might be destroyed, and we might no longer be enslaved to sin. ⁷For anyone who has died is freed from sin. ⁸But if we have died with Christ, we believe that we shall also live with Christ. ⁹For we know that Christ, being raised from the dead, will never die again; death no longer has dominion over Christ. ¹⁰The death Christ died, Christ died to sin, once for all; but the life Christ lives, Christ lives to God. ¹¹So you also must consider yourselves dead to sin and alive to God in Christ Jesus.

12 Let not sin therefore reign in your mortal bodies, to make you obey their passions. ¹³Do not yield your members to sin as instruments of wickedness, but yield yourselves to God as people who have been brought from death to life, and your members to God as instruments of righteousness. ¹⁴For sin will have no dominion over you, since you are not under law but under grace.

15 What then? Are we to sin because we are not under law but under grace? By no means! ¹⁶Do you not know that if you yield yourselves to anyone as obedient slaves, you are slaves of the one whom you obey, either of sin, which leads to death, or of obedience, which leads to righteousness? ¹⁷But thanks be to God, that you who were once slaves of sin have become obedient from the heart to the standard of teaching to which you were committed, ¹⁸and, having been set free from sin, have become slaves of righteousness. ¹⁹I am speaking in human terms, because of your natural limitations. For just as you once yielded your members as slaves to impurity and to greater and greater iniquity, so now yield your members as slaves to righteousness for sanctification.

20 When you were slaves to sin, you were free in regard to righ-

teousness. [21]But then what return did you get from the things of which you are now ashamed? The end of those things is death. [22]But now that you have been set free from sin and have become slaves of God, the return you get is sanctification and its end, eternal life. [23]For the wages of sin is death, but the free gift of God is eternal life in Christ Jesus our Lord.

7 Do you not know, sisters and brothers—for I am speaking to those who know the law—that the law is binding on people only during their life? [2]Thus a married woman is bound by law to her husband as long as he lives; but if her husband dies she is discharged from the law concerning the husband. [3]Accordingly, she will be called an adulteress if she lives with another man while her husband is alive. But if her husband dies, she is free from that law, and if she marries another man she is not an adulteress.

4 Likewise, my friends, you have died to the law through the body of Christ, so that you may belong to another, to the one who has been raised from the dead in order that we may bear fruit for God. [5]While we were living in the flesh, our sinful passions, aroused by the law, were at work in our members to bear fruit for death. [6]But now we are discharged from the law, dead to that which held us captive, so that we serve not under the old written code but in the new life of the Spirit.

7 What then shall we say? That the law is sin? By no means! Yet, if it had not been for the law, I would not have known sin. I would not have known what it is to covet if the law had not said, "You shall not covet." [8]But sin, finding opportunity in the commandment, wrought in me all kinds of covetousness. Apart from the law sin lies dead. [9]I was once alive apart from the law, but when the commandment came, sin revived and I died; [10]the very commandment which promised life proved to be death to me. [11]For sin, finding opportunity in the commandment, deceived me and by it killed me. [12]So the law is holy, and the commandment is holy and just and good.

13 Did that which is good, then, bring death to me? By no means! It was sin, working death in me through what is good, in order that sin might be shown to be sin, and through the commandment might become sinful beyond measure. [14]We know that the law is spiritual; but I am carnal, sold under sin. [15]I do not understand my own actions. For I do not do what I want, but I do the very thing I hate. [16]Now if I do what I do not want, I agree that the law is good. [17]So then it is no longer I that do it, but sin which dwells within me. [18]For I know that nothing good dwells within me, that is, in my flesh. I can will what is right, but I cannot do it. [19]For I do not do the good I want, but the evil I do not want is what I do. [20]Now if I do what I do not want, it is no longer I that do it, but sin which dwells within me.

21 So I find it to be a law that when I want to do right, evil lies close at

hand. 22For I delight in the law of God, in my inmost self, 23but I see in my members another law at war with the law of my mind and making me captive to the law of sin which dwells in my members. 24How wretched I am! Who will deliver me from this body of death? 25Thanks be to God through Jesus Christ our Lord! So then, I of myself serve the law of God with my mind, but with my flesh I serve the law of sin.

8 There is therefore now no condemnation for those who are in Christ Jesus. 2For the law of the Spirit of life in Christ Jesus has set me free from the law of sin and death. 3For God has done what the law, weakened by the flesh, could not do; sending God's own Child in the likeness of sinful flesh and for sin, God condemned sin in the flesh, 4in order that the just requirement of the law might be fulfilled in us, who walk not according to the flesh but according to the Spirit. 5For those who live according to the flesh set their minds on the things of the flesh, but those who live according to the Spirit set their minds on the things of the Spirit. 6To set the mind on the flesh is death, but to set the mind on the Spirit is life and peace. 7For the mind that is set on the flesh is hostile to God; it does not submit to God's law, indeed it cannot; 8and those who are in the flesh cannot please God.

9 But you are not in the flesh, you are in the Spirit, if in fact the Spirit of God dwells in you. Anyone who does not have the Spirit of Christ does not belong to Christ. 10But if Christ is in you, although your bodies are dead because of sin, your spirits are alive because of righteousness. 11If the Spirit of the one who raised Jesus from the dead dwells in you, the one who raised Christ Jesus from the dead will give life to your mortal bodies also through that same Spirit dwelling in you.

12 So then, brothers and sisters, we are debtors, not to the flesh, to live according to the flesh—13for if you live according to the flesh you will die, but if by the Spirit you put to death the deeds of the body you will live. 14For all who are led by the Spirit of God are daughters and sons of God. 15For you did not receive a spirit of slavery to fall back into fear, but you have received a spirit of adoption as children of God. When we cry, "God! Mother and Father!" 16it is the Spirit bearing witness with our spirit that we are children of God, 17and if children, then heirs, heirs of God and joint heirs with Christ, provided we suffer with Christ in order that we may also be glorified with Christ.

18 I consider that the sufferings of this present time are not worth comparing with the glory that is to be revealed to us. 19For the creation waits with eager longing for the revealing of the children of God; 20for the creation was subjected to futility, not of its own will but by the will of the one who subjected it in hope; 21because the creation itself will be set free from its bondage to decay and obtain the glorious liberty of the children of God. 22We know that the whole creation has been groaning

in travail together until now; ²³and not only the creation, but we ourselves, who have the firstfruits of the Spirit, groan inwardly as we wait for adoption as children of God, the redemption of our bodies. ²⁴For in this hope we were saved. Now hope that is seen is not hope. For who hopes for what is already seen? ²⁵But if we hope for what we do not see, we wait for it with patience.

26 The Spirit helps us in our weakness; for we do not know how to pray as we ought, but that very Spirit intercedes for us with sighs too deep for words. ²⁷And the one who searches human hearts knows what is the mind of the Spirit, because the Spirit intercedes for the saints according to the will of God.

28 We know that in everything God works for good with those who love God, who are called according to God's purpose. ²⁹For those whom God foreknew were also predestined to be conformed to the image of God's Child, in order that Christ might be the firstborn among many believers. ³⁰And those whom God predestined, God also called; and those whom God called, God also justified; and those whom God justified, God also glorified.

31 What then shall we say to this? If God is for us, who is against us? ³²God who did not spare God's own Child but gave up that Child for us all, will not God also give us all things with Christ? ³³Who shall bring any charge against God's elect? It is God who justifies; ³⁴who is to condemn? Is it Christ Jesus, who died, yes, who was raised from the dead, who is at the right hand of God, who indeed intercedes for us? ³⁵Who will separate us from the love of Christ? Shall tribulation, or distress, or persecution, or famine, or nakedness, or peril, or sword? ³⁶As it is written,

> "For your sake we are being killed all the day long;
> we are regarded as sheep to be slaughtered."

³⁷No, in all these things we are more than conquerors through the one who loved us. ³⁸For I am sure that neither death, nor life, nor angels, nor principalities, nor things present, nor things to come, nor powers, ³⁹nor height, nor depth, nor anything else in all creation, will be able to separate us from the love of God in Christ Jesus our Lord.

9 I am speaking the truth in Christ, I am not lying; my conscience bears me witness in the Holy Spirit, ²that I have great sorrow and unceasing anguish in my heart. ³For I could wish that I myself were accursed and cut off from Christ for the sake of my own people, my kindred by race. ⁴They are Israelites, and to them belong the relationship of children to God, the glory, the covenants, the giving of the law, the worship, and the promises; ⁵to them belong the ancestors in faith, and from them, ac-

cording to the flesh, is the Christ. God who is over all be blessed forever. Amen.

6 But it is not as though the word of God had failed. For not all who are descended from Israel belong to Israel, ⁷and not all are children of Abraham and Sarah because they are their descendants; but "Through Isaac shall your descendants be named." ⁸This means that it is not the children of the flesh who are the children of God, but the children of the promise are reckoned as descendants. ⁹For this is what the promise said, "About this time I will return and Sarah shall have a son." ¹⁰And not only so, but also when Rebecca had conceived children by one man, our ancestor Isaac, ¹¹though they were not yet born and had done nothing either good or bad, in order that God's purpose of election might continue, not because of works but because of God's call, ¹²she was told, "The elder will serve the younger." ¹³As it is written, "Jacob I loved, but Esau I hated."

14 What shall we say then? Is there injustice on God's part? By no means! ¹⁵For God says to Moses, "I will have mercy on whom I have mercy, and I will have compassion on whom I have compassion." ¹⁶So it depends not upon human will or exertion, but upon God's mercy. ¹⁷For the scripture says to Pharaoh, "I have raised you up for the very purpose of showing my power in you, so that my name may be proclaimed in all the earth." ¹⁸So then God has mercy on whomever God wills, and God hardens the heart of whomever God wills.

19 You will say to me then, "Why does God still find fault? For who can resist God's will?" ²⁰But who are you, a human being, to answer back to God? Will what is molded say to its molder, "Why have you made me thus?" ²¹Has the potter no right over the clay, to make out of the same lump one vessel for beauty and another for menial use? ²²What if God, desiring to show wrath and to make known God's power, has endured with much patience the vessels of wrath made for destruction, ²³in order to make known the riches of God's glory for the vessels of mercy, prepared beforehand for glory, ²⁴even us whom God has called, not from the Jews only but also from the Gentiles? ²⁵As indeed God says in Hosea,

> "Those who were not my people
> I will call 'my people,'
> and the one who was not my beloved
> I will call 'my beloved.' "
> ²⁶"And in the very place where it was said to them, 'You are not
> my people,'
> they will be called 'children of the living God.' "

27 And Isaiah cries out concerning Israel: "Though the number of the children of Israel be as the sand of the sea, only a remnant of them

will be saved; [28]for the Lord will pass sentence upon the earth with rigor and dispatch." [29]And as Isaiah predicted,

"If the Lord of hosts had not left us children,
we would have fared like Sodom and been made like
    Gomorrah."

30 Then what shall we say? Gentiles who did not pursue righteousness have attained it, that is, righteousness through faith; [31]but Israel, who pursued the righteousness which is based on law, did not succeed in fulfilling that law. [32]Why? Because they did not pursue it through faith, but as if it were based on works. They have stumbled over the stumbling stone, [33]as it is written,

"See, I am laying in Zion a stone that will make people stumble,
a rock that will make them fall;
and the one who believes in that rock will not be put to shame."

10 Friends, my heart's desire and prayer to God for them is that they may be saved. [2]I bear them witness that they have a zeal for God, but it is not enlightened. [3]For, being ignorant of the righteousness that comes from God, and seeking to establish their own, they did not submit to God's righteousness. [4]For Christ is the end of the law, that everyone who has faith may be justified.

5 Moses writes that whoever practices the righteousness which is based on the law shall live by it. [6]But the righteousness based on faith says, Do not say in your heart, "Who will ascend into heaven?" (that is, to bring Christ down), [7]or "Who will descend into the abyss?" (that is, to bring Christ up from the dead). [8]But what does it say? The word is near you, on your lips and in your heart (that is, the word of faith which we preach); [9]because, if you confess with your lips that Jesus is Lord and believe in your heart that God raised Jesus from the dead, you will be saved. [10]For if it is believed with the heart, there is righteousness, and if it is confessed with the mouth there is salvation. [11]The scripture says, "No one who believes in the coming one will be put to shame." [12]For there is no distinction between Jew and Greek; the same Lord is Lord of all and bestows riches upon all who call on that Lord. [13]For, "everyone who calls upon the name of the Lord will be saved."

14 But how are people to call upon one in whom they have not believed? And how are they to believe in one of whom they have never heard? And how are they to hear without the preaching? [15]And how can they preach unless they are sent? As it is written "How beautiful are the feet of those who preach good news!" [16]But they have not all heeded the gospel; for Isaiah says, "Lord, who has believed our preach-

ing?" ¹⁷So faith comes from what is heard, and what is heard comes by the preaching of Christ.

18 But I ask, have they not heard? Indeed they have, for

"Their voice has gone out to all the earth
and their words to the ends of the world."

¹⁹Again I ask, did Israel not understand? First Moses says,

"I will make you jealous of those who are not a nation;
with a foolish nation I will make you angry."

²⁰Then Isaiah is so bold as to say,

"I have been found by those who did not seek me
I have shown myself to those who did not ask for me."

²¹But of Israel it is said, "All day long I have held out my hands to a disobedient and contrary people."

11 I ask, then, has God rejected God's own people? By no means! I myself am an Israelite, a descendant of Abraham, a member of the tribe of Benjamin. ²God has not rejected the people whom God foreknew. Do you not know what the scripture says of Elijah, how he pleads with God against Israel? ³"Lord, they have killed your prophets, they have demolished your altars, and I alone am left, and they seek my life." ⁴But what is God's reply to Elijah? "I have kept for myself seven thousand people who have not bowed the knee to Baal." ⁵So too at the present time there is a remnant, chosen by grace. ⁶But if it is by grace, it is no longer on the basis of works; otherwise grace would no longer be grace.

7 What then? Israel failed to obtain what it sought. The elect obtained it, but the rest were hardened, ⁸as it is written,

"God gave them a spirit of stupor,
eyes that would not see and ears that would not hear,
down to this very day."
⁹And David says,
"Let their table become a snare and a trap,
a pitfall and a retribution for them;
¹⁰let their eyes be blinded so that they cannot see,
and bend their backs forever."

11 So I ask, have they stumbled so as to fall? By no means! But through their trespass salvation has come to the Gentiles, so as to make Israel jealous. ¹²Now if their trespass means riches for the world, and

if their failure means riches for the Gentiles, how much more will their full inclusion mean!

13 Now I am speaking to you Gentiles. Inasmuch then as I am an apostle to the Gentiles, I magnify my ministry [14]in order to make my own people jealous, and thus save some of them. [15]For if their rejection means the reconciliation of the world, what will their acceptance mean but life from the dead? [16]If the dough offered as firstfruits is holy, so is the whole lump; and if the root is holy, so are the branches.

17 But if some of the branches were broken off, and you, a wild olive shoot, were grafted in their place to share the richness of the olive tree, [18]do not boast over the branches. If you do boast, remember it is not you that support the root, but the root that supports you. [19]You will say, "Branches were broken off so that I might be grafted in." [20]That is true. They were broken off because of their unbelief, but you stand fast only through faith. So do not become proud, but stand in awe. [21]For if God did not spare the natural branches, neither will God spare you. [22]Note then the kindness and the severity of God: severity toward those who have fallen, but kindness to you, provided you continue in God's kindness; otherwise you too will be cut off. [23]And even the others, if they do not persist in their unbelief, will be grafted in, for God has the power to graft them in again. [24]For if you have been cut from what is by nature a wild olive tree, and grafted, contrary to nature, into a cultivated olive tree, how much more will these natural branches be grafted back into their own olive tree.

25 That you not be wise in your own estimation, I want you to understand this mystery, sisters and brothers: a hardening has come upon part of Israel, until the full number of the Gentiles come in, [26]and so all Israel will be saved; as it is written,

"The Deliverer will come from Zion,
 to banish ungodliness from Jacob";
[27]"and this will be my covenant with them
 when I take away their sins."

[28]As regards the gospel they are enemies of God, for your sake; but as regards election they are beloved for the sake of their forebears. [29]For the gifts and call of God are irrevocable. [30]Just as you were once disobedient to God but now have received mercy because of their disobedience, [31]so they have now been disobedient in order that by the mercy shown to you they also may receive mercy. [32]For God has consigned all people to disobedience, in order to have mercy on all.

33 O the depth of the riches and wisdom and knowledge of God! How unsearchable are God's judgments and how inscrutable God's ways!

³⁴"For who has known the mind of the Lord,
or who has been God's counselor?"
³⁵"Or who has given a gift to God
in order to be repaid?"

³⁶For from God and through God and to God are all things. To God be glory forever. Amen.

12 I appeal to you therefore, sisters and brothers, by the mercies of God, to present your bodies as a living sacrifice, holy and acceptable to God, which is your spiritual worship. ²Do not be conformed to this world but be transformed by the renewal of your mind, that you may prove what is the will of God, what is good and acceptable and perfect.

3 For by the grace given to me I bid everyone among you not to think of yourself more highly than you ought to think, but to think with sober judgment, each according to the measure of faith which God has assigned you. ⁴For as in one body we have many members, and all the members do not have the same function, ⁵so we, the many, are one body in Christ, and individually members one of another. ⁶Having gifts that differ according to the grace given to us, let us use them: if prophecy, in proportion to our faith; ⁷if service, in our serving; the one who teaches, in teaching; ⁸the one who exhorts, in exhortation; the one who contributes, in liberality; the one who gives aid, with zeal; the one who does acts of mercy, with cheerfulness.

9 Let love be genuine; hate what is evil, hold fast to what is good; ¹⁰be affectionately devoted to one another; outdo one another in showing honor. ¹¹Never flag in zeal, be aglow with the Spirit, serve the Lord. ¹²Rejoice in your hope, be patient in tribulation, be constant in prayer. ¹³Contribute to the needs of the saints, practice hospitality.

14 Bless those who persecute you; bless and do not curse them. ¹⁵Rejoice with those who rejoice, weep with those who weep. ¹⁶Live in harmony with one another; do not be haughty, but associate with the lowly; never be conceited. ¹⁷Repay no one evil for evil, but take thought for what is noble in the sight of all. ¹⁸If possible, so far as it depends on you, live peaceably with everyone. ¹⁹Beloved, never avenge yourselves, but leave it to the wrath of God; for it is written, "Vengeance is mine, I will repay, says the Lord." ²⁰No, "if your enemies are hungry, feed them; if they are thirsty, give them drink; for by so doing you will heap burning coals upon their heads." ²¹Do not be overcome by evil, but overcome evil with good.

13 Let every person be subject to the governing authorities. For there is no authority except from God, and those that exist have

been instituted by God. ²Therefore whoever resists the authorities resists what God has appointed, and those who resist will incur judgment. ³For rulers are not a terror to good conduct, but to bad. Would you have no fear of authority? Then do what is good, and you will receive approval, ⁴for the one in authority is God's servant for your good. But if you do wrong, be afraid, for the one in authority does not bear the sword in vain, but is the servant of God to execute God's wrath on the wrongdoer. ⁵Therefore one must be subject, not only to avoid God's wrath but also for the sake of conscience. ⁶For the same reason you also pay taxes, for the authorities are ministers of God, attending to this very thing. ⁷Pay all of them their dues, taxes to whom taxes are due, revenue to whom revenue is due, respect to whom respect is due, honor to whom honor is due.

8 Owe no one anything, except to love one another, for whoever loves one's neighbor has fulfilled the law. ⁹The commandments, "You shall not commit adultery, You shall not kill, You shall not steal, You shall not covet," and any other commandment, are summed up in this sentence, "You shall love your neighbor as yourself" ¹⁰Love does no wrong to a neighbor; therefore love is the fulfilling of the law.

11 Besides this you know what hour it is, how the hour has already come for you to wake from sleep. For salvation is nearer to us now than when we first believed; ¹²the night has passed, the day is at hand. Let us then cast off the works of the night and put on the armor of the day; ¹³let us conduct ourselves becomingly as in the day, not in reveling and drunkenness, not in debauchery and licentiousness, not in quarreling and jealousy. ¹⁴But put on the Lord Jesus Christ, and make no provision for the flesh, to gratify its desires.

14 As for those who are weak in faith, welcome them, but not to have disputes about opinions. ²Some believe they may eat anything, while the weak eat only vegetables. ³Do not let those who eat despise those who abstain, and do not allow those who abstain to pass judgment on those who eat; for God has welcomed them. ⁴Who are you to pass judgment on servants of another? It is before their own lord that they stand or fall. And they will be upheld, for the Lord is able to make them stand.

5 Some people esteem one day as better than another, while others esteem all days alike. Let all be fully convinced in their own mind. ⁶Those who observe the day, observe it in honor of the Lord. Those also who eat, eat in honor of Christ, since they give thanks to God; while those who abstain, abstain in honor of Christ and give thanks to God. ⁷None of us live to ourselves, and none of us die to ourselves. ⁸If we live, we live to Christ, and if we die, we die to Christ; so then, whether we

live or whether we die, we are Christ's. [9]For to this end, Christ died and lived again, so as to be Lord both of the dead and of the living.

10 Why do you pass judgment on your brother or sister? Or you, why do you despise your sister or brother? For we shall all stand before the judgment seat of God; [11]for it is written,

> "As I live, says the Lord, every knee shall bow to me,
> and every tongue shall give praise to God."

[12]So each of us will give account of ourselves to God.

13 Then let us no longer pass judgment on one another, but rather decide never to put a stumbling block or hindrance in the way of a brother or sister. [14]I know and am persuaded in the Lord Jesus that nothing is unclean in itself; but it is unclean for anyone who thinks it unclean. [15]If your sister or brother is being injured by what you eat, you are no longer walking in love. Do not let what you eat cause the ruin of one for whom Christ died. [16]So do not let your good be spoken of as evil. [17]For the dominion of God is not food and drink, but righteousness and peace and joy in the Holy Spirit. [18]Those who thus serve Christ are acceptable to God and have human approval. [19]Let us then pursue what makes for peace and for mutual upbuilding. [20]Do not, for the sake of food, destroy the work of God. Everything is indeed clean, but it is wrong for anyone to make others fall by what one eats. [21]It is right not to eat meat or drink wine or do anything that makes your brother or sister stumble. [22]The faith that you have, keep between yourself and God. Blessed are those who have no reason to judge themselves for what they approve. [23]But those who have doubts are condemned, if they eat, because they do not act from faith; for whatever does not proceed from faith is sin.

15 We who are strong ought to bear with the failings of the weak, and not to please ourselves. [2]Let each of us please our neighbor for the neighbor's good and edification. [3]For Christ did not please Christ's self; but, as it is written, "The reproaches of those who reproached you fell on me." [4]Whatever was written in former days was written for our instruction, that by steadfastness and by the encouragement of the scriptures we might have hope. [5]May the God of steadfastness and encouragement grant you to live in such harmony with one another, in accord with Christ Jesus, [6]that together you may with one voice glorify God the Father and Mother of our Lord Jesus Christ.

7 Welcome one another, therefore, as Christ has welcomed you, for the glory of God. [8]For I tell you that Christ became a servant to the Jews to show God's truthfulness, in order to confirm the promises given to our ancestors in faith, [9]and in order that the Gentiles might glorify God for showing mercy. As it is written,

"Therefore I will praise you among the Gentiles,
and sing to your name";

¹⁰and again it is said,

"Rejoice, O Gentiles, with the people of God";

¹¹and again,

"Praise the Lord, all Gentiles,
and let all the people praise God";

¹²and further Isaiah says,

"The root of Jesse shall come,
the one who rises to rule the Gentiles,
in whom the Gentiles shall hope."

¹³May the God of hope fill you with all joy and peace in believing, so that by the power of the Holy Spirit you may abound in hope.

14 I myself am satisfied about you, sisters and brothers, that you yourselves are full of goodness, filled with all knowledge, and able to instruct one another. ¹⁵But on some points I have written to you very boldly by way of reminder, because of the grace given me by God ¹⁶to be a minister of Christ Jesus to the Gentiles in the priestly service of the gospel of God, so that the offering of the Gentiles may be acceptable, sanctified by the Holy Spirit. ¹⁷In Christ Jesus, then, I have reason to be proud of my work for God. ¹⁸For I will not venture to speak of anything except what Christ has wrought through me to win obedience from the Gentiles, by word and deed, ¹⁹by the power of signs and wonders, by the power of the Holy Spirit, so that from Jerusalem and as far around as Illyricum I have fully preached the gospel of Christ, ²⁰thus making it my ambition to preach the gospel, not where Christ has already been named, lest I build on someone else's foundation, ²¹but as it is written,

"They shall see who have never been told of the coming one,
and those who have never heard shall understand."

22 This is the reason why I have so often been hindered from coming to you. ²³But now, since I no longer have any room for work in these regions, and since I have longed for many years to come to you, ²⁴I hope to see you in passing as I go to Spain, and to be sped on my journey there by you, once I have enjoyed your company for a little. ²⁵At present, however, I am going to Jerusalem with aid for the saints. ²⁶For Macedonia and Achaia have been pleased to make some contribution for the poor among the saints at Jerusalem. ²⁷They were pleased to do it, and indeed they are in debt to them, for if the Gentiles have come to share in their spiritual blessings, they ought also to be of service to them in material

blessings. [28]When therefore I have completed this, and have delivered to them what has been raised, I shall go on by way of you to Spain; [29]and I know that when I come to you I will come in the fullness of the blessing of Christ.

30 I appeal to you, brothers and sisters, by our Lord Jesus Christ and by the love of the Spirit, to strive together with me in your prayers to God on my behalf, [31]that I may be delivered from the unbelievers in Judea, and that my service for Jerusalem may be acceptable to the saints, [32]so that by God's will I may come to you with joy and be refreshed in your company. [33]The God of peace be with you all. Amen.

16 I commend to you our sister Phoebe, a deacon of the church at Cenchreae, [2]that you may receive her in the Lord as befits the saints, and help her in whatever she may require from you, for she has been a helper of many and of myself as well.

3 Greet Prisca and Aquila, my coworkers in Christ Jesus, [4]who risked their necks for my life, to whom not only I but also all the churches of the Gentiles give thanks; [5]greet also the church in their house. Greet my beloved Epaenetus, who was the first convert in Asia for Christ. [6]Greet Mary, who has worked hard among you. [7]Greet Andronicus and Junia, my kinsfolk and prisoners with me; they are noteworthy among the apostles, and they were in Christ before me. [8]Greet Ampliatus, my beloved in the Lord. [9]Greet Urbanus, our coworker in Christ, and my beloved Stachys. [10]Greet Apelles, who is approved in Christ. Greet those who belong to the family of Aristobulus. [11]Greet my relative Herodion. Greet those in the Lord who belong to the family of Narcissus. [12]Greet those women who are workers in the Lord, Tryphaena and Tryphosa. Greet the beloved Persis. She has worked hard in the Lord. [13]Greet Rufus, eminent in the Lord, also his mother and mine. [14]Greet Asyncritus, Phlegon, Hermes, Patrobas, Hermas, and the brothers and sisters who are with them. [15]Greet Philologus, Julia, Nereus and his sister, and Olympas, and all the saints who are with them. [16]Greet one another with a holy kiss. All the churches of Christ greet you.

17 I appeal to you, sisters and brothers, to take note of those who create dissensions and difficulties, in opposition to the doctrine which you have been taught; avoid them. [18]For such people do not serve our Lord Christ, but their own appetites, and by smooth speech and flattery they deceive the hearts of the unsuspecting. [19]For while your obedience is known to all, so that I rejoice over you, I would have you wise as to what is good, and guileless as to what is evil; [20]then the God of peace will soon crush Satan under your feet. The grace of our Lord Jesus Christ be with you.

21 Timothy, my coworker, greets you; so do Lucius and Jason and Sosipater, my kindred.

22 I Tertius, the writer of this letter, greet you in the Lord.

23 Gaius, who is host to me and to the whole church, greets you. Erastus, the city treasurer, and our brother Quartus, greet you.

25 Now to the one who is able to strengthen you according to my gospel and the preaching of Jesus Christ, according to the revelation of the mystery which was kept secret for long ages, 26but is now disclosed and through the prophetic writings is made known to all nations, according to the command of the eternal God, to bring about the obedience of faith—27to the only wise God be glory forevermore through Jesus Christ! Amen.

1 Corinthians

1 Paul, called by the will of God to be an apostle of Christ Jesus, and our brother Sosthenes,

2 To the church of God which is at Corinth, to those sanctified in Christ Jesus, called to be saints together with all those who in every place call on the name of our Lord Jesus Christ, both their Lord and ours:

3 Grace to you and peace from God our Father and Mother and from the Lord Jesus Christ.

4 I give thanks to God always for you because of the grace of God which was given you in Christ Jesus, ⁵that in every way you were enriched in Christ with all speech and all knowledge—⁶even as the testimony to Christ was confirmed among you—⁷so that you are not lacking in any spiritual gift, as you wait for the revealing of our Lord Jesus Christ, ⁸who will sustain you to the end, guiltless in the day of our Lord Jesus Christ. ⁹God is faithful, by whom you were called into the community of God's Child, Jesus Christ our Lord.

10 I appeal to you, sisters and brothers, by the name of our Lord Jesus Christ, that all of you agree and that there be no dissensions among you, but that you be united in the same mind and the same judgment. ¹¹For it has been reported to me by Chloe's people that there is quarreling among you, my friends. ¹²What I mean is that each one of you says, "I belong to Paul," or "I belong to Apollos," or "I belong to Cephas," or "I belong to Christ." ¹³Is Christ divided? Was Paul crucified for you? Or were you baptized in the name of Paul? ¹⁴I am thankful that I baptized none of you except Crispus and Gaius; ¹⁵lest anyone should say that you were baptized in my name. ¹⁶(I did baptize also the household of Stephanas. Beyond that, I do not know whether I baptized anyone

else.) ¹⁷For Christ did not send me to baptize but to preach the gospel, and not with eloquent wisdom, lest the cross of Christ be emptied of its power.

18 For the word of the cross is folly to those who are perishing, but to us who are being saved it is the power of God. ¹⁹For it is written,

"I will destroy the wisdom of the wise,
and the cleverness of the clever I will thwart."

²⁰Where is the wise person? Where is the scribe? Where is the debater of this age? Has not God made foolish the wisdom of the world? ²¹For since, in the wisdom of God, the world did not know God through wisdom, it pleased God through the folly of what we preach to save those who believe. ²²For Jews demand signs and Greeks seek wisdom, ²³but we preach Christ crucified, a stumbling block to Jews and folly to Gentiles, ²⁴but to those who are called, both Jews and Greeks, Christ the power of God and the wisdom of God. ²⁵For the foolishness of God is wiser than human wisdom, and the weakness of God is stronger than human strength.

26 For consider your call, my friends; not many of you were wise according to worldly standards, not many were powerful, not many were of noble birth; ²⁷but God chose what is foolish in the world to shame the wise, God chose what is weak in the world to shame the strong, ²⁸God chose what is low and despised in the world, even things that are not, to bring to nothing things that are, ²⁹so that no human being might boast in the presence of God. ³⁰God is the source of your life in Christ Jesus, whom God made our wisdom, our righteousness and sanctification and redemption; ³¹therefore, as it is written, "Let the one who boasts, boast of the Lord."

2 When I came to you, brothers and sisters, I did not come proclaiming to you the testimony of God in lofty words or wisdom. ²For I decided to know nothing among you except Jesus Christ, and that very one crucified. ³I was with you in weakness and in much fear and trembling; ⁴and my speech and my message were not in plausible words of wisdom, but in demonstration of the Spirit and of power, ⁵that your faith might not rest in human wisdom but in the power of God.

6 Yet among the mature we do impart wisdom, although it is not a wisdom of this age or of the rulers of this age, who are doomed to pass away. ⁷But we impart a secret and hidden wisdom of God, which God decreed before the ages for our glorification. ⁸Not one of the rulers of this age understood that; for if they had, they would not have crucified the Lord of glory. ⁹But, as it is written,

"What no eye has seen, nor ear heard,
nor the human heart conceived,
what God has prepared for those who love God,"

[10]God has revealed to us through the Spirit. For the Spirit searches everything, even the depths of God. [11]For who knows a person's thoughts except the person's own spirit which is within? So also no one comprehends the thoughts of God except the Spirit of God. [12]Now we have received not the spirit of the world, but the Spirit which is from God, that we might understand the gifts bestowed on us by God. [13]And we impart this in words not taught by human wisdom, but taught by the Spirit, interpreting spiritual truths to those who possess the Spirit.

14 Those who are unspiritual do not receive the gifts of the Spirit of God, for such gifts are folly to them, and they are not able to understand them because they are spiritually discerned. [15]Those who are spiritual judge all things, but are themselves to be judged by no one. [16]"For who has known the mind of the Lord so as to instruct the Lord?" But we have the mind of Christ.

3 But I, sisters and brothers, could not address you as spiritual people, but as people of the flesh, as children in Christ. [2]I fed you with milk, not solid food; for you were not ready for it; and even yet you are not ready, [3]for you are still of the flesh. For while there is jealousy and strife among you, are you not of the flesh, and behaving in human ways? [4]For when one says, "I belong to Paul," and another, "I belong to Apollos," are you not merely human?

5 What then is Apollos? What is Paul? Servants through whom you believed, as the Lord assigned to each. [6]I planted, Apollos watered, but God gave the growth. [7]So neither the one who plants nor the one who waters is anything, but only God who gives the growth. [8]The one who plants and the one who waters are equal, and shall receive wages according to their labor. [9]For we are God's coworkers; you are God's field, God's building.

10 According to the grace of God given to me, like an expert builder I laid a foundation, and another is building upon it. Let each one take care how it is built upon. [11]For no other foundation can anyone lay than that which is laid, which is Jesus Christ. [12]Now if anyone builds on the foundation with gold, silver, precious stones, wood, hay, straw—[13]the work of each one will become manifest; for the Day will disclose it, because it will be revealed with fire, and the fire will test what sort of work each one has done. [14]If the work which anyone has built on the foundation survives, the builder will receive a reward. [15]If anyone's work is burned up, one will suffer loss, though one will, oneself, be saved, but only as through fire.

16 Do you not know that you are God's temple and that God's Spirit dwells in you? [17]Whoever destroys God's temple, God will destroy. For God's temple is holy, and you are that temple.

18 Let none deceive themselves. If any among you think that they are wise in this age, let them become fools that they may become wise. [19]For the wisdom of this world is folly with God. For it is written, "God catches the wise in their craftiness," [20]and again, "The Lord knows that the thoughts of the wise are futile." [21]So let no one boast of mere human beings. For all things are yours, [22]whether Paul or Apollos or Cephas or the world or life or death or the present or the future, all are yours; [23]and you are Christ's; and Christ is God's.

4 This is how one should regard us, as servants of Christ and stewards of the mysteries of God. [2]Moreover it is required of stewards that they be found trustworthy. [3]But with me it is a very small thing that I should be judged by you or by any human court. I do not even judge myself. [4]I am not aware of anything against myself, but I am not thereby acquitted. It is the Lord who judges me. [5]Therefore do not pronounce judgment before the time, before the Lord comes, who will bring to light the things now hidden and will disclose the purposes of the heart. Then all will receive their commendation from God.

6 I have applied all this to myself and Apollos for your benefit, sisters and brothers, that you may learn by us not to go beyond what is written, that none of you may be puffed up in favor of one against another. [7]For who sees anything different in you? What have you that you did not receive? If then you received it, why do you boast as if it were not a gift?

8 Already you are filled! Already you have become rich! Without us you have become kings and queens! And would that you did reign, so that we might share the rule with you! [9]For I think that God has exhibited us apostles as last of all, like people sentenced to death, because we have become a spectacle to the world, to angels and to human beings. [10]We are fools for Christ's sake, but you are wise in Christ. We are weak, but you are strong. You are held in honor, but we in disrepute. [11]To the present hour we hunger and thirst, we are ill-clad and buffeted and homeless, [12]and we labor, working with our own hands. When reviled, we bless; when persecuted, we endure; [13]when slandered, we try to conciliate; we have become, and are now, as the refuse of the world, the scum of all things.

14 I do not write this to make you ashamed, but to admonish you as my beloved children. [15]For though you have countless guides in Christ, you do not have many fathers or mothers. For I became your father in Christ Jesus through the gospel. [16]I urge you, then, be imitators of me. [17]Therefore I sent to you Timothy, my beloved and faithful child in the Lord, to remind you of my ways in Christ, as I teach them everywhere

in every church. [18]Some are arrogant, thinking that I am not coming to you. [19]But I will come to you soon, if the Lord wills, and I will find out not the talk of these arrogant people but their power. [20]For the dominion of God does not consist in talk but in power. [21]What do you wish? Shall I come to you with a rod, or with love in a spirit of gentleness?

5 It is actually reported that there is immorality among you, and of a kind that is not found even among pagans; for a man is living with his father's wife. [2]And you are arrogant! Ought you not rather to mourn? Let whoever has done this be removed from among you.

3 For though absent in body I am present in spirit, and as if present, I have already pronounced judgment [4]in the name of the Lord Jesus on the man who has done such a thing. When you are assembled, and my spirit is present, with the power of our Lord Jesus, [5]you are to deliver this man to Satan for the destruction of the flesh, that his spirit may be saved in the day of the Lord Jesus.

6 Your boasting is not good. Do you not know that a little leaven leavens the whole lump? [7]Cleanse out the old leaven that you may be a new lump, as you really are unleavened. For Christ, our paschal lamb, has been sacrificed. [8]Let us, therefore, celebrate the festival, not with the old leaven, the leaven of malice and evil, but with the unleavened bread of sincerity and truth.

9 I wrote to you in my letter not to associate with immoral people; [10]not at all meaning the immoral of this world, or the greedy and robbers, or idolaters, since then you would need to go out of the world. [11]But rather I wrote to you not to associate with anyone who bears the name of a sister or brother, who is guilty of immorality or greed, or is an idolater, reviler, drunkard, or robber—not even to eat with such a person. [12]For what have I to do with judging outsiders? Is it not those inside the church whom you are to judge? [13]God judges those outside. "Drive out the wicked person from among you."

6 When one of you has a grievance against another, do you dare go to court before the unrighteous instead of the saints? [2]Do you not know that the saints will judge the world? And if the world is to be judged by you, are you incompetent to try trivial cases? [3]Do you not know that we are to judge angels? How much more, matters pertaining to this life! [4]If then you have such cases, why do you lay them before those who are least esteemed by the church? [5]I say this to your shame. Can it be that there is no person among you wise enough to decide between believers, [6]but one goes to court against another, and before unbelievers at that?

7 To have lawsuits at all with one another is a defeat for you. Why not rather suffer wrong? Why not rather be defrauded? [8]But you yourselves wrong and defraud—even believers!

9 Do you not know that the unrighteous will not inherit the dominion of God? Do not be deceived; neither the immoral, nor idolaters, nor adulterers, nor catamites, nor pederasts, [10]nor thieves, nor the greedy, nor drunkards, nor revilers, nor robbers will inherit the dominion of God. [11]And such were some of you. But you were washed, you were sanctified, you were justified in the name of the Lord Jesus Christ and in the Spirit of our God.

12 "All things are lawful for me," but not all things are helpful. "All things are lawful for me," but I will not be enslaved by anything. [13]"Food is meant for the stomach and the stomach for food"—and God will destroy both one and the other. The body is not meant for immorality, but for the Lord, and the Lord for the body. [14]And God raised the Lord and will also raise us up by God's power. [15]Do you not know that your bodies are members of Christ? Shall I therefore take the members of Christ and make them members of a prostitute? Never! [16]Do you not know that one who joins oneself to a prostitute becomes one body with the prostitute? For, as it is written, "The two shall become one flesh." [17]But one who is united to Christ becomes one spirit with Christ. [18]Shun immorality. Every other sin which a person commits is outside the body; but immoral people sin against their own bodies. [19]Do you not know that your body is a temple of the Holy Spirit within you, which you have from God? You are not your own; [20]you were bought with a price. So glorify God in your body.

7 Now concerning the matters about which you wrote. "It is well for a man not to touch a woman." [2]But because of the temptation to immorality, each man should have his own wife and each woman her own husband. [3]The husband should give to his wife her conjugal rights, and likewise the wife to her husband. [4]For the wife does not rule over her own body, but the husband does; likewise the husband does not rule over his own body, but the wife does. [5]Do not refuse one another except perhaps by agreement for a season, that you may devote yourselves to prayer; but then come together again, lest Satan tempt you through lack of self-control. [6]I say this by way of concession, not of command. [7]I wish that all were as I myself am. But each has a special gift from God, one of one kind and one of another.

8 To the unmarried and the widows I say that it is well for them to remain single as I do. [9]But if they cannot exercise self-control, they should marry. For it is better to marry than to be aflame with passion.

10 To the married I give charge, not I but the Lord, that the wife should not separate from her husband [11](but if she does, let her remain single or else be reconciled to her husband)—and that the husband should not divorce his wife.

12 To the rest I say, not the Lord, that if any brother has a wife who is an unbeliever, and she consents to live with him, he should not divorce her. [13]If any woman has a husband who is an unbeliever, and he consents to live with her, she should not divorce him. [14]For the unbelieving husband is consecrated through his wife, and the unbelieving wife is consecrated through her husband. Otherwise, your children would be unclean, but as it is they are holy. [15]But if the unbelieving partner desires to separate, let it be so; in such a case the brother or sister is not bound. For God has called us to peace. [16]Wife, how do you know whether you will save your husband? Husband, how do you know whether you will save your wife?

17 Only, let everyone lead the life which the Lord has assigned, and in which God has called you. [18]Was any of you at the time of your call already circumcised? Then do not seek to remove the marks of circumcision. Was any of you at the time of your call uncircumcised? Then do not seek circumcision. [19]For neither circumcision counts for anything nor uncircumcision, but keeping the commandments of God. [20]Everyone of you should remain in the state in which you were called. [21]Were you a slave when called? Never mind. But if you can gain your freedom, avail yourself of the opportunity. [22]For whoever was called in the Lord as a slave is a freed person of the Lord. Likewise whoever was free when called is a slave of Christ. [23]You were bought with a price; do not becomes slaves of anybody. [24]So, brothers and sisters, in whatever state each of you was called, remain there with God.

25 Now concerning the unmarried, I have no command of the Lord, but I give my opinion as one who by the Lord's mercy is trustworthy. [26]I think that in view of the present distress it is well for people to remain as they are. [27]Are you bound to a wife? Do not seek to be free. Are you free from a wife? Do not seek marriage. [28]But if you marry, you do not sin, and if an unmarried woman marries she does not sin. Yet those who marry will have worldly troubles, and I would spare you that. [29]I mean, sisters and brothers, the appointed time has grown very short; from now on, let those who are married live as though they were not, [30]and those who mourn as though they were not mourning, and those who rejoice as though they were not rejoicing, and those who buy as though they had no goods, [31]and those who deal with the world as though they had no dealings with it. For the form of this world is passing away.

32 I want you to be free from anxieties. The unmarried man is anxious about the affairs of the Lord, how to please the Lord; [33]but the married man is anxious about worldly affairs, how to please his wife, [34]and his interests are divided. And the unmarried woman or young girl is anxious about the affairs of the Lord, how to be holy in body and spirit; but the married woman is anxious about worldly affairs, how to please her husband. [35]I say this for your own benefit, not to lay any restraint

upon you, but to promote good order and to secure your undivided devotion to the Lord.

36 If any of you think that you are not behaving properly toward your betrothed, if your passions are strong, and it has to be, then do as you wish: marry—it is not a sin. [37]But any of you who are firmly established in your heart, being under no necessity but having your desire under control, and have determined this in your heart, to keep your spouse as your betrothed, you will do well. [38]So that one who marries one's betrothed does well; and one who refrains from marriage will do better.

39 A wife is bound to her husband as long as he lives. If the husband dies, she is free to be married to whom she wishes, only in the Lord. [40]But in my judgment she is happier if she remains as she is. And I think that I have the Spirit of God.

8 Now concerning food offered to idols: we know that "all of us possess knowledge." "Knowledge" puffs up, but love builds up. [2]If any imagine that they know something, they do not yet know as they ought to know. [3]But if one loves God, one is known by God.

4 Hence, as to the eating of food offered to idols, we know that "an idol has no real existence," and that "there is no God but one." [5]For although there may be so-called gods in heaven or on earth—as indeed there are many "gods" and many "lords"—[6]yet for us there is one God, the Father and Mother, from whom are all things and for whom we exist, and one Lord, Jesus Christ, through whom are all things and through whom we exist.

7 However, not all possess this knowledge. But some, through being hitherto accustomed to idols, eat food as really offered to an idol; and their conscience, being weak, is defiled. [8]Food will not commend us to God. We are no worse off if we do not eat, and no better off if we do. [9]Only take care lest this liberty of yours somehow become a stumbling block to the weak. [10]For if anyone, having a weak conscience, sees you, a person of knowledge, at table in an idol's temple, might that one not be encouraged to eat food offered to idols? [11]And so by your knowledge that weak person is destroyed, the sister or brother for whom Christ died. [12]Thus, sinning against your brothers or sisters and wounding their conscience when it is weak, you sin against Christ. [13]Therefore, if food is a cause of my sister's or brother's falling, I will never eat meat, lest I cause that person to fall.

9 Am I not free? Am I not an apostle? Have I not seen Jesus our Lord? Are not you my work in the Lord? [2]If to others I am not an apostle, at least I am to you; for you are the seal of my apostleship in the Lord.

3 This is my defense to those who would examine me. ⁴Do we not have the right to our food and drink? ⁵Do we not have the right to be accompanied by a wife, as the other apostles and the brothers of the Lord and Cephas? ⁶Or is it only Barnabas and I who have no right to refrain from working for a living? ⁷Do any people serve as soldiers at their own expense? Do they plant a vineyard without eating any of its fruit? Do they tend a flock without getting some of the milk?

8 Do I say this on human authority? Does not the law say the same? ⁹For it is written in the law of Moses, "You shall not muzzle an ox when it is treading out the grain." Is it for oxen that God is concerned? ¹⁰Does God not speak entirely for our sake? It was written for our sake, because the plower should plow in hope and the thresher thresh in hope of a share in the crop. ¹¹If we have sown spiritual good among you, is it too much if we reap your material benefits? ¹²If others share this rightful claim on you, do not we still more?

Nevertheless, we have not made use of this right, but we endure anything rather than put an obstacle in the way of the gospel of Christ. ¹³Do you not know that those who are employed in the temple service get their food from the temple, and those who serve at the altar share in the sacrificial offerings? ¹⁴In the same way, the Lord commanded that those who proclaim the gospel should get their living by the gospel.

15 But I have made no use of any of these rights, nor am I writing this to secure any such provision. For I would rather die than have anyone deprive me of my ground for boasting. ¹⁶For if I preach the gospel, that gives me no ground for boasting. For necessity is laid upon me. Woe to me if I do not preach the gospel! ¹⁷For if I do this of my own will, I have a reward; but if not of my own will, I am entrusted with a commission. ¹⁸What then is my reward? Just this: that in my preaching I may offer the gospel free of charge, not making full use of my right in the gospel.

19 For though I am free from all people, I have made myself a slave to all, that I might win the more. ²⁰To the Jews I became as a Jew, in order to win Jews; to those under the law I became as one under the law—though not being myself under the law—that I might win those under the law. ²¹To those outside the law I became as one outside the law—not being without law toward God but under the law of Christ—that I might win those outside the law. ²²To the weak I became weak, that I might win the weak. I have become all things to all people, that I might by all means save some. ²³I do it all for the sake of the gospel, that I may share in its blessings.

24 Do you not know that in a race all the runners compete, but only one receives the prize? So run that you may obtain it. ²⁵Every athlete exercises self-control in all things. They do it to receive a perishable wreath, but we an imperishable. ²⁶Well, I do not run aimlessly, I do not box as

one beating the air; [27]but I pommel my body and subdue it, lest after preaching to others I myself should be disqualified.

10 I want you to know, sisters and brothers, that our ancestors were all under the cloud, and all passed through the sea, [2]and all were baptized into Moses in the cloud and in the sea, [3]and all ate the same supernatural food [4]and all drank the same supernatural drink. For they drank from the supernatural Rock which followed them, and the Rock was Christ. [5]Nevertheless with most of them God was not pleased; for they were overthrown in the wilderness.

6 Now these things are warnings for us, not to desire evil as they did. [7]Do not be idolaters as some of them were; as it is written, "The people sat down to eat and drink and rose up to dance." [8]We must not indulge in immorality as some of them did, and twenty-three thousand fell in a single day. [9]We must not put the Lord to the test, as some of them did and were destroyed by serpents; [10]nor grumble, as some of them did and were destroyed by the Destroyer. [11]Now these things happened to them as a warning, but they were written down for our instruction, upon whom the end of the ages has come. [12]Therefore let any who think that they stand take heed lest they fall. [13]No temptation has overtaken you that is not common to everyone. God is faithful, and will not let you be tempted beyond your strength; but with the temptation God will also provide the way of escape, so that you may be able to endure it.

14 Therefore, my beloved, shun the worship of idols. [15]I speak as to sensible people; judge for yourselves what I say. [16]The cup of blessing which we bless, is it not a participation in the blood of Christ? The bread which we break, is it not a participation in the body of Christ? [17]Because there is one bread, we who are many are one body, for we all partake of the one bread. [18]Consider the people of Israel; are not those who eat the sacrifices partners in the altar? [19]What do I imply then? That food offered to idols is anything, or that an idol is anything? [20]No, I imply that what pagans sacrifice they sacrifice to demons and not to God. I do not want you to be partners with demons. [21]You cannot drink the cup of the Lord and the cup of demons. You cannot partake of the table of the Lord and the table of demons. [22]Shall we provoke the Lord to jealousy? Are we stronger than the Lord?

23 "All things are lawful," but not all things are helpful. "All things are lawful," but not all things build up. [24]Do not seek your own advantage but the good of your neighbor. [25]Eat whatever is sold in the meat market without raising any question on the ground of conscience. [26]For "the earth is the Lord's, and everything in it." [27]If one of the unbelievers invites you to dinner and you are disposed to go, eat whatever is set before you without raising any question on the ground of conscience. [28](But if someone says to you, "This has been offered in sacrifice," then out

of consideration for the person who informed you, and for conscience' sake—29I mean the conscience of the other, not yours—do not eat it.) For why should my liberty be determined by another person's scruples? 30If I partake with thankfulness, why am I denounced because of that for which I give thanks?

31 So, whatever you eat or drink, or whatever you do, do all to the glory of God. 32Give no offense to Jews or to Greeks or to the church of God, 33just as I try to please everyone in everything I do, not seeking my 11 own advantage, but that of everyone else, that they may be saved. 1Be imitators of me, as I am of Christ.

2 I commend you because you remember me in everything and maintain the traditions even as I have delivered them to you. 3But I want you to understand that the head of every man is Christ, and the head of a woman is her husband, and the head of Christ is God. 4Any man who prays or prophesies with his head covered dishonors his head, 5but any woman who prays or prophesies with her head unveiled dishonors her head—it is the same as if her head were shaven. 6For if a woman will not veil herself, then she should cut off her hair; but if it is disgraceful for a woman to be shorn or shaven, let her wear a veil. 7For a man ought not to cover his head, since he is the image and glory of God; but woman is the glory of man. 8(For man was not made from woman, but woman from man. 9Neither was man created for woman, but woman for man.) 10That is why a woman ought to have a veil on her head, because of the angels. 11(Nevertheless, in the Lord woman is not independent of man nor man of woman; 12for as woman is made from man, so man comes through woman. And all things are from God.) 13Judge for yourselves; is it proper for a woman to pray to God with her head uncovered? 14Does not nature itself teach you that for a man to wear long hair is degrading to him, 15but if a woman has long hair, it is her pride? For her hair is given to her for a covering. 16If anyone is disposed to be contentious, we recognize no other practice, nor do the churches of God.

17 But in the following instructions I do not commend you, because when you come together it is not for the better but for the worse. 18For, in the first place, when you assemble as a church, I hear that there are divisions among you; and I partly believe it, 19for there must be factions among you in order that those who are genuine among you may be recognized. 20When you meet together, it is not the Lord's supper that you eat. 21For in eating, each of you goes ahead with your own meal, and one is hungry and another is drunk. 22What! Do you not have houses to eat and drink in? Or do you despise the church of God and humiliate those who have nothing? What shall I say to you? Shall I commend you in this? No, I will not.

23 For I received from the Lord what I also delivered to you, that the Lord Jesus on the night of the betrayal took bread, ²⁴and after giving thanks, broke it, and said, "This is my body which is for you. Do this in remembrance of me." ²⁵In the same way also the cup, after supper, saying, "This cup is the new covenant in my blood. Do this, as often as you drink it, in remembrance of me." ²⁶For as often as you eat this bread and drink the cup, you proclaim the Lord's death until the Lord comes.

27 Whoever, therefore, eats the bread or drinks the cup of the Lord in an unworthy manner will be guilty of profaning the body and blood of the Lord. ²⁸Examine yourselves, and only then eat of the bread and drink of the cup. ²⁹For all who eat and drink without discerning the body, eat and drink judgment on themselves. ³⁰That is why many of you are weak and ill, and some have died. ³¹But if we judged ourselves truly, we would not be judged. ³²But when we are judged by the Lord, we are chastened so that we may not be condemned along with the world.

33 So then, my sisters and brothers, when you come together to eat, wait for one another—³⁴anyone who is hungry should eat at home—lest you come together to be condemned. About the other things I will give directions when I come.

12 Now concerning spiritual gifts, brothers and sisters, I do not want you to be uninformed. ²You know that when you were heathen, you were led astray to speechless idols. ³Therefore I want you to understand that no one speaking by the Spirit of God ever says "Jesus be cursed!" and no one can say "Jesus is Lord" except by the Holy Spirit.

4 Now there are varieties of gifts, but the same Spirit; ⁵and there are varieties of service, but the same Lord; ⁶and there are varieties of activities, but it is the same God who inspires them all in everyone. ⁷To each is given the manifestation of the Spirit for the common good. ⁸To one is given through the Spirit the utterance of wisdom, and to another the utterance of knowledge according to the same Spirit, ⁹to another faith by the same Spirit, to another gifts of healing by the one Spirit, ¹⁰to another the working of miracles, to another prophecy, to another the ability to distinguish between spirits, to another various kinds of tongues, to another the interpretation of tongues. ¹¹All these are inspired by one and the same Spirit, who apportions to each one individually as the Spirit wills.

12 For just as the body is one and has many members, and all the members of the body, though many, are one body, so it is with Christ. ¹³For by one Spirit we were all baptized into one body—Jews or Greeks, slaves or free—and all were made to drink of one Spirit.

14 For the body does not consist of one member but of many. ¹⁵If the foot should say, "Because I am not a hand, I do not belong to the body," that would not make it any less a part of the body. ¹⁶And if the

ear should say, "Because I am not an eye, I do not belong to the body," that would not make it any less a part of the body. ¹⁷If the whole body were an eye, where would be the hearing? If the whole body were an ear, where would be the sense of smell? ¹⁸But as it is, God arranged the organs in the body, each one of them, as God chose. ¹⁹If all were a single organ, where would the body be? ²⁰As it is, there are many parts, yet one body. ²¹The eye cannot say to the hand, "I have no need of you," nor again the head to the feet, "I have no need of you." ²²On the contrary, the parts of the body which seem to be weaker are indispensable, ²³and those parts of the body which we think less honorable we invest with the greater honor, and our unpresentable parts are treated with greater modesty, ²⁴which our more presentable parts do not require. But God has so composed the body, giving the greater honor to the inferior part, ²⁵that there may be no discord in the body, but that the members may have the same care for one another. ²⁶If one member suffers, all suffer together; if one member is honored, all rejoice together.

27 Now you are the body of Christ and individually members of it. ²⁸And God has appointed in the church first apostles, second prophets, third teachers, then workers of miracles, then healers, helpers, administrators, speakers in various kinds of tongues. ²⁹Are all apostles? Are all prophets? Are all teachers? Do all work miracles? ³⁰Do all possess gifts of healing? Do all speak with tongues? Do all interpret? ³¹But earnestly desire the higher gifts.

And I will show you a still more excellent way.

13 If I speak in human tongues or the tongues of angels, but have not love, I am a noisy gong or a clanging cymbal. ²And if I have prophetic powers, and understand all mysteries and all knowledge, and if I have all faith, so as to remove mountains, but have not love, I am nothing. ³If I give away all I have, and if I deliver my body to be burned, but have not love, I gain nothing.

4 Love is patient and kind; love is not jealous or boastful; ⁵it is not arrogant or rude. Love does not insist on its own way; it is not irritable or resentful; ⁶it does not rejoice at wrong, but rejoices in the right. ⁷Love bears all things, believes all things, hopes all things, endures all things.

8 Love never ends; as for prophecies, they will pass away; as for tongues, they will cease; as for knowledge, it will pass away. ⁹For our knowledge is imperfect and our prophecy is imperfect; ¹⁰but when the perfect comes, the imperfect will pass away. ¹¹When I was a child, I spoke like a child, I thought like a child, I reasoned like a child; when I became an adult, I gave up childish ways. ¹²For now we see in a mirror dimly, but then face to face. Now I know in part; then I shall understand fully, even as I have been fully understood. ¹³So faith, hope, love abide, these three; but the greatest of these is love.

14 Make love your aim, and earnestly desire the spiritual gifts, especially that you may prophesy. [2]For those who speak in a tongue speak not to human beings but to God; for no one understands them, but they utter mysteries in the Spirit. [3]On the other hand, those who prophesy speak to human beings for their upbuilding and encouragement and consolation. [4]Those who speak in a tongue edify themselves, but those who prophesy edify the church. [5]Now I want you all to speak in tongues, but even more to prophesy. One who prophesies is greater than one who speaks in tongues, unless someone interprets, so that the church may be edified.

6 Now, brothers and sisters, if I come to you speaking in tongues, how shall I benefit you unless I bring you some revelation or knowledge or prophecy or teaching? [7]If even lifeless instruments, such as the flute or the harp, do not give distinct notes, how will anyone know what is played? [8]And if the bugle gives an indistinct sound, who will get ready for battle? [9]So with yourselves; if you in a tongue utter speech that is not intelligible, how will anyone know what is said? For you will be speaking into the air. [10]There are doubtless many different languages in the world, and none is without meaning; [11]but if I do not know the meaning of the language, I will be a foreigner to the speaker and the speaker a foreigner to me. [12]So with yourselves; since you are eager for manifestations of the Spirit, strive to excel in building up the church.

13 Therefore, one who speaks in a tongue should pray for the power to interpret. [14]For if I pray in a tongue, my spirit prays but my mind is unfruitful. [15]What am I to do? I will pray with the spirit and I will pray with the mind also; I will sing with the spirit and I will sing with the mind also. [16]Otherwise, if you bless with the spirit, how can anyone in the position of an outsider say the "Amen" to your thanksgiving, not knowing what you are saying? [17]For you may give thanks well enough, but the other person is not edified. [18]I thank God that I speak in tongues more than you all; [19]nevertheless, in church I would rather speak five words with my mind, in order to instruct others, than ten thousand words in a tongue.

20 Dear friends, do not be children in your thinking; be babes in evil, but in thinking be mature. [21]In the law it is written, "By people of strange tongues and by the lips of foreigners will I speak to this people, and even then they will not listen to me, says the Lord." [22]Thus, tongues are a sign not for believers but for unbelievers, while prophecy is not for unbelievers but for believers. [23]If, therefore, the whole church assembles and all speak in tongues, and outsiders or unbelievers enter, will they not say that you are mad? [24]But if all prophesy, an unbeliever or outsider who enters is convicted by all, is called to account by all, [25]the secrets of the unbeliever's heart are disclosed and, bowing down, that person will worship God and declare that God is really among you.

26 What then, brothers and sisters? When you come together, each one has a hymn, a lesson, a revelation, a tongue, or an interpretation. Let all things be done for edification. ²⁷If any speak in a tongue, let there be only two or at most three, and each in turn; and let one person interpret. ²⁸But if there is no one to interpret, then let the people keep silent in church and speak to themselves and to God. ²⁹Let two or three prophets speak, and let the others weigh what is said. ³⁰If a revelation is made to another sitting by, let the first be silent. ³¹For you can all prophesy one by one, so that all may learn and all be encouraged; ³²and the spirits of prophets are subject to prophets. ³³For God is not a God of confusion but of peace.

As in all the churches of the saints, ³⁴the women should keep silent in the churches. For they are not permitted to speak, but should be subordinate, as even the law says. ³⁵If there is anything they desire to know, let them ask their husbands at home. For it is shameful for a woman to speak in church. ³⁶What! Did the word of God originate with you, or are you the only ones it has reached?

37 If any of you think you are a prophet, or spiritual, you should acknowledge that what I am writing to you is a command of the Lord. ³⁸Anyone who does not recognize this is not to be recognized. ³⁹So, my sisters and brothers, earnestly desire to prophesy, and do not forbid speaking in tongues; ⁴⁰but all things should be done decently and in order.

15 Now I would remind you, sisters and brothers, in what terms I preached to you the gospel, which you received, in which you stand, ²by which you are saved, if you hold it fast—unless you believed in vain.

3 For I delivered to you as of first importance what I also received, that Christ died for our sins in accordance with the scriptures, ⁴that Christ was buried, and was raised on the third day in accordance with the scriptures, ⁵and that Christ appeared to Cephas, then to the twelve. ⁶Then Christ appeared to more than five hundred followers at one time, most of whom are still alive, though some have fallen asleep. ⁷Then Christ appeared to James, then to all the apostles. ⁸Last of all, as to one untimely born, Christ appeared also to me. ⁹For I am the least of the apostles, unfit to be called an apostle, because I persecuted the church of God. ¹⁰But by the grace of God I am what I am, and God's grace toward me was not in vain. On the contrary, I worked harder than any of them, though it was not I, but the grace of God which is with me. ¹¹Whether then it was I or they, so we preach and so you believed.

12 Now if Christ is preached as raised from the dead, how can some of you say that there is no resurrection of the dead? ¹³But if there is no resurrection of the dead, then Christ has not been raised; ¹⁴if Christ has

not been raised, then our preaching is in vain and your faith is in vain. ¹⁵We are even found to be misrepresenting God, because we testified of God that God raised Christ, whom God did not raise if it is true that the dead are not raised. ¹⁶For if the dead are not raised, then Christ has not been raised. ¹⁷If Christ has not been raised, your faith is futile and you are still in your sins. ¹⁸Then those also who have fallen asleep in Christ have perished. ¹⁹If for only this life we have hoped in Christ, we are of all people most to be pitied.

20 But in fact Christ has been raised from the dead, the firstfruits of those who have fallen asleep. ²¹For as by a human being came death, by a human being has come also the resurrection of the dead. ²²For as in Adam all die, so also in Christ shall all be made alive. ²³But each in the proper order: Christ the first fruits, then at Christ's coming those who belong to Christ. ²⁴Then comes the end, when Christ delivers the dominion to God the Father and Mother, after destroying every rule and every authority and power. ²⁵For Christ must reign until all enemies are put under Christ's feet. ²⁶The last enemy to be destroyed is death. ²⁷"For God has put all things in subjection under Christ's feet." But when it says, "All things are put in subjection," it is clear that the one who put all things under Christ is not included. ²⁸When all things are subjected to Christ, then Christ also will be subjected to God who put all things under Christ, that God may be everything to everyone.

29 Otherwise, what do people mean be being baptized on behalf of the dead? If the dead are not raised at all, why are people baptized on their behalf? ³⁰Why am I in peril every hour? ³¹I protest, brothers and sisters, by my pride in you which I have in Christ Jesus our Lord, I die every day! ³²What do I gain if, humanly speaking, I fought with beasts at Ephesus? If the dead are not raised, "Let us eat and drink, for tomorrow we die." ³³Do not be deceived: "Bad company ruins good morals." ³⁴Come to your right mind, and sin no more. For some have no knowledge of God. I say this to your shame.

35 But someone will ask, "How are the dead raised? With what kind of body do they come?" ³⁶You fool! What you sow does not come to life unless it dies. ³⁷And what you sow is not the body which is to be, but a bare kernel, perhaps of wheat or of some other grain. ³⁸But God gives it a body as God has chosen, and to each kind of seed its own body. ³⁹For not all flesh is alike, but there is one kind for human beings, another for animals, another for birds, and another for fish. ⁴⁰There are celestial bodies and there are terrestrial bodies; but the glory of the celestial is one, and the glory of the terrestrial is another. ⁴¹There is one glory of the sun, and another glory of the moon, and another glory of the stars; for star differs from star in glory.

42 So is it with the resurrection of the dead. What is sown is perishable, what is raised is imperishable. ⁴³It is sown in dishonor, it is raised

in glory. It is sown in weakness, it is raised in power. ⁴⁴It is sown a physical body, it is raised a spiritual body. If there is a physical body, there is also a spiritual body. ⁴⁵Thus it is written, "The first Adam became a living being"; the last Adam became a life-giving spirit. ⁴⁶But it is not the spiritual which is first but the physical, and then the spiritual. ⁴⁷The first was from the earth, made of dust; the second is from heaven. ⁴⁸As was the one made of dust, so are those who are of the dust; and as is the one of heaven, so are those who are of heaven. ⁴⁹Just as we have borne the image of the one of dust, we shall also bear the image of the one of heaven. ⁵⁰I tell you this, friends: flesh and blood cannot inherit the dominion of God, nor does the perishable inherit the imperishable.

51 I tell you a mystery. We shall not all sleep, but we shall all be changed, ⁵²in a moment, in the twinkling of an eye, at the last trumpet. For the trumpet will sound, and the dead will be raised imperishable, and we shall be changed. ⁵³For this perishable nature must put on the imperishable, and this mortal nature must put on immortality. ⁵⁴When the perishable puts on the imperishable, and the mortal puts on immortality, then shall come to pass the saying that is written:

"Death is swallowed up in victory."
⁵⁵"O death, where is your victory?
O death, where is your sting?"

⁵⁶The sting of death is sin, and the power of sin is the law. ⁵⁷But thanks be to God, who gives us the victory through our Lord Jesus Christ.

58 Therefore, my beloved friends, be steadfast, immovable, always abounding in the work of the Lord, knowing that in the Lord, your labor is not in vain.

16 Now concerning the contribution for the saints: as I directed the churches of Galatia, so you also are to do. ²On the first day of every week, each of you is to put something aside and store it up, as each may prosper, so that contributions need not be made when I come. ³And when I arrive, I will send those whom you accredit by letter to carry your gift to Jerusalem. ⁴If it seems advisable that I should go also, they will accompany me.

5 I will visit you after passing through Macedonia, for I intend to pass through Macedonia, ⁶and perhaps I will stay with you or even spend the winter, so that you may speed me on my journey, wherever I go. ⁷For I do not want to see you now just in passing; I hope to spend some time with you, if the Lord permits. ⁸But I will stay in Ephesus until Pentecost, ⁹for a wide door for effective work has opened to me, and there are many adversaries.

10 When Timothy comes, see that you put him at ease among you, for he is doing the work of the Lord, as I am. ¹¹So let no one despise

him. Speed him on his way in peace, that he may return to me; for I am expecting him with the others.

12 As for our brother Apollos, I strongly urged him to visit you with the others, but it was not at all his will to come now. He will come when he has opportunity.

13 Be watchful, stand firm in your faith, be courageous, be strong. [14]Let all that you do be done in love.

15 Now, friends, you know that the household of Stephanas were the first converts in Achaia, and they have devoted themselves to the service of the saints; [16]I urge you to be subject to such people and to every coworker and laborer. [17]I rejoice at the coming of Stephanas and Fortunatus and Achaicus, because they have made up for your absence; [18]for they refreshed my spirit as well as yours. Give recognition to such people.

19 The churches of Asia send greetings. Aquila and Prisca, together with the church in their house, send you hearty greetings in the Lord. [20]All the sisters and brothers send greetings. Greet one another with a holy kiss.

21 I, Paul, write this greeting with my own hand. [22]Let anyone who has no love for the Lord be accursed. Our Lord, come. [23]The grace of the Lord Jesus be with you. [24]My love be with you all in Christ Jesus. Amen.

2 Corinthians

1 Paul, an apostle of Christ Jesus by the will of God, and Timothy our brother.

To the church of God which is at Corinth, with all the saints who are in the whole of Achaia:

2 Grace to you and peace from God our Father and Mother and from the Lord Jesus Christ.

3 Blessed be the God, and Father and Mother, of our Lord Jesus Christ, the Mother and Father of all mercies and the God of all comfort, ⁴who comforts us in all our affliction, so that we may be able to comfort those who are in any affliction, with the comfort with which we ourselves are comforted by God. ⁵For as we share abundantly in Christ's sufferings, so through Christ we share abundantly in comfort too. ⁶If we are afflicted, it is for your comfort and salvation; and if we are comforted, it is for your comfort, which you experience when you patiently endure the same sufferings that we suffer. ⁷Our hope for you is unshaken; for we know that as you share in our sufferings, you will also share in our comfort.

8 For we do not want you to be ignorant, brothers and sisters, of the affliction we experienced in Asia; for we were so utterly, unbearably crushed that we despaired of life itself. ⁹Why, we felt that we had received the sentence of death; but that was to make us rely not on ourselves but on God who raises the dead, ¹⁰who delivered us from so deadly a peril, and who will deliver us. On God we have set our hope that we will be delivered again. ¹¹You also must help us by prayer, so that many will give thanks on our behalf for the blessing granted us in answer to many prayers.

12 For our boast is this, the testimony of our conscience that we have behaved in the world, and still more toward you, with holiness and

197

godly sincerity, not by earthly wisdom but by the grace of God. [13]For we write you nothing but what you can read and understand; I hope you will understand fully, [14]as you have understood in part, that you can be proud of us as we can be of you, on the day of the Lord Jesus.

15 Because I was sure of this, I wanted to come to you first, so that you might have a double pleasure; [16]I wanted to visit you on my way to Macedonia, and to come back to you from Macedonia and have you send me on my way to Judea. [17]Was I vacillating when I wanted to do this? Do I make my plans like a worldly person, ready to say Yes and No at once? [18]As surely as God is faithful, our word to you has not been Yes and No. [19]For the Child of God, Jesus Christ, whom we preached among you, Silvanus and Timothy and I, was not Yes and No; but in Christ it is always Yes. [20]For all the promises of God find their Yes in Christ. That is why we utter the Amen through Jesus Christ, to the glory of God. [21]But it is God who establishes us with you in Christ, and has commissioned us; [22]God has put God's seal upon us and given us the Spirit of God in our hearts as a guarantee.

23 But I call God to witness against me—it was to spare you that I refrained from coming to Corinth. [24]Not that we lord it over your faith; we work with you for your joy, for you stand firm in your faith. 2 [1]For I made up my mind not to make you another painful visit. [2]For if I cause you pain, who is there to make me glad but the one whom I have pained? [3]And I wrote as I did, so that when I came I might not suffer pain from those who should have made me rejoice, for I felt sure of all of you, that my joy would be the joy of you all. [4]For I wrote you out of much affliction and anguish of heart and with many tears, not to cause you pain but to let you know the abundant love that I have for you.

5 But if anyone has caused pain, it has been caused not to me, but in some measure—not to put it too severely—to you all. [6]For such a person this punishment by the majority is enough; [7]so you should rather turn to forgive and comfort anyone who has caused pain, or the person may be overwhelmed by excessive sorrow. [8]So I beg you to reaffirm your love for such a human being. [9]For this is why I wrote, that I might test you and know whether you are obedient in everything. [10]Anyone whom you forgive, I also forgive. What I have forgiven, if I have forgiven anything, has been for your sake in the presence of Christ, [11]to keep Satan from gaining the advantage over us; for we are not ignorant of Satan's designs.

12 When I came to Troas to preach the gospel of Christ, a door was opened for me in the Lord; [13]but my mind could not rest because I did not find my brother Titus there. So I took leave of them and went on to Macedonia.

14 But thanks be to God, who in Christ always leads us in triumph, and through us spreads the fragrance of the knowledge of Christ every-

where. [15]For we are the aroma of Christ to God among those who are being saved and among those who are perishing, [16]to one a fragrance from death to death, to the other a fragrance from life to life. Who is sufficient for these things? [17]For we are not, like so many, peddlers of God's word; but as sincere people, as commissioned by God, in the sight of God we speak in Christ.

3 Are we beginning to commend ourselves again? Or do we need, as some do, letters of recommendation to you, or from you? [2]You yourselves are our letter of recommendation, written on your hearts, to be known and read by all; [3]and you show that you are a letter from Christ delivered by us, written not with ink but with the Spirit of the living God, not on tablets of stone but on tablets of human hearts.

4 Such is the confidence that we have through Christ toward God. [5]Not that we are competent of ourselves to claim anything as coming from us; our competence is from God, [6]who has made us competent to be ministers of a new covenant, not in a written code but in the Spirit; for the written code kills, but the Spirit gives life.

7 Now if the dispensation of death, carved in letters on stone, came with such splendor that the Israelites could not look at Moses' face because of its brightness, fading as this was, [8]will not the dispensation of the Spirit be attended with greater splendor? [9]For if there was splendor in the dispensation of condemnation, the dispensation of righteousness must far exceed it in splendor. [10]Indeed, in this case, what once had splendor has come to have no splendor at all, because of the splendor that surpasses it. [11]For if what faded away came with splendor, what is permanent must have much more splendor.

12 Since we have such a hope, we are very bold, [13]not like Moses, who put a veil over his face so that the Israelites might not see the end of the fading splendor. [14]But their minds were hardened; for to this day, when they read the old covenant, that same veil remains unlifted, because only through Christ is it taken away. [15]Yes, to this day whenever Moses is read a veil lies over their minds; [16]but when one turns to the Lord the veil is removed. [17]Now the Lord is the Spirit, and where the Spirit of the Lord is, there is freedom. [18]And we all, with unveiled face, beholding the glory of the Lord, are being changed into the same likeness from one degree of glory to another; for this comes from the Lord who is the Spirit.

4 Therefore, having this ministry by the mercy of God, we do not lose heart. [2]We have renounced disgraceful, underhanded ways; we refuse to practice cunning or to tamper with God's word, but by the open statement of the truth we would commend ourselves to everyone's conscience in the sight of God. [3]And even if our gospel is veiled,

it is veiled only to those who are perishing. ⁴In their case the god of this world has blinded the minds of the unbelievers, to keep them from seeing the light of the gospel of the glory of Christ, who is the likeness of God. ⁵For what we preach is not ourselves, but Jesus Christ as Lord, with ourselves as your servants for Jesus' sake. ⁶For it is the God who said, "Let light shine out of darkness," who has shone in our hearts to give the light of the knowledge of the glory of God in the face of Christ.

7 But we have this treasure in earthen vessels, to show that the transcendent power belongs to God and not to us. ⁸We are afflicted in every way, but not crushed; perplexed, but not driven to despair; ⁹persecuted, but not forsaken; struck down, but not destroyed; ¹⁰always carrying in the body the death of Jesus, so that the life of Jesus may also be manifested in our bodies. ¹¹For while we live we are always being given up to death for Jesus' sake, so that the life of Jesus may be manifested in our mortal flesh. ¹²So death is at work in us, but life in you.

13 Since we have the same spirit of faith as the psalmist who wrote, "I believed, and so I spoke," we too believe, and so we speak, ¹⁴knowing that the one who raised the Lord Jesus will raise us also with Jesus and will present us with you. ¹⁵For it is all for your sake, so that as grace extends to more and more people it may increase thanksgiving, to the glory of God.

16 So we do not lose heart. Though our outer nature is wasting away, our inner nature is being renewed every day. ¹⁷For this slight momentary affliction is preparing for us an eternal weight of glory beyond all comparison, ¹⁸because we look not to the things that are seen but to the things that are unseen; for the things that are seen are transient, but the things that are unseen are eternal.

5 For we know that if the earthly tent we live in is destroyed, we have a building from God, a house not made with hands, eternal in the heavens. ²Here indeed we groan, and long to put on our heavenly dwelling, ³so that by putting it on we may not be found naked. ⁴For while we are still in this tent, we sigh with anxiety; not that we would be unclothed, but that we would be further clothed, so that what is mortal may be swallowed up by life. ⁵The one who has prepared us for this very thing is God, who has given us the Spirit as a guarantee.

6 So we are always of good courage; we know that while we are at home in the body we are away from the Lord, ⁷for we walk by faith, not by sight. ⁸We are of good courage, and we would rather be away from the body and at home with the Lord. ⁹So whether we are at home or away, we make it our aim to please the Lord. ¹⁰For we must all appear before the judgment seat of Christ, so that each one may receive good or evil, according to what each has done in the body.

11 Therefore, knowing the fear of the Lord, we try to persuade other

people; but what we are is known to God, and I hope it is known also to your conscience. [12]We are not commending ourselves to you again, but giving you cause to be proud of us, so that you may be able to answer those who pride themselves on a person's position and not on the person's heart. [13]For if we are beside ourselves, it is for God; if we are in our right mind, it is for you. [14]For the love of Christ controls us, because we are convinced that one has died for all; therefore all have died. [15]And Christ died for all, that those who live might live no longer for themselves but for the one who for their sake died and was raised.

16 From now on, therefore, we regard no one from a human point of view; even though we once regarded Christ from a human point of view, we regard Christ thus no longer. [17]Therefore, if anyone is in Christ, there is a new creation; the old has passed away—the new has come. [18]All this is from God, who through Christ reconciled us to God's self and gave us the ministry of reconciliation; [19]that is, God was in Christ reconciling the world to God's self, not counting their trespasses against them, and entrusting to us the message of reconciliation. [20]So we are ambassadors for Christ, God making God's appeal through us. We beseech you on behalf of Christ, be reconciled to God. [21]For our sake God made to be sin the one who knew no sin, so that in that very one we might become the righteousness of God.

6 Working together with God, then, we entreat you not to accept the grace of God in vain. [2]For God says,

"At the acceptable time I have listened to you,
and helped you on the day of salvation."

Now is the acceptable time; now is the day of salvation. [3]We put no obstacle in anyone's way, so that no fault may be found with our ministry, [4]but as servants of God we commend ourselves in every way: through great endurance, in afflictions, hardships, calamities, [5]beatings, imprisonments, disturbances, labors, sleepless nights, hunger; [6]by purity, knowledge, forbearance, kindness, the Holy Spirit, genuine love, [7]truthful speech, and the power of God; with the weapons of righteousness for the right hand and for the left; [8]in honor and dishonor, in ill repute and good repute. We are treated as impostors, and yet are true; [9]as unknown, and yet well known; as dying, and yet we live; as punished, and yet not killed; [10]as sorrowful, yet always rejoicing; as poor, yet making many rich; as having nothing, and yet possessing everything.

11 Our words to you have been frank, Corinthians; our heart is wide open to you. [12]You are not restricted by us, but you are restricted in your own affections [13]In return—I speak as to children—widen your hearts also.

14 Do not be mismated with unbelievers. For what do righteousness and iniquity have in common? Or what partnership has day with night? [15]What agreement has Christ with Belial? Or what has a believer in common with an unbeliever? [16]What agreement has the temple of God with idols? For we are the temple of the living God; as God said,

> "I will live in them and move among them,
> and I will be their God,
> and they will be my people.
> [17]Therefore come out from them
> and be separate from them, says the Lord,
> and touch nothing unclean;
> then I will welcome you,
> [18]and I will be a father and mother to you,
> and you shall be my sons and daughters,
> says the Lord Almighty."

7 Since we have these promises, beloved, let us cleanse ourselves from every defilement of body and spirit, and make holiness perfect in the fear of God.

2 Open your hearts to us; we have wronged no one, we have corrupted no one, we have taken advantage of no one. [3]I do not say this to condemn you, for I said before that you are in our hearts, to die together and to live together. [4]I have great confidence in you; I have great pride in you; I am filled with comfort. With all our affliction, I am overjoyed.

5 For even when we came into Macedonia, our bodies had no rest but we were afflicted at every turn—quarrels without and fear within. [6]But God, who comforts the downcast, comforted us by the coming of Titus, [7]and not only by his coming, but also by the comfort with which he was comforted in you, as he told us of your longing, your mourning, your zeal for me, so that I rejoiced still more. [8]For even if I made you sorry with my letter, I do not regret it (though I did regret it), for I see that that letter grieved you, though only for a while. [9]As it is, I rejoice, not because you were grieved, but because you were grieved into repenting; for you felt a godly grief, so that you suffered no loss through us. [10]For godly grief produces a repentance that leads to salvation and brings no regret, but worldly grief produces death. [11]For see what earnestness this godly grief has produced in you, what eagerness to clear yourselves, what indignation, what alarm, what longing, what zeal, what punishment! At every point you have proved yourselves guiltless in the matter. [12]So although I wrote to you, it was not on account of the one who did the wrong, nor on account of the one who suffered the wrong, but in

order that your zeal for us might be revealed to you in the sight of God. ¹³Therefore we are comforted.

And besides our own comfort, we rejoiced still more at the joy of Titus, because his mind has been set at rest by you all. ¹⁴For if I have expressed to him some pride in you, I was not put to shame; but just as everything we said to you was true, so our boasting before Titus has proved true. ¹⁵And his heart goes out all the more to you, as he remembers the obedience of you all, and the fear and trembling with which you received him. ¹⁶I rejoice, because I have perfect confidence in you.

8 We want you to know, brothers and sisters, about the grace of God which has been shown in the churches of Macedonia, ²for in a severe test of affliction, their abundance of joy and their extreme poverty have overflowed in a wealth of liberality on their part. ³For they gave according to their means, as I can testify, and beyond their means, of their own free will, ⁴begging us earnestly for the favor of taking part in the relief of the saints—⁵and this, not as we expected, but first they gave themselves to the Lord and to us by the will of God. ⁶Accordingly we have urged Titus that as he had already made a beginning, he should also complete among you this gracious work. ⁷Now as you excel in everything—in faith, in speech, in knowledge, in all earnestness, and in your love for us—see that you excel in this generous undertaking also.

8 I say this not as a command, but to prove by the earnestness of others that your love also is genuine. ⁹For you know the grace of our Lord Jesus Christ, who though rich, yet for your sake became poor, so that by the poverty of Christ you might become rich. ¹⁰And in this matter I give my advice: it is best for you now to complete what a year ago you began not only to do but to desire, ¹¹so that your readiness in desiring it may be matched by your completing it out of what you have. ¹²For if the willingness to give is there, it is acceptable according to what one has, not according to what one has not. ¹³I do not mean that others should be eased and you burdened, ¹⁴but that as a matter of equality your abundance at the present time should supply their want, so that their abundance may supply your want, that there may be equality. ¹⁵As it is written, "The one who gathered much had nothing over, and the one who gathered little had no lack."

16 But thanks be to God who puts the same earnest care for you into the heart of Titus. ¹⁷For he not only accepted our appeal, but being himself very earnest he is going to you of his own accord. ¹⁸With him we are sending the brother who is famous among all the churches for his preaching of the gospel; ¹⁹and not only that, but he has been appointed by the churches to travel with us in this generous undertaking which we are carrying on, for the glory of the Lord and to show our good will. ²⁰We intend that no one should blame us about this liberal gift which

we are administering, [21]for we aim at what is honorable not only in the Lord's sight but also in the sight of human beings. [22]And with them we are sending our brother whom we have often tested and found diligent in many matters, but who is now more diligent than ever because of his great confidence in you. [23]As for Titus, he is my partner and coworker in your service; and as for our brothers and sisters, they are messengers of the churches, the glory of Christ. [24]So give proof, before the churches, of your love and of our boasting about you to the churches.

9 Now it is superfluous for me to write to you about the offering for the saints, [2]for I know your readiness, of which I boast about you to the people of Macedonia, saying that Achaia has been ready since last year; and your zeal has stirred up most of them. [3]But I am sending the brothers so that our boasting about you may not prove vain in this case, so that you may be ready, as I said you would be; [4]lest if some Macedonians come with me and find that you are not ready, we be humiliated—to say nothing of you—for being so confident. [5]So I thought it necessary to urge the believers to go on to you before me, and arrange in advance for this gift you have promised, so that it may be ready not as given grudgingly but as a willing gift.

6 The point is this: whoever sows sparingly will also reap sparingly, and whoever sows bountifully will also reap bountifully. [7]Each of you must do as you have decided, not reluctantly or under compulsion, for God loves a cheerful giver. [8]And God is able to provide you with every blessing in abundance, so that you may always have enough of everything and may provide in abundance for every good work. [9]As it is written,

> "God scattered abroad, and gave to the poor;
> God's righteousness endures forever."

[10]The one who supplies seed to the sower and bread for food will supply and multiply your resources and increase the harvest of your righteousness. [11]You will be enriched in every way for great generosity, which through us will produce thanksgiving to God; [12]for the rendering of this service not only supplies the wants of the saints but also overflows in many thanksgivings to God. [13]Under the test of this service, you will glorify God by your obedience in acknowledging the gospel of Christ, and by the generosity of your contribution for them and for all others; [14]while they long for you and pray for you, because of the surpassing grace of God in you. [15]Thanks be to God for God's inexpressible gift!

10 I, Paul, myself entreat you, by the meekness and gentleness of Christ—I who am humble when face to face with you, but bold to you when I am away!—[2]I beg of you that when I am present I may

not have to show boldness with such confidence as I count on showing against some who suspect us of living in a worldly way. ³For though we live in the world we are not carrying on a worldly war, ⁴for the weapons of our warfare are not worldly but have divine power to destroy fortresses. ⁵We destroy arguments and every proud obstacle to the knowledge of God, and take every thought captive to obey Christ, ⁶being ready to punish every disobedience, when your obedience is complete.

7 Look at what is before your eyes. If you are confident that you are Christ's, remind yourself that as you are Christ's, so are we. ⁸For even if I boast a little too much of our authority, which the Lord gave for building you up and not for destroying you, I shall not be put to shame. ⁹I would not seem to be frightening you with letters. ¹⁰For they say, "His letters are weighty and strong, but his bodily presence is weak, and his speech of no account." ¹¹Let such people understand that what we say by letter when absent, we do when present. ¹²Not that we venture to class or compare ourselves with some of those who commend themselves. But when they measure themselves by one another, and compare themselves with one another, they are without understanding.

13 But we will not boast beyond limit, but will keep to the limits God has apportioned us, to reach even as far as you. ¹⁴For we are not overextending ourselves, as though we did not reach you; we were the first to come all the way to you with the gospel of Christ. ¹⁵We do not boast beyond limit, in the labors of others; but our hope is that as your faith increases, our field of action among you may be greatly enlarged, ¹⁶so that we may preach the gospel in lands beyond you, without boasting of work already done in another's field. ¹⁷"Let one who boasts, boast of the Lord." ¹⁸For it is not those who commend themselves that are accepted, but those whom the Lord commends.

11 I wish you would bear with me in a little foolishness. Do bear with me! ²I feel a divine jealousy for you, for I betrothed you to Christ to present you as a pure bride to her one husband. ³But I am afraid that as the serpent deceived Eve by cunning, your thoughts will be led astray from a sincere and pure devotion to Christ. ⁴For if someone comes and preaches another Jesus than the one we preached, or if you receive a different spirit from the one you received, or if you accept a different gospel from the one you accepted, you submit to it readily enough. ⁵I think that I am not in the least inferior to these superlative apostles. ⁶Even if I am unskilled in speaking, I am not in knowledge; in every way we have made this plain to you in all things.

7 Did I commit a sin in abasing myself so that you might be exalted, because I preached God's gospel without cost to you? ⁸I robbed other churches by accepting support from them in order to serve you.

⁹And when I was with you and was in want, I did not burden anyone, for my needs were supplied by friends who came from Macedonia. So I refrained and will refrain from burdening you in any way. ¹⁰As the truth of Christ is in me, this boast of mine shall not be silenced in the regions of Achaia. ¹¹And why? Because I do not love you? God knows I do!

12 And what I do I will continue to do, in order to undermine the claim of those who would like to claim that in their boasted mission they work on the same terms as we do. ¹³For such people are false apostles, deceitful workers, disguising themselves as apostles of Christ. ¹⁴And no wonder, for even Satan puts on a disguise as an angel of light. ¹⁵So it is not strange if Satan's servants also disguise themselves as servants of righteousness. Their end will correspond to their deeds.

16 I repeat, let no one think me foolish; but even if you do, accept me as a fool, so that I too may boast a little. ¹⁷(What I am saying I say not with the Lord's authority but as a fool, in this boastful confidence; ¹⁸since many boast of worldly things, I too will boast.) ¹⁹For you gladly bear with fools, being wise yourselves! ²⁰For you bear it if someone makes slaves of you, or preys upon you, or takes advantage of you, or puts on airs, or strikes you in the face. ²¹To my shame, I must say, we were too weak for that!

But whatever anyone dares to boast of—I am speaking as a fool—I also dare to boast of that. ²²Are they Hebrews? So am I. Are they Israelites? So am I. Are they descendants of Abraham? So am I. ²³Are they servants of Christ? I am a better one—I am talking like a mad person—with far greater labors, far more imprisonments, with countless beatings, and often near death. ²⁴Five times I have received at the hands of the Jews the forty lashes less one. ²⁵Three times I have been beaten with rods; once I was stoned. Three times I have been shipwrecked; a night and a day I have been adrift at sea; ²⁶on frequent journeys, in danger from rivers, danger from robbers, danger from my own people, danger from Gentiles, danger in the city, danger in the wilderness, danger at sea, danger from false brothers and sisters; ²⁷in toil and hardship, through many a sleepless night, in hunger and thirst, often without food, in cold and exposure. ²⁸And, apart from other things, there is the daily pressure upon me of my anxiety for all the churches. ²⁹Who is weak, and I am not weak? Who is made to fall, and I am not indignant?

30 If I must boast, I will boast of the things that show my weakness. ³¹The God, and Father and Mother of the Lord Jesus, the one who is blessed forever, knows that I do not lie. ³²At Damascus, the governor under King Aretas guarded the city of Damascus in order to seize me, ³³but I was let down in a basket through a window in the wall, and escaped his hands.

12 I must boast; there is nothing to be gained by it, but I will go on to visions and revelations of the Lord. ²I know someone in Christ who fourteen years ago was caught up to the third heaven—whether in the body or out of the body I do not know, God knows. ³And I know that this person was caught up into Paradise—whether in the body or out of the body I do not know, God knows—⁴and there heard things that cannot be told, which may not be uttered. ⁵On behalf of this one I will boast, but on my own behalf I will not boast, except of my weaknesses. ⁶Though if I wish to boast, I will not be a fool, for I will be speaking the truth. But I refrain from it, so that no one may think more of me than can be seen in me or heard from me. ⁷And to keep me from being too elated by the abundance of revelations, a thorn was given me in the flesh, a messenger of Satan, to harass me, to keep me from being too elated. ⁸Three times I besought the Lord about this, that it should leave me; ⁹but the Lord said to me, "My grace is sufficient for you, for my power is made perfect in weakness." I will all the more gladly boast of my weaknesses, that the power of Christ may rest upon me. ¹⁰For the sake of Christ, then, I am content with weaknesses, insults, hardships, persecutions, and calamities; for when I am weak, then I am strong.

11 I have been a fool! You forced me to it, for I ought to have been commended by you. For I was not at all inferior to these superlative apostles, even though I am nothing. ¹²The signs of a true apostle were performed among you with great patience, with signs and wonders and mighty works. ¹³For in what were you less favored than the rest of the churches, except that I myself did not burden you? Forgive me this wrong!

14 Here for the third time I am ready to come to you. And I will not be a burden, for I seek not what is yours but you; for children ought not to lay up for their parents, but parents for their children. ¹⁵I will most gladly spend and be spent for your souls. If I love you the more, am I to be loved the less? ¹⁶But granting that I myself did not burden you, I was crafty, you say, and got the better of you by guile. ¹⁷Did I take advantage of you through any of those whom I sent to you? ¹⁸I urged Titus to go, and sent the believer with him. Did Titus take advantage of you? Did we not act in the same spirit? Did we not take the same steps?

19 Have you been thinking all along that we have been defending ourselves before you? It is in the sight of God that we have been speaking in Christ, and all for your upbuilding, beloved. ²⁰For I fear that perhaps I may come and find you not what I wish, and that you may find me not what you wish; that perhaps there may be quarreling, jealousy, anger, selfishness, slander, gossip, conceit, and disorder. ²¹I fear that when I come again my God may humble me before you, and I may have to mourn over many of those who sinned before and have not re-

pented of the impurity, immorality, and licentiousness which they have practiced.

13 This is the third time I am coming to you. Any charge must be sustained by the evidence of two or three witnesses. [2]I warned those who sinned before and all the others, and I warn them now while absent, as I did when present on my second visit, that if I come again I will not spare them—[3]since you desire proof that Christ is speaking in me. Christ is not weak in dealing with you, but is powerful in you. [4]For Christ was crucified in weakness, but lives by the power of God. For we are weak in Christ, but in dealing with you we will live with Christ by the power of Christ.

5 Examine yourselves, to see whether you are holding to your faith. Test yourselves. Do you not realize that Jesus Christ is in you?—unless indeed you fail to meet the test! [6]I hope you will find out that we have not failed. [7]But we pray God that you may not do wrong—not that we may appear to have met the test, but that you may do what is right, though we may seem to have failed. [8]For we cannot do anything against the truth, but only for the truth. [9]For we are glad when we are weak and you are strong. What we pray for is your improvement. [10]I write this while I am away from you, in order that when I come I may not have to be severe in my use of the authority which the Lord has given me for building up and not for tearing down.

11 Finally, my friends, farewell. Mend your ways, heed my appeal, agree with one another, live in peace, and the God of love and peace will be with you. [12]Greet one another with a holy kiss. [13]All the saints greet you.

14 The grace of the Lord Jesus Christ and the love of God and the communion of the Holy Spirit be with you all.

Galatians

1 Paul an apostle—not from human beings nor through any person, but through Jesus Christ and God the Father and Mother, who raised Christ from the dead—²and all the coworkers who are with me,

To the churches of Galatia:

3 Grace to you and peace from God the Father and Mother and from the Lord Jesus Christ, ⁴who gave up Christ's life for our sins to deliver us from the present evil age, according to the will of our God the Mother and Father, ⁵to whom be the glory forever and ever. Amen.

6 I am astonished that you are so quickly deserting the one who called you in the grace of Christ and turning to a different gospel—⁷not that there is another gospel, but there are some who trouble you and want to pervert the gospel of Christ. ⁸But even if we, or an angel from heaven, should preach to you a gospel contrary to that which we preached to you, let that one be accursed. ⁹As we have said before, so now I say again, if anyone is preaching to you a gospel contrary to that which you received, let that one be accursed.

10 Am I now seeking human favor, or the favor of God? Or am I trying to please human beings? If I were still pleasing them, I should not be a servant of Christ.

11 For I would have you know, sisters and brothers, that the gospel which was preached by me is not a human gospel. ¹²For I did not receive it from a human being, nor was I taught it, but it came through a revelation of Jesus Christ. ¹³For you have heard of my former life in Judaism, how I persecuted the church of God violently and tried to destroy it; ¹⁴and I advanced in Judaism beyond many of my own age among my people, so extremely zealous was I for the traditions of my ancestors. ¹⁵But when God, who had set me apart before I was born and had called me through grace, ¹⁶was pleased to reveal God's Child to me, in order

that I might preach that one among the Gentiles, I did not confer with any human being, [17]nor did I go up to Jerusalem to those who were apostles before me, but I went away into Arabia; and again I returned to Damascus.

18 Then after three years I went up to Jerusalem to visit Cephas, and remained with him fifteen days. [19]But I saw none of the other apostles except James the Lord's brother. [20](In what I am writing to you, before God, I do not lie!) [21]Then I went into the regions of Syria and Cilicia. [22]And I was still not known by sight to the churches of Christ in Judea; [23]they only heard it said, "He who once persecuted us is now preaching the faith he once tried to destroy." [24]And they glorified God because of me.

2 Then after fourteen years I went up again to Jerusalem with Barnabas, taking Titus along with me. [2]I went up by revelation; and I laid before them (but privately before those who were of repute) the gospel which I preach among the Gentiles, lest somehow I should be running or had run in vain. [3]But even Titus, who was with me, was not compelled to be circumcised, though he was a Greek. [4]But because of false Christians secretly brought in, who slipped in to spy out our freedom which we have in Christ Jesus, that they might bring us into bondage—[5]to them we did not yield in submission even for a moment, that the truth of the gospel might be preserved for you. [6]And from those who were reputed to be something (what they were makes no difference to me; God shows no partiality)—those, I say, who were of repute added nothing to me; [7]but on the contrary, when they saw that I had been entrusted with the gospel to those outside the law, just as Peter had been entrusted with the gospel to those under the law [8](for the one who worked through Peter for the mission to those under the law worked also through me for the Gentiles), [9]and when they perceived the grace that was given to me, James and Cephas and John, who were reputed to be pillars, shook hands with Barnabas and me, that we should go to the Gentiles and they to those under the law; [10]only they would have us remember the poor, which indeed I was eager to do.

11 But when Cephas came to Antioch I opposed him to his face, because he stood condemned. [12]For before certain people came from James, Cephas ate with the Gentiles; but when they came, he drew back and separated himself, fearing those advocating being under the law. [13]And with him the rest of the Jews acted insincerely, so that even Barnabas was carried away by their insincerity. [14]But when I saw that they were not straightforward about the truth of the gospel, I said to Cephas before them all, "If you, though a Jew, live like a Gentile and not like a Jew, how can you compel the Gentiles to live like Jews?" [15]We ourselves, who are Jews by birth and not Gentile sinners, [16]yet who know that a

person is not justified by works of the law but through faith in Jesus Christ, even we have believed in Christ Jesus, in order to be justified by faith in Christ, and not by works of the law, because by works of the law shall no one be justified. [17]But if, in our endeavor to be justified in Christ, we ourselves were found to be sinners, is Christ then an agent of sin? Certainly not! [18]But if I build up again those things which I tore down, then I prove myself a transgressor. [19]For I through the law died to the law, that I might live to God. [20]I have been crucified with Christ; it is no longer I who live, but Christ who lives in me; and the life I now live in the flesh, I live by faith in the Child of God, who loved me and gave up life for me. [21]I do not nullify the grace of God; for if justification were through the law, then Christ died to no purpose.

3 O foolish Galatians! Who has bewitched you, before whose eyes Jesus Christ was publicly portrayed as crucified? [2]Let me ask you only this: Did you receive the Spirit by works of the law, or by hearing with faith? [3]Are you so foolish? Having begun with the Spirit, are you now ending with the flesh? [4]Did you experience so many things in vain?—if it really is in vain. [5]Does the one who supplies the Spirit to you and works miracles among you do so by works of the law, or by hearing with faith?

6 Thus Abraham "believed God, and it was reckoned to him as righteousness." [7]So you see that it is people of faith who are the children of Abraham and Sarah. [8]And the scripture, foreseeing that God would justify the Gentiles by faith, preached the gospel beforehand to Abraham, saying, "In you shall all the nations be blessed." [9]So then, those who are people of faith are blessed with Abraham who had faith.

10 For all who rely on works of the law are under a curse; for it is written, "Cursed be everyone who does not abide by all things written in the book of the law, and do them." [11]Now it is evident that no one is justified before God by the law; for "The one who through faith is righteous shall live"; [12]but the law does not rest on faith, for "The one who does them shall live by them." [13]Christ redeemed us from the curse of the law, having become a curse for us—for it is written, "Cursed be everyone who hangs on a tree"—[14]that in Christ Jesus the blessing of Abraham might come upon the Gentiles, that we might receive the promise of the Spirit through faith.

15 To give a human example, brothers and sisters: no one annuls even a human will, or adds to it, once it has been ratified. [16]Now the promises were made to Abraham and to his offspring. It does not say, "And to offsprings," referring to many; but, referring to one, "And to your offspring," which is Christ. [17]This is what I mean: the law, which came four hundred and thirty years afterward, does not annul a covenant previously ratified by God, so as to make the promise void. [18]For

if the inheritance is by the law, it is no longer by promise; but God gave it to Abraham by a promise.

19 Why then the law? It was added because of transgressions, till the offspring should come to whom the promise had been made; and it was ordained by angels through an intermediary. 20Now an intermediary implies more than one; but God is one.

21 Is the law then against the promises of God? Certainly not; for if a law had been given which could make alive, then righteousness would indeed be by the law. 22But the scripture consigned all things to sin, that what was promised to faith in Jesus Christ might be given to those who believe.

23 Now before faith came, we were confined under the law, kept under restraint until faith should be revealed. 24So that the law was our custodian until Christ came, that we might be justified by faith. 25But now that faith has come, we are no longer under a custodian; 26for in Christ Jesus you are all sons and daughters of God, through faith. 27For as many of you as were baptized into Christ have put on Christ. 28There is not Jew or Greek, there is not slave or free, there is not male and female; for you are all one in Christ Jesus. 29And if you are Christ's, then you are offspring of Abraham and Sarah, heirs according to promise.

4 I mean that the heirs, while children, are no better than slaves, though they are the owners of all the estate; 2but they are under guardians and trustees until the date set by the parent. 3So with us; when we were children, we were slaves to the elemental spirits of the universe. 4But when the time had fully come, God sent forth God's Child, born of woman, born under the law, 5to redeem.those who were under the law, so that we might receive adoption as children of God. 6And because you are children, God has sent the Spirit of God's Child into our hearts, crying, "God! Mother and Father!" 7So through God you are no longer a slave but a child, and if a child then an heir.

8 Formerly, when you did not know God, you were in bondage to beings that by nature are not gods; 9but now that you have come to know God, or rather to be known by God, how can you turn back again to the weak and beggarly elemental spirits, whose slaves you want to be once more? 10You observe days, and months, and seasons, and years! 11I am afraid I have labored over you in vain.

12 Sisters and brothers, I beseech you, become as I am, for I also have become as you are. You did me no wrong; 13you know it was because of a bodily ailment that I preached the gospel to you at first; 14and though my condition was a trial to you, you did not scorn or despise me, but received me as an angel of God, as Christ Jesus. 15What has become of the satisfaction you felt? For I bear witness to you, that if possible, you would have plucked out your eyes and given them to me. 16Have I then

become your enemy by telling you the truth? [17]They make much of you, but for no good purpose; they want to shut you out, that you may make much of them. [18]For a good purpose it is always good to be made much of, and not only when I am present with you. [19]My little children, with whom I am again in travail until Christ be formed in you, [20]I could wish to be present with you now and to change my tone, for I am perplexed about you.

21 Tell me, you who desire to be under law, do you not hear the law? [22]For it is written that Abraham had two children, one by a slave and one by a free woman. [23]But the son of the slave was born according to the flesh, the son of the free woman through promise. [24]Now this is an allegory: these women are two covenants. One is from Mount Sinai, bearing children for slavery; she is Hagar. [25]Now Hagar is Mount Sinai in Arabia; she corresponds to the present Jerusalem, for she is in slavery with her children. [26]But the Jerusalem above is free, and it is our mother. [27]For it is written,

> "Rejoice, O barren one who does not bear;
> break forth and shout, you who are not in travail;
> for the children of the desolate one are many more than the
>   children of her that is married."

[28]Now we, brothers and sisters, like Isaac, are children of the promise. [29]But as at that time the child who was born according to the flesh persecuted the child who was born according to the Spirit, so it is now. [30]But what does the scripture say? "Cast out the slave and her son; for the son of the slave will not inherit with the son of the free woman." [31]So, sisters and brothers, we are not children of the slave but of the free woman.

5 For freedom Christ has set us free; stand fast therefore, and do not submit again to a yoke of slavery.

2 Now I, Paul, say to you that if you receive circumcision, Christ will be of no advantage to you. [3]I testify again to all who receive circumcision that they are bound to keep the whole law. [4]You are severed from Christ, you who would be justified by the law; you have fallen away from grace. [5]For through the Spirit, by faith, we wait for the hope of righteousness. [6]For in Christ Jesus neither being under the law nor being outside the law is of any avail, but faith working through love. [7]You were running well; who kept you from obeying the truth? [8]This persuasion is not from the one who calls you. [9]A little leaven leavens the whole lump. [10]I have confidence in the Lord that you will take no other view than mine; and the one who is troubling you will be condemned, whoever it is. [11]But, friends, if I still preach circumcision, why am I still persecuted? In that case the stumbling block of the cross has been removed. [12]I wish those who unsettle you would mutilate themselves!

13 For you were called to freedom, sisters and brothers; only do not use your freedom as an opportunity for the flesh, but through love serve one another. [14]For the whole law is fulfilled in one word, "You shall love your neighbor as yourself." [15]But if you bite and devour one another, take heed that you are not consumed by one another.

16 But I say, walk by the Spirit, and do not gratify the desires of the flesh. [17]For the desires of the flesh are against the Spirit, and the desires of the Spirit are against the flesh; for these are opposed to each other, to prevent you from doing what you would like. [18]But if you are led by the Spirit, you are not under the law. [19]Now the works of the flesh are plain: fornication, impurity, licentiousness, [20]idolatry, sorcery, enmity, strife, jealousy, anger, selfishness, dissension, party spirit, [21]envy, drunkenness, carousing, and the like. I warn you, as I warned you before, that those who do such things shall not inherit the dominion of God. [22]But the fruit of the Spirit is love, joy, peace, patience, kindness, goodness, faithfulness, [23]gentleness, self-control; against such there is no law. [24]And those who belong to Christ Jesus have crucified the flesh with its passions and desires.

25 If we live by the Spirit, let us also walk by the Spirit. [26]Let us have no self-conceit, no provoking of one another, no envy of one another.

6 Sisters and brothers, if a person is overtaken in any trespass, you who are spiritual should restore such a one in a spirit of gentleness. Look to yourselves, lest you too be tempted. [2]Bear one another's burdens, and so fulfill the law of Christ. [3]For if people think they are something, when they are nothing, they deceive themselves. [4]For all should test their own work, and then their reason to boast will be in themselves alone and not in their neighbors. [5]For all will have to bear their own load.

6 Let each person who is taught the word share all good things with the one who teaches.

7 Do not be deceived; God is not mocked, for whatever you sow, you will also reap. [8]For if you sow to your own flesh, you will from the flesh reap corruption; but if you sow to the Spirit, you will from the Spirit reap eternal life. [9]And let us not grow weary in well-doing, for in due season we will reap, if we do not lose heart. [10]So then, as we have opportunity, let us do good to all people, and especially to those who are of the household of faith.

11 See with what large letters I am writing to you with my own hand. [12]It is those who want to make a good showing in the flesh that would compel you to be circumcised, and only in order that they may not be persecuted for the cross of Christ. [13]For even those who receive circumcision do not themselves keep the law, but they desire to have you

circumcised that they may glory in your flesh. ¹⁴But far be it from me to glory except in the cross of our Lord Jesus Christ, by which the world has been crucified to me, and I to the world. ¹⁵For neither circumcision counts for anything, nor uncircumcision, but a new creation. ¹⁶Peace and mercy be upon all who walk by this rule, upon the Israel of God.

17 Henceforth let no one trouble me; for I bear on my body the marks of Jesus.

18 The grace of our Lord Jesus Christ be with your spirit, my friends. Amen.

Ephesians

1 Paul, an apostle of Christ Jesus by the will of God,
To the saints who are also faithful in Christ Jesus:
2 Grace to you and peace from God our Father and Mother and from the Lord Jesus Christ.

3 Blessed be the God, and Father and Mother, of our Lord Jesus Christ, who has blessed us in Christ with every spiritual blessing in the heavenly places, ⁴even as God chose us in Christ before the foundation of the world, that we should be holy and blameless before God, ⁵who destined us in love to be God's children through Jesus Christ, according to the purpose of God's will, ⁶to the praise of God's glorious grace freely bestowed on us in the Beloved, ⁷in whom we have redemption by blood, the forgiveness of our trespasses, according to the riches of God's grace ⁸lavished upon us. ⁹For God has made known to us in all wisdom and insight the mystery of God's will, according to God's purpose set forth in Christ ¹⁰as a plan for the fullness of time, to unite all things in Christ, things in heaven and things on earth.

11 In Christ, according to the purpose of the one who accomplishes all things according to the counsel of the divine will, ¹²we who first hoped in Christ have been destined and appointed to live for the praise of God's glory. ¹³In Christ you also, who have heard the word of truth, the gospel of your salvation, and have become believers, were sealed with the promised Holy Spirit, ¹⁴which is the guarantee of our inheritance until we acquire possession of it, to the praise of God's glory.

15 For this reason, because I have heard of your faith in the Lord Jesus and your love toward all the saints, ¹⁶I do not cease to give thanks

for you, remembering you in my prayers, [17]that the God of our Lord Jesus Christ, the Father and Mother of glory, may give you a spirit of wisdom and of revelation in the knowledge of God, [18]having the eyes of your hearts enlightened, that you may know what is the hope to which you have been called, what are the riches of God's glorious inheritance in the saints, [19]and what is the immeasurable greatness of God's power in us who believe, according to the working of God's great might [20]which was accomplished in Christ when God raised Christ from the dead and made Christ sit at God's right hand in the heavenly places, [21]far above all rule and authority and power and dominion, and above every name that is named, not only in this age but also in that which is to come; [22]and God has put all things under Christ's feet and has made Christ the head over all things for the church, [23]which is Christ's body, the fullness of the one who fills all in all.

2 And you God made alive, when you were dead through the trespasses and sins [2]in which you once walked, following the course of this world, following the prince of the power of the air, the spirit that is now at work in the children of disobedience. [3]Among these we all once lived in the passions of our flesh, following the desires of body and mind, and so we were by nature children of wrath, like the rest of humankind. [4]But God, who is rich in mercy, out of the great love with which God loved us, [5]even when we were dead through our trespasses, made us alive together with Christ (by grace you have been saved), [6]and raised us up with Christ, and made us sit with Christ in the heavenly places in Christ Jesus, [7]that in the coming ages God might show the immeasurable riches of God's grace in kindness toward us in Christ Jesus. [8]For by grace you have been saved through faith; and this is not your own doing, it is the gift of God—[9]not because of works, lest anyone should boast. [10]For we are God's handiwork, created in Christ Jesus for good works, which God prepared beforehand, that we should walk in them.

11 Therefore remember that at one time you Gentiles in the flesh, called the uncircumcision by what is called the circumcision, which is made in the flesh by hands—[12]remember that you were at that time separated from Christ, alienated from the commonwealth of Israel, and strangers to the covenants of promise, having no hope and without God in the world. [13]But now in Christ Jesus you who once were far off have been brought near in the blood of Christ. [14]For Christ is our peace, who has made us both one, and has broken down the dividing wall of hostility, [15]by abolishing in Christ's own flesh the law with its commandments and ordinances, in order to create in Christ one new humanity in place of the two, so making peace, [16]and in order to reconcile us both to God in one body through the cross, thereby bringing the hostility to an end.

17And Christ came and preached peace to you who were far off and peace to those who were near; 18for through Christ we both have access in one Spirit to God the Mother and Father. 19So then you are no longer strangers and sojourners, but you are citizens together with the saints and members of the household of God, 20built upon the foundation of the apostles and prophets, Christ Jesus being the cornerstone, 21in whom the whole structure is joined together and grows into a holy temple in the Lord; 22in whom you also are built into it for a dwelling place of God in the Spirit.

3 For this reason I, Paul, a prisoner for Christ Jesus on behalf of you Gentiles—2assuming that you have heard of the stewardship of God's grace that was given to me for you, 3how the mystery was made known to me by revelation, as I have written briefly. 4When you read this you can perceive my insight into the mystery of Christ, 5which was not made known to the human race in other generations as it has now been revealed to Christ's holy apostles and prophets by the Spirit; 6that is, how the Gentiles are joint heirs, members of the same body, and partakers of the promise in Christ Jesus through the gospel.

7 Of this gospel I was made a minister according to the gift of God's grace which was given me by the working of God's power. 8To me, though I am the very least of all the saints, this grace was given, to preach to the Gentiles the unsearchable riches of Christ, 9and to make everyone see what is the plan of the mystery hidden for ages in God who created all things; 10that through the church the manifold wisdom of God might now be made known to the principalities and powers in the heavenly places. 11This was according to the eternal purpose which God has realized in Christ Jesus our Lord, 12in whom we have boldness and confidence of access through our faith in Christ. 13So I ask you not to lose heart over what I am suffering for you, which is your glory.

14 For this reason I bow my knees before God the Father and Mother, 15from whom every family in heaven and on earth is named, 16that according to the riches of God's glory God may grant you to be strengthened with might through God's Spirit in the inner person, 17and that Christ may dwell in your hearts through faith; that you, being rooted and grounded in love, 18may have power to comprehend with all the saints what is the breadth and length and height and depth, 19and to know the love of Christ which surpasses knowledge, that you may be filled with all the fullness of God.

20 Now to the one who by the power at work within us is able to do far more abundantly than all that we ask or think, 21to God be glory in the church and in Christ Jesus to all generations, forever and ever. Amen.

4 I therefore, a prisoner for the Lord, beg you to lead a life worthy of the calling to which you have been called, ²with all lowliness and meekness, with patience, forbearing one another in love, ³eager to maintain the unity of the Spirit in the bond of peace. ⁴There is one body and one Spirit, just as you were called to the one hope that belongs to your call, ⁵one Lord, one faith, one baptism, ⁶one God, Mother and Father of us all, who is above all and through all and in all. ⁷But grace was given to each of us according to the measure of Christ's gift. ⁸Therefore it is said,

"That one ascended on high, led a host of captives,
and gave gifts to people."

⁹(In saying, "That one ascended," it is also implied that that one descended into the lower parts of the earth. ¹⁰The one who descended is the same one who also ascended far above all the heavens, so that all things might be fulfilled.) ¹¹And the gifts given were that some should be apostles, some prophets, some evangelists, some pastors and teachers, ¹²to equip the saints for the work of ministry, for building up the body of Christ, ¹³until we all attain to the unity of the faith and of the knowledge of the Child of God, to a mature humanity, to the measure of the fullness of Christ; ¹⁴so that we may no longer be children, tossed to and fro and carried about with every wind of doctrine, by human cunning and craftiness in deceitful wiles. ¹⁵Rather, speaking the truth in love, we are to grow up in every way into the one who is the head, into Christ, ¹⁶from whom the whole body, joined and knit together by every joint with which it is supplied, when each part is working properly, makes bodily growth and upbuilds itself in love.

17 Now this I affirm and testify in the Lord, that you must no longer live as the Gentiles do, in the futility of their minds; ¹⁸they are darkened in their understanding, alienated from the life of God because of the ignorance that is in them, due to their hardness of heart; ¹⁹they have become callous and have given themselves up to licentiousness, greedy to practice every kind of uncleanness. ²⁰You did not so learn Christ!— ²¹assuming that you have heard about Christ and were taught in Christ, as the truth is in Jesus. ²²Put off your old nature which belongs to your former manner of life and is corrupt through deceitful lusts, ²³and be renewed in the spirit of your minds, ²⁴and put on the new nature, created after the likeness of God in true righteousness and holiness.

25 Therefore, putting away falsehood, let all of us speak the truth with our neighbors, for we are members one of another. ²⁶Be angry but do not sin; do not let the sun go down on your anger, ²⁷and give no opportunity to the devil. ²⁸Let the thief no longer steal, but rather labor, doing honest manual work, in order to be able to give to those in need. ²⁹Let no evil talk come out of your mouths, but only such as is good for edifying, as fits the occasion, that it may impart grace to those who hear.

³⁰And do not grieve the Holy Spirit of God, in whom you were sealed for the day of redemption. ³¹Let all bitterness and wrath and anger and quarreling and slander be put away from you, with all malice, ³²and be kind to one another, tenderhearted, forgiving one another, as God in Christ forgave you.

5 Therefore be imitators of God, as beloved children. ²And walk in love, as Christ loved us and gave up Christ's self for us, a fragrant offering and sacrifice to God.

3 But fornication and all impurity or covetousness must not even be named among you, as is fitting among saints. ⁴Let there be no filthiness, nor silly talk, nor buffoonery, which are not fitting; but instead let there be thanksgiving. ⁵Be sure of this, that no fornicator or impure person, or one who is covetous (that is, an idolater), has any inheritance in the dominion of Christ and of God. ⁶Let no one deceive you with empty words, for it is because of these things that the wrath of God comes upon the children of disobedience. ⁷Therefore do not associate with them, ⁸for once you were stumbling in the night, but now you are light in the Lord; walk as children of light ⁹(for the fruit of light is found in all that is good and right and true), ¹⁰and try to learn what is pleasing to the Lord. ¹¹Take no part in unfruitful works, but instead expose them. ¹²For it is a shame even to speak of the things that are done in secret; ¹³but all things exposed by the light are revealed, for everything that is revealed is light. ¹⁴Therefore it is said,

"Awake, O sleeper, and arise from the dead,
and Christ shall give you light."

15 Look carefully then how you walk, not unwisely but wisely, ¹⁶making the most of the time, because the days are evil. ¹⁷Therefore do not be foolish, but understand what the will of the Lord is. ¹⁸And do not get drunk with wine, for that is debauchery; but be filled with the Spirit, ¹⁹addressing one another in psalms and hymns and spiritual songs, singing and making melody to the Lord with all your heart, ²⁰always and for everything giving thanks in the name of our Lord Jesus Christ to God the Father and Mother.

21 Be subject to one another out of reverence for Christ. ²²Wives, be subject to your husbands, as to the Lord. ²³For the husband is the head of the wife as Christ is the head of the church, the body, and is its Savior. ²⁴As the church is subject to Christ, so let wives also be subject in everything to their husbands. ²⁵Husbands, love your wives, as Christ loved the church and gave up Christ's self for it, ²⁶in order to sanctify it, having cleansed it by the washing of water with the word, ²⁷so as to present the church to Christ in splendor, without spot or wrinkle or any such thing, that it might be holy and without blemish. ²⁸Even so

husbands should love their wives as their own bodies. He who loves his wife loves himself. ²⁹For never does one eat one's own flesh, but one nourishes it and cherishes it, as Christ does the church, ³⁰because we are members of Christ's body. ³¹"For this reason a man shall leave his father and mother and be joined to his wife, and the two shall become one flesh." ³²This is a profound mystery, and I am saying that it refers to Christ and the church; ³³however, let each one of you love his wife as himself, and let the wife see that she respects her husband.

6 Children, obey your parents in the Lord, for this is right. ²"Honor your father and mother" (this is the first commandment with a promise), ³"that it may be well with you and that you may live long on the earth." ⁴Parents, do not provoke your children to anger, but bring them up in the guidance and instruction of the Lord.

5 Slaves, be obedient to those who are your earthly masters, with fear and trembling, in singleness of heart, as to Christ; ⁶not to attract attention, and to please people, but as servants of Christ, doing the will of God from the heart, ⁷rendering service with a good will as to the Lord and not to human beings, ⁸knowing that whoever does good will receive the same again from the Lord, whether a slave or free. ⁹Masters, do the same to them, and forbear threatening, knowing that the one who is both their Master and yours is in heaven, and with that one there is no partiality.

10 Finally, be strong in the Lord and in the strength of the Lord's might. ¹¹Put on the whole armor of God, that you may be able to stand against the wiles of the devil. ¹²For we are not contending against flesh and blood, but against the principalities, against the powers, against the world rulers of this present evil age, against the spiritual hosts of wickedness in the heavenly places. ¹³Therefore take the whole armor of God, that you may be able to withstand in the evil day, and having done all, to stand. ¹⁴Stand therefore, having girded your loins with truth, and having put on the breastplate of righteousness, ¹⁵and having shod your feet with the equipment of the gospel of peace; ¹⁶besides all these, taking the shield of faith, with which you can quench all the flaming darts of the evil one. ¹⁷And take the helmet of salvation, and the sword of the Spirit, which is the word of God. ¹⁸Pray at all times in the Spirit, with all prayer and supplication. To that end keep alert with all perseverance, making supplications for all the saints, ¹⁹and also for me, that a message may be given me in opening my mouth boldly to proclaim the mystery of the gospel, ²⁰for which I am an ambassador in chains; that I may declare it boldly, as I ought to speak.

21 Now that you also may know how I am and what I am doing, Tychicus the beloved brother and faithful minister in the Lord will tell

you everything. [22]I have sent him to you for this very purpose, that you may know how we are, and that he may encourage your hearts.

23 Peace be to the sisters and brothers, and love with faith, from God the Father and Mother and from the Lord Jesus Christ. [24]Grace be with all who love our Lord Jesus Christ with love undying.

Philippians

1 Paul and Timothy, servants of Christ Jesus,
To all the saints in Christ Jesus who are at Philippi, with the bishops and deacons:
2 Grace to you and peace from God our Father and Mother and from the Lord Jesus Christ.

3 I thank my God in all my remembrance of you, ⁴always in every prayer of mine for you all making my prayer with joy, ⁵thankful for your partnership in the gospel from the first day until now. ⁶And I am sure that the one who began a good work in you will bring it to completion at the day of Jesus Christ. ⁷It is right for me to feel thus about you all, because I hold you in my heart, for you are all partakers with me of grace, both in my imprisonment and in the defense and confirmation of the gospel. ⁸For God is my witness, how I yearn for you all with the affection of Christ Jesus. ⁹And it is my prayer that your love may abound more and more, with knowledge and all discernment, ¹⁰so that you may approve what is excellent, and may be pure and blameless for the day of Christ, ¹¹filled with the fruits of righteousness which come through Jesus Christ, to the glory and praise of God.

12 I want you to know, brothers and sisters, that what has happened to me has really served to advance the gospel, ¹³so that it has become known throughout the whole praetorian guard and to everybody else that my imprisonment is for Christ; ¹⁴and most of the believers have been made confident in the Lord because of my imprisonment, and are much more bold to speak the word without fear.

15 Some indeed preach Christ from envy and rivalry, but others from good will. ¹⁶The latter do it out of love, knowing that I am put

here for the defense of the gospel; [17]the former proclaim Christ out of partisanship, not sincerely but thinking that they afflict me in my imprisonment. [18]What then? Only that in every way, whether in pretense or in truth, Christ is proclaimed; and in that I rejoice.

19 Yes, and I shall rejoice. For I know that through your prayers and the help of the Spirit of Jesus Christ this will turn out for my deliverance, [20]as it is my eager expectation and hope that I shall not be at all ashamed, but that with full courage now as always Christ will be honored in my body, whether by life or by death. [21]For to me to live is Christ, and to die is gain. [22]If it is to be life in the flesh, that means fruitful labor for me. Yet which I will choose I cannot tell. [23]I am hard pressed between the two. My desire is to depart and be with Christ, for that is far better. [24]But to remain in the flesh is more necessary on your account. [25]Convinced of this, I know that I shall remain and continue with you all, for your progress and joy in the faith, [26]so that in me you may have ample cause to glory in Christ Jesus, because of my coming to you again.

27 Only let your manner of life be worthy of the gospel of Christ, so that whether I come and see you or am absent, I may hear of you that you stand firm in one spirit, with one mind striving side by side for the faith of the gospel. [28]and not frightened in anything by your opponents. This is a clear omen to them of their destruction, but of your salvation, and that from God. [29]For it has been granted to you that for the sake of Christ you should not only believe in Christ but also suffer for Christ's sake, [30]engaged in the same conflict which you saw and now hear to be mine.

2 So if there is any encouragement in Christ, any incentive of love, any participation in the Spirit, any affection and sympathy, [2]complete my joy by being of the same mind, having the same love, being in full accord and of one mind. [3]Do nothing from selfishness or conceit, but in humility count others better than yourselves. [4]Let each of you look not only to your own interests but also to the interests of others. [5]Have this mind among yourselves, which is yours in Christ Jesus [6]who, though being in the form of God, did not count equality with God a thing to be grasped, [7]but emptied Christ's self, taking the form of a servant, being born in the likeness of human beings. [8]And being found in human form, Christ humbled Christ's self and became obedient unto death, even death on a cross. [9]Therefore God has highly exalted Jesus and bestowed on Jesus the name which is above every name, [10]that at the name of Jesus every knee should bow, in heaven and on earth and under the earth, [11]and every tongue confess that Jesus Christ is Lord, to the glory of God the Father and Mother.

12 Therefore, my beloved, as you have always obeyed, so now, not only as in my presence but much more in my absence, work out your

own salvation with fear and trembling; ¹³for God is at work in you, both to will and to work for God's good pleasure.

14 Do all things without grumbling or questioning, ¹⁵that you may be blameless and innocent, children of God without blemish in the midst of a crooked and perverse generation, among whom you shine as lights in the world, ¹⁶holding fast the word of life, so that in the day of Christ I may be proud that I did not run in vain or labor in vain. ¹⁷Even if I am to be poured as a libation upon the sacrificial offering of your faith, I am glad and rejoice with you all. ¹⁸Likewise you also should be glad and rejoice with me.

19 I hope in the Lord Jesus to send Timothy to you soon, so that I may be cheered by news of you. ²⁰I have no one like him, who will be genuinely anxious for your welfare. ²¹They all look after their own interests, not those of Jesus Christ. ²²But Timothy's worth you know, how as a son with a father he has served with me in the gospel. ²³I hope therefore to send him just as soon as I see how it will go with me; ²⁴and I trust in the Lord that shortly I myself will come also.

25 I have thought it necessary to send to you Epaphroditus my brother and coworker and comrade in arms, and your messenger and minister to my need, ²⁶for he has been longing for you all, and has been distressed because you heard that he was ill. ²⁷Indeed he was ill, near death. But God had mercy on him, and not only on him but on me also, lest I should have sorrow upon sorrow. ²⁸I am the more eager to send him, therefore, that you may rejoice at seeing him again, and that I may be less anxious. ²⁹So receive him in the Lord with all joy; and honor such people, ³⁰for he nearly died for the work of Christ, risking his life to complete your service to me.

3 Finally, my sisters and brothers, rejoice in the Lord. To write the same things to you is not irksome to me, and is safe for you.

2 Look out for the dogs, look out for the evil-workers, look out for those who mutilate the flesh. ³For we are the true circumcision, who worship God in spirit, and glory in Christ Jesus, and put no confidence in the flesh. ⁴Though I myself have reason for confidence in the flesh also. If anyone has reason to have confidence in the flesh, I have more: ⁵circumcised on the eighth day, of the people of Israel, of the tribe of Benjamin, a Hebrew born of Hebrews; as to the law a Pharisee, ⁶as to zeal a persecutor of the church, as to righteousness under the law blameless. ⁷But whatever gain I had, I counted as loss for the sake of Christ. ⁸Indeed I count everything as loss because of the surpassing worth of knowing Christ Jesus my Lord, for whose sake I have suffered the loss of all things, and count them as refuse, in order that I may gain Christ ⁹and be found in Christ, not having a righteousness of my own, based on law, but that which is through faith in Christ, the righteousness from

God that depends on faith; [10]that I may know Christ and the power of Christ's resurrection, and may share Christ's sufferings, taking the same form that Christ took in death, [11]that if possible I may attain the resurrection from the dead.

12 Not that I have already obtained the goal or am already perfect; but I press on to make it my own, because I have been taken hold of by Christ Jesus. [13]Sisters and brothers, I do not consider that I have made it my own; but one thing I do, forgetting what lies behind and straining forward to what lies ahead, [14]I press on toward the goal for the prize of the upward call of God in Christ Jesus. [15]Let those of us who are mature be thus minded; and if in anything you are otherwise minded, God will reveal that also to you. [16]Only let us hold true to what we have attained.

17 Brothers and sisters, join in imitating me, and mark those who live according to the example you have in us. [18]For many, of whom I have often told you and now tell you even with tears, live as enemies of the cross of Christ. [19]Their end is destruction, their god is the belly, and they glory in their shame, with minds set on earthly things. [20]But our commonwealth is in heaven, and from it we await a Savior, the Lord Jesus Christ, [21]who will change our lowly body to be like Christ's glorious body, by the power which enables Christ even to subject all things to Christ's self.

4 Therefore, my sisters and brothers, whom I love and long for, my joy and crown, stand firm thus in the Lord, my beloved.

2 I entreat Euodia and I entreat Syntyche to agree in the Lord. [3]And I ask you also, true companion, help these women, for they have labored side by side with me in the gospel together with Clement and the rest of my coworkers, whose names are in the book of life.

4 Rejoice in the Lord always; again I will say, Rejoice. [5]Let everyone know your forbearance. The Lord is at hand. [6]Have no anxiety about anything, but in everything, by prayer and supplication with thanksgiving, let your requests be made known to God. [7]And the peace of God, which passes all understanding, will keep your hearts and your minds in Christ Jesus.

8 Finally, my friends, whatever is true, whatever is honorable, whatever is just, whatever is pure, whatever is pleasing, whatever is praiseworthy, if there is any excellence, if there is anything worthy of praise, think about these things. [9]What you have learned and received and heard and seen in me, do; and the God of peace will be with you.

10 I rejoice in the Lord greatly that now at length you have revived your concern for me; you were indeed concerned for me, but had no opportunity. [11]Not that I complain of want; for I have learned, in whatever state I am, to be content. [12]I know how to be abased, and I know how to abound; in any and all circumstances I have learned the secret

of facing plenty and hunger, abundance and want. [13]I can do all things in Christ who strengthens me.

14 Yet it was kind of you to share my trouble. [15]As you Philippians yourselves know that in the beginning of the gospel, when I left Macedonia, no church entered into partnership with me in giving and receiving except you only; [16]for even in Thessalonica you sent me help more than once. [17]Not that I seek the gift; but I seek the fruit which increases to your credit. [18]I have received full payment, and more; I am filled, having received from Epaphroditus the gifts you sent, a fragrant offering, a sacrifice acceptable and pleasing to God. [19]And my God will supply every need of yours according to God's riches in glory in Christ Jesus. [20]To our God, Mother and Father, be glory forever and ever. Amen.

21 Greet every saint in Christ Jesus. The believers who are with me greet you. [22]All the saints greet you, especially those of Caesar's household.

23 The grace of the Lord Jesus Christ be with your spirit.

Colossians

1 Paul, an apostle of Christ Jesus by the will of God, and Timothy our brother,
2 To the saints and faithful brothers and sisters in Christ at Colossae: Grace to you and peace from God our Father and Mother.

3 When we pray for you, we always thank God, the Father and Mother of our Lord Jesus Christ, ⁴because we have heard of your faith in Christ Jesus and of the love which you have for all the saints, ⁵because of the hope laid up for you in heaven. Of this you have heard before in the word of the truth, the gospel ⁶which has come to you, as indeed in the whole world it is bearing fruit and growing—so among yourselves, from the day you heard and understood the grace of God in truth, ⁷as you learned it from our beloved Epaphras, a servant with us. He is a faithful minister of Christ on our behalf ⁸and has made known to us your love in the Spirit.
9 And so, from the day we heard of it, we have not ceased to pray for you, asking that you may be filled with the knowledge of God's will in all spiritual wisdom and understanding, ¹⁰to lead a life worthy of the Lord, pleasing in everything, bearing fruit in every good work and increasing in the knowledge of God. ¹¹May you be strengthened with all power, according to God's glorious might, for all endurance and patience with joy, ¹²giving thanks to God the Mother and Father, who has qualified us to share in the inheritance of the saints in light. ¹³God has delivered us from the power of evil and transferred us to the dominion of God's beloved Child, ¹⁴in whom we have redemption, the forgiveness of sins.
15 Christ is the image of the invisible God, the firstborn of all creation. ¹⁶For in Christ all things were created, in heaven and on earth, visible and invisible, whether thrones or dominions or principalities

or authorities—all things were created through Christ and for Christ. [17]Christ is before all things, the one in whom all things hold together. [18]Christ is the head of the body, the church, and is the beginning, the firstborn from the dead, that in everything Christ might be preeminent. [19]For in Christ all the fullness of God was pleased to dwell, [20]and through Christ to reconcile for Christ all things, whether on earth or in heaven, making peace by the blood of the cross.

21 And you, who once were estranged and hostile in mind, doing evil deeds, [22]have now been reconciled in Christ's body of flesh by Christ's death, in order to present you holy and blameless and irreproachable before God, [23]provided that you continue in the faith, stable and steadfast, not shifting from the hope of the gospel which you heard, which has been preached to every creature under heaven, and of which I, Paul, became a minister.

24 Now I rejoice in my sufferings for your sake, and in my flesh I complete what is lacking in Christ's afflictions for the sake of Christ's body, that is, the church, [25]of which I became a minister according to the divine office which was given to me for you, to make the word of God fully known, [26]the mystery hidden for ages and generations but now made manifest to the saints. [27]To them God chose to make known how great among the Gentiles are the riches of the glory of this mystery, which is Christ in you, the hope of glory. [28]Christ we proclaim, warning everyone and teaching everyone in all wisdom, that we may present everyone mature in Christ. [29]For this I work, striving with all the energy which God mightily inspires within me.

2 For I want you to know how greatly I strive for you, and for those at Laodicea, and for all who have not seen my face, [2]that their hearts may be encouraged as they are knit together in love, to have all the riches of assured understanding and the knowledge of God's mystery, of Christ, [3]in whom are hid all the treasures of wisdom and knowledge. [4]I say this in order that no one may delude you with beguiling speech. [5]For though I am absent in body, yet I am with you in spirit, rejoicing to see your orderliness and the firmness of your faith in Christ.

6 As therefore you received Christ Jesus the Lord, so live in Christ, [7]rooted and built up in Christ and established in the faith, just as you were taught, abounding in thanksgiving.

8 See to it that no one makes a prey of you by philosophy and empty deceit, according to human tradition, according to the elemental spirits of the universe, and not according to Christ. [9]For in Christ the whole fulness of deity dwells bodily, [10]and you have come to fulness of life in Christ, who is the head of all rule and authority, [11]and in whom also you were circumcised with a circumcision made without hands, by

putting off the body of flesh in the circumcision of Christ; [12]and you were buried with Christ in baptism, in which you were also raised with Christ through faith in the working of God, who raised Christ from the dead. [13]And you, who were dead in trespasses and the uncircumcision of your flesh, God made alive together with Christ, having forgiven us all our trespasses, [14]having canceled the bond which stood against us with its legal demands; this God set aside, nailing it to the cross, [15]disarming the principalities and powers, and making a public example of them, triumphing over them in Christ.

16 Therefore let no one pass judgment on you in questions of food and drink, or with regard to a festival or a new moon or a sabbath. [17]These are only a shadow of what is to come; but the substance belongs to Christ. [18]Let no one disqualify you, insisting on self-abasement and worship of angels, taking a stand on visions, puffed up without reason by thinking in a worldly way, [19]and not holding fast to the Head, from whom the whole body, nourished and knit together through its joints and ligaments, grows with a growth that is from God.

20 If with Christ you died to the elemental spirits of the universe, why do you live as if you still belonged to the world? Why do you submit to regulations, [21]"Do not handle, Do not taste, Do not touch" [22](referring to things which all perish as they are used), according to human precepts and doctrines? [23]These have indeed an appearance of wisdom in promoting rigor of devotion and self-abasement and severity to the body, but they are of no value in checking the indulgence of the flesh.

3 If then you have been raised with Christ, seek the things that are above, where Christ is, seated at the right hand of God. [2]Set your minds on things that are above, not on things that are on earth. [3]For you have died, and your life is hid with Christ in God. [4]When Christ who is our life appears, then you also will appear with Christ in glory.

5 Put to death therefore what is earthly in you: fornication, impurity, passion, evil desire, and covetousness, which is idolatry. [6]On account of these the wrath of God is coming. [7]In these you once walked, when you lived in them. [8]But now put them all away: anger, wrath, malice, slander, and filthy talk from your mouth. [9]Do not lie to one another, seeing that you have put off the old nature with its practices [10]and have put on the new nature, which is being renewed in knowledge after the image of its creator. [11]Here there cannot be Greek and Jew, those who are under the law and those who are not, barbarian, Scythian, slave or free, but Christ is all, and in all.

12 Put on then, as God's chosen ones, holy and beloved, compassion, kindness, lowliness, meekness, and patience, [13]forbearing one another and, if one has a complaint against another, forgiving each other; as the Lord has forgiven you, so you also must forgive. [14]And above all

these put on love, which binds everything together in perfect harmony. ¹⁵And let the peace of Christ rule in your hearts, to which indeed you were called in the one body. And be thankful. ¹⁶Let the word of Christ dwell in you richly, teach and admonish one another in all wisdom, and sing psalms and hymns and spiritual songs with thankfulness in your hearts to God. ¹⁷And whatever you do, in word or deed, do everything in the name of the Lord Jesus, giving thanks to God the Father and Mother through Jesus Christ.

18 Wives, be subject to your husbands, as is fitting in the Lord. ¹⁹Husbands, love your wives, and do not be harsh with them. ²⁰Children, obey your parents in everything, for this pleases the Lord. ²¹Fathers, do not provoke your children, lest they become discouraged. ²²Slaves, obey in everything those who are your earthly masters, not to attract attention, and to please people, but in singleness of heart, fearing the Lord. ²³Whatever your task, work heartily, as serving the Lord and not human beings, ²⁴knowing that from the Lord you will receive the inheritance as your reward; you are serving the Lord Christ. ²⁵For wrongdoers will be paid back for the wrong they have done, and there is no partiality.

4 Masters, treat your slaves justly and fairly, knowing that you also have a Master in heaven.

2 Continue steadfastly in prayer, being watchful in it with thanksgiving; ³and pray for us also, that God may open to us a door for the word, to declare the mystery of Christ, on account of which I am in prison, ⁴that I may make it clear, as I ought to.

5 Conduct yourselves wisely toward outsiders, making the most of the time. ⁶Let your speech always be gracious, seasoned with salt, so that you may know how you ought to answer everyone.

7 Tychicus will tell you all about my affairs; he is a beloved brother and faithful minister and servant with me in the Lord. ⁸I have sent him to you for this very purpose, that you may know how we are and that he may encourage your hearts, ⁹and with him Onesimus, the faithful and beloved brother, who is one of yourselves. They will tell you of everything that has taken place here.

10 Aristarchus, who is with me in prison, greets you, and Mark the cousin of Barnabas (concerning whom you have received instructions— if he comes to you, receive him), ¹¹and Jesus who is called Justus. These are the only people of the circumcision among my coworkers for the dominion of God, and they have been a comfort to me. ¹²Epaphras, who is one of yourselves, a servant of Christ Jesus, greets you, always remembering you earnestly in his prayers, that you may stand mature and fully assured in the whole will of God. ¹³For I bear Epaphras witness that he has worked hard for you and for those in Laodicea and in Hierapolis.

¹⁴Luke the beloved physician and Demas greet you. ¹⁵Give my greetings to the believers at Laodicea, and to Nympha and the church in her house. ¹⁶And when this letter has been read among you, have it read also in the church of the Laodiceans; and see that you read also the letter from Laodicea. ¹⁷And say to Archippus, "See that you fulfill the ministry which you have received in the Lord."

18 I, Paul, write this greeting with my own hand. Remember my chains. Grace be with you.

1 Thessalonians

1 Paul, Silvanus, and Timothy,
To the church of the Thessalonians in God the Mother and Father and in the Lord Jesus Christ:
Grace to you and peace.

2 We give thanks to God always for you all, constantly mentioning you in our prayers, ³remembering before God our Father and Mother your work of faith and labor of love and steadfastness of hope in our Lord Jesus Christ. ⁴For we know, friends beloved by God, that God has chosen you; ⁵for our gospel came to you not only in word, but also in power and in the Holy Spirit and with full conviction. You know what kind of people we proved to be among you for your sake. ⁶And you became imitators of us and of the Lord, for you received the word in much affliction, with joy inspired by the Holy Spirit; ⁷so that you became an example to all the believers in Macedonia and in Achaia. ⁸For not only has the word of the Lord sounded forth from you in Macedonia and Achaia, but your faith in God has gone forth everywhere, so that we need not say anything. ⁹For they themselves report concerning us what a welcome we had among you, and how you turned to God from idols, to serve a living and true God, ¹⁰and to wait for God's Child from heaven, whom God raised from the dead, Jesus who delivers us from the wrath to come.

2 For you yourselves know, my friends, that our visit to you was not in vain; ²but though we had already suffered and been shamefully treated at Philippi, as you know, we had courage in our God to declare to you the gospel of God in the face of great opposition. ³For our appeal does not spring from error or uncleanness, nor is it made with guile; ⁴but

just as we have been approved by God to be entrusted with the gospel, so we speak, not to please human beings, but to please God who tests our hearts. [5]For we never used either words of flattery, as you know, or a pretext for greed, as God is witness; [6]nor did we seek glory from anyone, whether from you or from others, though we might have made demands as apostles of Christ. [7]But we were gentle among you, like a nurse taking care of children. [8]So being affectionately desirous of you, we were ready to share with you not only the gospel of God but also our own selves, because you had become very dear to us.

9 For you remember our labor and toil, my friends; we worked night and day, that we might not burden any of you, while we preached to you the gospel of God. [10]You are witnesses, and God also, how holy and righteous and blameless was our behavior to you believers; [11]for you know how, like a parent with a child, we exhorted each one of you and encouraged you and charged you [12]to lead a life worthy of God, who calls you into God's own dominion and glory.

13 And we also thank God constantly for this, that when you received the word of God which you heard from us, you accepted it not as a human word but as what it really is, the word of God, which is at work in you believers. [14]For you, sisters and brothers, became imitators of the churches of God in Christ Jesus which are in Judea; for you suffered the same things from your own compatriots as they did from the Jews, [15]who killed both the Lord Jesus and the prophets, and drove us out, and displease God and oppose everybody [16]by hindering us from speaking to the Gentiles that they may be saved—so as always to fill up the measure of their sins. But God's wrath has come upon them at last.

17 But since for a short time, brothers and sisters, we were bereft of you, in person not in heart, we endeavored the more eagerly and with great desire to see you face to face, [18]because we wanted to come to you—I, Paul, again and again—but Satan hindered us. [19]For what is our hope or joy or crown of boasting before our Lord Jesus at the Lord's coming? Is it not you? [20]For you are our glory and joy.

3 Therefore when we could bear it no longer, we were willing to be left behind at Athens alone, [2]and we sent Timothy, our brother and God's helper in the gospel of Christ, to establish you in your faith and to exhort you, [3]so that no one would be disturbed by these afflictions. You yourselves know that this is to be our lot. [4]For when we were with you, we told you beforehand that we were to suffer affliction; just as it has come to pass, as you know. [5]For this reason, when I could bear it no longer, I sent that I might know your faith, for fear that somehow the tempter had tempted you and that our labor would be in vain.

6 But now that Timothy has come to us from you, and has brought us the good news of your faith and love, and has reported that you al-

ways remember us kindly and long to see us, as we long to see you—[7]for this reason, brothers and sisters, in all our distress and affliction we have been comforted about you through your faith; [8]for now we live, if you stand fast in the Lord. [9]For what thanksgiving can we render to God for you, for all the joy which we feel because of you before our God, [10]praying earnestly night and day that we may see you face to face and supply what is lacking in your faith?

11 Now may God, even God's own self, our Mother and Father, and our Lord Jesus, direct our way to you; [12]and may the Lord make you increase and abound in love to one another and to all people, as we do to you, [13]in order to establish your hearts unblamable in holiness before God our Father and Mother, at the coming of our Lord Jesus with all the saints.

4 Finally, sisters and brothers, we beseech and exhort you in the Lord Jesus, that as you learned from us how you ought to live and to please God, just as you are doing, you do so more and more. [2]For you know what instructions we gave you through the Lord Jesus. [3]For this is the will of God, your sanctification: that you abstain from unchastity; [4]that each one of you know how to control your own body in holiness and honor, [5]not in the passion of lust like heathen who do not know God; [6]that no one transgress and wrong another human being in this matter, because the Lord is an avenger in all these things, as we solemnly forewarned you. [7]For God has not called us for uncleanness, but in holiness. [8]Therefore whoever disregards this, disregards not human beings but God, who gives the Holy Spirit to you.

9 But concerning love of the brothers and sisters you have no need to have anyone write to you, for you yourselves have been taught by God to love one another; [10]and indeed you do love all the sisters and brothers throughout Macedonia. But we exhort you, friends, to do so more and more, [11]to aspire to live quietly, to mind your own affairs, and to work with your hands, as we charged you; [12]so that you may command the respect of outsiders, and be dependent on no one.

13 But we would not have you ignorant, sisters and brothers, concerning those who are asleep, that you may not grieve as others do who have no hope. [14]For since we believe that Jesus died and rose again, even so, through Jesus, God will bring with Jesus those who have fallen asleep. [15]For this we declare to you by the word of the Lord, that we who are alive, who are left until the coming of the Lord, will not precede those who have fallen asleep. [16]For the Lord, indeed, will descend from heaven with a cry of command, with the archangel's call, and with the sound of the trumpet of God. And the dead in Christ will rise first; [17]then we who are alive, who are left, will be caught up together with them in the clouds to meet the Lord in the air; and so we will

always be with the Lord. [18]Therefore comfort one another with these words.

5 But as to the times and the seasons, friends, you have no need to have anything written to you. [2]For you yourselves know well that the day of the Lord will come like a thief in the night. [3]When people say, "There is peace and security," then sudden destruction will come upon them as travail comes upon a woman with child, and there will be no escape. [4]But you are not in the night, sisters and brothers, for that day to surprise you like a thief [5]For you are all children of light and children of the day; we are not of the night. [6]So then let us not sleep, as others do, but let us keep awake and be sober. [7]For those who sleep, sleep at night, and those who get drunk are drunk at night. [8]But, since we belong to the day, let us be sober, and put on the breastplate of faith and love, and for a helmet the hope of salvation. [9]For God has not destined us for wrath, but to obtain salvation through our Lord Jesus Christ, [10]who died for us so that whether we wake or sleep we might live with Christ. [11]Therefore encourage one another and build one another up, just as you are doing.

12 But we beseech you, brothers and sisters, to respect those who labor among you and are over you in the Lord, and admonish you, [13]and to esteem them very highly in love because of their work. Be at peace among yourselves. [14]And we exhort you, beloved, admonish the idlers, encourage the fainthearted, help the weak, be patient with them all. [15]See that none of you repays evil for evil, but always seek to do good to one another and to all. [16]Rejoice always, [17]pray constantly, [18]give thanks in all circumstances; for this is the will of God in Christ Jesus for you. [19]Do not quench the Spirit, [20]do not despise prophesying, [21]but test everything; hold fast what is good, [22]abstain from every form of evil.

23 May the God of peace sanctify you wholly; and may your spirit and soul and body be kept sound and blameless at the coming of our Lord Jesus Christ. [24]The one who calls you is faithful, and will do it.

25 Beloved, pray for us.

26 Greet all the brothers and sisters with a holy kiss.

27 I adjure you by the Lord that this letter be read to all of them.

28 The grace of our Lord Jesus Christ be with you.

2 Thessalonians

1 Paul, Silvanus, and Timothy,
To the church of the Thessalonians in God our Father and Mother and in the Lord Jesus Christ:

2 Grace to you and peace from God the Father and Mother and the Lord Jesus Christ.

3 We are bound to give thanks to God always for you, brothers and sisters, as is fitting, because your faith is growing abundantly, and the love of every one of you for one another is increasing. ⁴Therefore we ourselves boast of you in the churches of God for your steadfastness and faith in all your persecutions and in the afflictions which you are enduring.

5 This is evidence of the righteous judgment of God, that you may be made worthy of the dominion of God, for which you are suffering— ⁶since indeed God deems it just to repay with affliction those who afflict you, ⁷and to grant rest with us to you who are afflicted, when the Lord Jesus is revealed from heaven with the mighty angels in flaming fire, ⁸inflicting vengeance upon those who do not know God and upon those who do not obey the gospel of our Lord Jesus. ⁹They shall suffer the punishment of eternal destruction and exclusion from the Lord's presence and from the glory of the Lord's might, ¹⁰when on that day the Lord comes to be glorified in the saints, and to be marveled at in all who have believed, because our testimony to you was believed. ¹¹To this end we always pray for you, that our God may make you worthy of God's call, and may fulfill every good resolve and work of faith with power, ¹²so that the name of our Lord Jesus may be glorified in you, and you in the Lord, according to the grace of our God and the Lord Jesus Christ.

2 Now concerning the coming of our Lord Jesus Christ and our assembling to meet the Lord, we beg you, sisters and brothers, [2]not to
be quickly shaken in mind or excited, either by spirit or by word, or by
a letter purporting to be from us, to the effect that the day of the Lord
has come. [3]Let no one deceive you in any way; for that day will not
come, unless the rebellion comes first, and the lawless one is revealed,
the one destined for destruction, [4]who is the adversary and self-exalter
over every so-called god or object of worship, so as to take a seat in the
temple of God, and claim to be God. [5]Do you not remember that when
I was still with you I told you this? [6]And you know what the restraining
power is now, so that the lawless one may be revealed at the right time.
[7]For the mystery of lawlessness is already at work; but only until the one
who now restrains it is out of the way. [8]And then the lawless one will
be revealed, and will be slain by the breath of the mouth of the Lord
Jesus, and will be destroyed by Jesus' appearing and coming. [9]The coming of the lawless one by the activity of Satan will be with all power and
with pretended signs and wonders, [10]and with all wicked deception for
those who are to perish, because they refused to love the truth and so
be saved. [11]Therefore God sends upon them a strong delusion, to make
them believe what is false, [12]so that all may be condemned who did not
believe the truth but had pleasure in unrighteousness.

13 But we are bound to give thanks to God always for you, brothers and sisters beloved by the Lord, because God chose you from the
beginning to be saved, through sanctification by the Spirit and belief in
the truth. [14]To this God called you through our gospel, so that you may
obtain the glory of our Lord Jesus Christ. [15]So then, beloved, stand firm
and hold to the traditions which you were taught by us, either by word
of mouth or by letter.

16 Now may our Lord Jesus Christ, and God our Mother and Father,
who loved us and gave us eternal comfort and good hope through grace,
[17]comfort your hearts and establish them in every good work and word.

3 Finally, sisters and brothers, pray for us, that the word of the Lord
may speed on and triumph, as it did among you, [2]and that we may
be delivered from wicked and evil people; for not all have faith. [3]But the
Lord is faithful, and will strengthen you and guard you from evil. [4]And
we have confidence in the Lord about you, that you are doing and will
do the things which we command. [5]May the Lord direct your hearts to
the love of God and to the steadfastness of Christ.

6 Now we command you, friends, in the name of our Lord Jesus
Christ, that you keep away from any brother or sister who is living in
idleness and not in accord with the tradition that you received from us.
[7]For you yourselves know how you ought to imitate us; we were not
idle when we were with you, [8]we did not eat anyone's bread without

paying, but with toil and labor we worked night and day, that we might not burden any of you. [9]It was not because we have not that right, but to give you in our conduct an example to imitate. [10]For even when we were with you, we gave you this command: Anyone who will not work is not to eat. [11]For we hear that some of you are living in idleness, mere busybodies, not doing any work. [12]Now such persons we command and exhort in the Lord Jesus Christ to do their work in quietness and to earn their own living. [13]Friends, do not be weary in well-doing.

14 If there are any who refuse to obey what we say in this letter, note them, and have nothing to do with them, that they may be ashamed. [15]Do not look on them as enemies, but warn them as brothers and sisters.

16 Now may the Lord of peace give you peace at all times in all ways. The Lord be with you all.

17 I, Paul, write this greeting with my own hand. This is the mark in every letter of mine; it is the way I write. [18]The grace of our Lord Jesus Christ be with you all.

Philemon

1 Paul, a prisoner for Christ Jesus, and Timothy our brother,
To Philemon our beloved coworker ²and Apphia our sister and
Archippus our companion in struggle, and the church in your house:

3 Grace to you and peace from God our Father and Mother and from
the Lord Jesus Christ.

4 I thank my God always when I remember you in my prayers, ⁵because I hear of your love and of the faith which you have toward the
Lord Jesus and all the saints, ⁶and I pray that the sharing of your faith
may promote the knowledge of all the good that is ours in Christ. ⁷For I
have derived much joy and comfort from your love, my brother, because
the hearts of the saints have been refreshed through you.

8 Accordingly, though I am bold enough in Christ to command you
to do what is required, ⁹yet for love's sake I prefer to appeal to you—I,
Paul, an ambassador and now a prisoner also for Christ Jesus—¹⁰I appeal to you for my child, Onesimus, whose father I have become in my
imprisonment. ¹¹(Formerly he was useless to you, but now he is indeed
useful to you and to me.) ¹²I am sending Onesimus back to you, sending my very heart. ¹³I would have been glad to keep him with me, in
order that he might serve me on your behalf during my imprisonment
for the gospel; ¹⁴but I preferred to do nothing without your consent in
order that your goodness might not be by compulsion but of your own
free will.

15 Perhaps this is why Onesimus was parted from you for a while,
that you might have him back forever, ¹⁶no longer as a slave but more
than a slave, as a beloved brother, especially to me but how much more
to you, both in the flesh and in the Lord. ¹⁷So if you consider me your
partner, receive Onesimus as you would receive me. ¹⁸If he has wronged

you at all, or owes you anything, charge that to my account. [19]I, Paul, write this with my own hand, I will repay it—to say nothing of your owing me even your own self. [20]Yes, brother, I want some benefit from you in the Lord. Refresh my heart in Christ.

21 Confident of your obedience, I write to you, knowing that you will do even more than I say. [22]At the same time, prepare a guest room for me, for I am hoping through your prayers to be granted to you.

23 Epaphras, a prisoner with me in Christ Jesus, sends greetings to you, [24]as do Mark, Aristarchus, Demas, and Luke, my coworkers.

25 The grace of the Lord Jesus Christ be with your spirit.

Appendix

The following is a brief discussion of the major inclusive terms that appear in this translation.

"God the Father and Mother" for "God the Father"
Frequently in the New Testament God is referred to as "Father." "Father" provides a lens through which to see God. When it was first said that God is "Father," the statement was understood as a metaphor, not as a proposition.

A metaphor is a figure of speech used to extend meaning through comparison of dissimilars. In the metaphor "God is Father," two dissimilars, "God" and "Father," are juxtaposed, and the meaning of "God" is extended. Metaphors disclose a new way of seeing; they speak indirectly and evoke a wide range of associations that vary with the hearer. They are imprecise and open-ended; and it is not true that there is only one "right" metaphor, and all others are "wrong." In that case all metaphors but one would be superfluous. Metaphors do not "correspond" to what is, but are appropriate to one's experience and provide a fresh way of perceiving it.

But by repetition, the dissimilarities of metaphors become more and more similar, until the metaphor finally disappears and we are left with a simple proposition that is not literally true.

Now, if one were to say, "God is our Mother," the statement would be clearly understood as a metaphor, not a proposition. To put up the screen "mother" through which to see God would elicit the response of a true metaphor for us. Of course, God *is* not, literally, our Mother; but neither *is* God, literally, our Father. A metaphor for God that balances the less familiar female imagery with the very familiar male imagery

243

is provided in this translation. We speak, then, of God as "Father and Mother" or "Mother and Father," thus extending the biblical metaphor, and at the same time reminding us of the metaphorical character of the biblical reference to God as "Father" when it was first said and heard.

In the Gospel of John, where the metaphor "Father" occurs most often, as well as occasionally elsewhere, "Father" is sometimes rendered "God."

"Child" for "Son"

Very frequently in the New Testament Jesus is designated "Son" of God. A son is a man, and of course the historical person Jesus was a man. But in the Gospels Jesus' maleness is not assumed to have significance for the salvation of either men or women. It is the fact that Jesus was *human* that is so clear in the Gospels and that became of such crucial importance in the church for its understanding of Jesus' work of salvation. When Jesus is called "Son of God," it is not Jesus' maleness that is being underscored, but Jesus' intimate relationship to God (see Matt. 11:25–27). Sonship also has other connotations in the New Testament, such as divine authority (see Matt. 28:18–20) and freedom (see Rom. 8:21).

If then the fact that Jesus was *male* has no christological significance in the New Testament, then neither does the fact that Jesus was a *son* and not a *daughter*. Therefore, in this translation, the formal equivalent "Child" or "Child of God" (occasionally "Offspring") is used for "Son" when it occurs in a christological sense, and gender-specific pronouns referring to the "Child" are avoided; thus, all readers will be enabled to identify themselves with Jesus' *humanity*.

When Jesus is identified as "Son," believers become "sons," and therefore heirs. In this translation, Jesus as "Child" allows believers— men and women—to understand themselves as "children" of God and therefore heirs.

While the word "child" may imply a minor, or childishness, in the New Testament it clearly refers to "adults" in more than half of its occurrences. For example, the word "child" (or "children") is used for adult descendants (Acts 13:33; Rom. 9:8); or for adults who are "children" of a teacher or apostle (1 Cor. 4:14; 2 Cor. 6:13); or for adult Christians (2 John 1, 4); or for adults who are "children of God" (John 11:52; Rom. 8:16). In these and many other passages, "child" or "children" connotes primarily close relationship, and more often of adults than of minors. The canon itself, therefore, provides the church with a substitute for the word "son" that is not gender specific. These meanings of "child" in the New Testament are also consistent with contemporary usage, in which the term "child" refers not only to minors but also to a relationship to parents without reference to age.

"The Human One" for "the Son of Man"

The term "the Son of Man" occurs often in the Gospels, and almost nowhere else in the New Testament. It occurs only on Jesus' lips (with one exception), and only as Jesus speaks about himself. How do the gospel authors understand its meaning?

Much light would be shed on the meaning of the term if there were clear antecedents for its use in the Gospels, but any such antecedents are impossible to demonstrate. It cannot be shown that Jewish use of the term "the Son of Man" has influenced its use in the Gospels; in fact the term does not appear to have functioned as a title at all prior to its application to Jesus by the church. Furthermore, its meaning in the Gospels varies in different contexts. The term, however, is subject to misinterpretation as a reference to a male human being, "the son" of "the Man." And so we have used "the Human One" as the formal equivalent for "the Son of Man" in this translation. That formal equivalent is not derived from or dependent on any particular judgment as to the background of "the Son of Man" in Judaism and is not intended to prejudice in any way the ongoing discussion of that issue. We believe, however, that the title "the Human One" is open to the same nuances of interpretation allowed by the title "the Son of Man." These nuances are to be derived from the context in which the term is used, rather than from the term itself.

Gender-Specific Pronouns for God and Christ

Because English pronouns are inherently gender-specific, they are not used in this translation to refer either to God or to the preexistent or postcrucifixion Christ.

"Dominion of God" for "Kingdom of God"

The Greek word *basileia*, traditionally translated as "kingdom" (for example, kingdom of God, kingdom of heaven), is here translated "dominion." There are two reasons for this:

(1) The Greek word *basileia* means both "rule" or "reign" *and* "realm"; it refers both to the exercise of authority and to the place where the authority is exercised. "*Basileia* of God," therefore, can refer either to the *exercise* of God's authority or to the *place* over which God exercises authority.

Now it is evident that "kingdom," in contemporary usage, refers only to place, not to action, while "dominion" may refer to either: one may have dominion over and one may enter into a dominion. So "dominion" is a very close English approximation of the Greek *basileia*.

(2) Because "kingdom" is such a blatantly androcentric and patriarchal word, "dominion" is preferable when used in connection with God, though, of course, it is true that etymologically "dominion" is a

male-oriented word (not atypical of Latin words relating to the exercise of power).

"Ruler" for "King"

The word "king" is used in the Bible both in reference to earthly royal figures and as a metaphor for God. Here when "King" is used as a metaphor for God it is rendered usually as "Ruler."

Teacher

Epistatēs, a Greek word used only by Luke in the New Testament and rendered "Master" in the Revised Standard Version, is translated here as "Teacher." It had a wide variety of connotations, such as supervisor, administrator, or governor, but no specific religious connotations. Luke uses it in passages where parallels in Matthew and Mark have "Lord," "Teacher," or "Rabbi."

Sisters and Brothers, Friends, Neighbors, Beloved

In Greek usage the word "brother" refers not only to a male sibling, but also to a more distant relative, a friend, a neighbor, or even a member of one's community or race, irrespective of sex. Paul reflects such a broad use of the word "brethren" ("brothers") in a phrase he uses in Rom. 9:3, where in the Revised Standard Version "my brethren" is the equivalent of "my kinsmen by race." Here the whole phrase is rendered "my own people [for my brethren], my kindred by race."

In the New Testament, the word "brothers" sometimes also includes "sisters." For example, in Luke 21:16, which the Revised Standard Version renders "You will be delivered up even by parents and brothers and kinsmen and friends," "brothers" is certainly intended to designate "brothers and sisters": *everyone* will "deliver up," and sisters are surely not excluded. And when Paul writes to the Christians in Corinth and calls them "brothers" or "brethren" ("When I came to you, brethren," RSV of 1 Cor. 2:1), he is most assuredly addressing the women in the church as well as the men. In such cases of direct address, "brethren" has been rendered here either as "sisters and brothers" ("brothers and sisters") or as "friends," "neighbors," or rarely as "beloved," depending on context. In postcrucifixion sayings attributed to Jesus, "brethren" is translated as "followers" (as in Matt. 28:10) or as "friends" (as in John 20:17) to make clear that the reference is to early Christians and not to Jesus' siblings.

Sarah's Name

The name "Sarah" has been included with Abraham's name in contexts where the generation or origin of the people of Israel is the major concern; thus, both male and female are implied.

"The Jews" in the Gospel of John

The term "the Jews" occurs very frequently in the Fourth Gospel. Sometimes it refers in a straightforward, historical way to the ethnic people of whom Jesus was one and among whom Jesus lived out his life. Sometimes, however, it is used almost as a code word for religious leaders who misunderstand the true identity of Christ. When "the Jews" is used in the former sense it remains unchanged in this translation. When it is used in the latter sense it is rendered "the religious authorities" or simply "the authorities" or "leaders" so as to minimize what could be perceived as a warrant for anti-Semitism in the Gospel of John.